SUPERPLONK
2004

MALCOLM GLUCK

SUPERPLONK

2004

THE TOP
1000

Collins

First published in 2003 by
Collins, an imprint of
HarperCollins*Publishers*
77–85 Fulham Palace Road
Hammersmith
London W6 8JB

The Collins website address is www.collins.co.uk

Collins is a registered trademark of HarperCollins Publishers Ltd

09 08   07   06   05   04   03
7 6   5   4   3   2   1

Editor: Susan Fleming
Design: Stuart Brill and Bob Vickers
Indexer: Laura Hicks

A catalogue record for this book is available from the British Library

ISBN 0-00-716040-2

Printed and bound in Great Britain by Clays Ltd, St Ives plc.

To
ARTHUR SEYMOUR JOHN TESSIMOND,
poet and adman,
1902–1962

'We have many grave things to worry about, but if we look round for a sturdy thing proved to be able to take knocks, the eye rests with relief upon the English language; a great nuisance to handle, of course, but one we need hardly fear that it is in decay.'

William Empson, *Times Literary Supplement*, 20 September 1960 (as published in *Argufying*, Chatto & Windus, 1987)

CONTENTS

ACKNOWLEDGEMENTS

I would like to thank everyone who has helped make this book possible: publishing director Denise Bates and my editor Susan Fleming (both of whom stayed unflappable during many a last-minute hiccup), Jane Rose (who directs marketing) and Jane Hollyman (who manages it), Nick Ford (who directs the sales team), and Bob Vickers who has made such an elegant job of the design.

I also thank my literary agent Felicity Rubinstein, my computer consultant Richard Darsa and Sue Gluck and Sue Bolton who inputted all my tasting notes (from handwriting which few would recognise as English).

INTRODUCTION

WELCOME TO MY BRAVE NEW WORLD OF GLUGGING

Thirteen years I've been writing this annual wine guide. I've filled bottle banks with more empties than any other single individual in the UK (maybe the world). I've written hundreds of thousand of words (over the past two years for my website alone, superplonk.com, my iMac word-counter tells me I've churned out 241,513 words).

Enough, gentle reader, is enough. Or rather enough is enough as far as the way I approach writing this book is concerned. I have read and digested what my correspondents say. I have listened attentively to the views of my readers. I have buttonholed wine drinkers from Arbroath to Zennor. Above all, I have obeyed my instincts.

The result is *Superplonk 2004 – The Top 1000*. It is the new approach to the Superplonk book for the new millennium. It is much simpler to use, much crisper in its opinions, richer in its concentration on the best wines, and, above all, it is more compact, concentrated and entertaining. I have revised my whole approach to the book, except in one crucial aspect: value for money is still the essential criterion for any wine's inclusion. I am still the only wine writer who rates wines on this humane basis and I suspect I always will be. For me, there is no romance in expensive wine unless the liquid in the bottle is sublime. How else could a rationalist proceed?

The book, you will readily note, is still divided into retailer sections but no longer sub-divided by countries of origin. This information is important at point of sale, yes, but here you need the information only as part of much else. The usual suspects are here. The supermarkets are Asda, Booths, Budgens, Marks & Spencer, Morrisons, Safeway, Sainsbury's, Somerfield, Tesco and Waitrose. The wine shops are Majestic, Oddbins, and the Thresher Group. But there are also wines from e-tailers, London stores and small merchants.

You will note also that I have done away with listing all wines under 16 points. The website, superplonk.com, carries details and ratings of all the wines I taste, but the book will concentrate solely on the top raters. These are the ones scoring 16+ points out of 20 – red, white, rosé, sparkling and fortified. Nothing could be simpler. But immediately you ask: how does this rating system work? This is how:

HOW I RATE A WINE. WHAT MAKES A SUPERPLONK A SUPERPLONK

It is worth repeating: value for money is my single unwavering focus. I drink with my readers' pockets in my mouth. I do not see the necessity of paying a lot for a bottle of everyday drinking wine and only rarely do I consider it worth paying a high price for, say, a wine for a special occasion or because you want to experience what a so-called 'grand' wine may be like.

I do taste expensive wines regularly. I do not, regularly, find them worth the money. That said, there are some pricey bottles in these pages. They are here because the wines are genuinely worth every penny (which is what the definition of a Superplonk is). A wine of magnificent complexity, thrilling fruit, superb aroma, great depth and finesse is worth drinking. Such a wine challenges the intellect as much as the palate and its value lies, like a great theatrical performance or outstanding novel, in its unforgettableness. I will rate it highly. Even though it costs a lot, the lot it costs is justified.

20 points Life rarely throws up perfection. Indeed, some aesthetes regard true beauty as always revealing a small flaw. I do not. There is no flaw in a 20-point wine. It has perfect balance, finesse, flavour and finish – dull terms to describe the sum of an unforgettable experience. A perfect wine is also perfectly affordable. That is not to say (necessarily) £2.99 or even £4.99, but a sum related to common sense. Even if such a wine costs £100 it is still worth 20 points and the possible pain of acquisition. I exclude from this auction-antiques which cost thousands of pounds, for these are the perverted passions of wine collectors and the prices paid rarely bear any relation to the quality of the liquid in the bottles. No wine is truly worth thousands of pounds and no civilised individual would pay it.

19 points What's a point between friends? Or between one wine and another? 19 points represents a superb wine of towering individuality and impact. Almost perfect and well worth the expense (even if it is an expensive bottle), such a wine will flood the senses with myriad smells, tastes and flavours and provide a tantalising glimpse, whilst it lasts, of the sheer textured genius of great wine. Such a wine is individual, rich, subtle yet potent, and overwhelmingly delicious. It can start, and finish, a conversation.

18 points This is an excellent wine but lacking that ineffable sublimity of richness and complexity to achieve the very highest rating. Such a wine offers superb drinking and thundering good value and it must exhibit a remarkably well-textured richness. True, I do emphasise texture above other aspects of complexity (like all those fruits some tasters are determined to find in a wine), and here the texture is so well married to the acids and sugars that it is all of a piece. Such a wine is remarkable, immensely drinkable, complex and compelling.

17 points An exciting, well-made wine, almost invariably hugely affordable, which offers real glimpses of multi-layered richness. It will demonstrate individuality and incisiveness and it will offer a seductive mouthfeel and sense of luxury. It may be a more immediate wine than those rating higher, but it will still linger in the memory the day after it is drunk – for it will have given a delightful and impressive performance.

16 points This is a very good wine indeed. Good enough for any dinner party and any level of drinker (with the possible exception of those most toffee-nosed of snobs for whom pleasure usually comes associated with a fat price-tag). Not necessarily an expensive wine is implied here but it will be a terrifically drinkable, satisfying and multi-dimensional one. It will be properly balanced and often be excellent with particular kinds of dishes (which it enhances).

HOW TO BECOME A WORLD-CLASS WINE TASTER IN 7 EASY LESSONS

You have a palate, don't you? You have a memory. You know what you like. Okay. Do you want to be a bit smarter around wine?

Then you can become a wine taster (like Amy Wislocki of *Decanter Magazine* for example, who kindly published a portion of these tasting thoughts of mine a few Christmases ago). All that stands in your way is confidence. Rid yourself of your reservations and bingo!. . . the mysteries of wine tasting will dissolve like magic.

Look at yourself in the mirror. Stick out your tongue. If only you could count the number of tastebuds on it you would know, just as surely as you know also whether you are sufficiently musical to possess the skill to play an instrument, whether you can be a world-class taster or not. It is because of your tongue that you are able to taste wine – we'll leave out the importance of your nose at this point.

One reason why different people have a different reaction to the same glass of wine is because not everyone has the same number of tastebuds on his or her tongue (and also because each individual's saliva is unique). The number of tastebuds crucially affects the ability to taste brilliantly, adequately, or with downright mediocrity. As a result of this disparity in basic equipment, there must be many people in the wine trade who lack a sufficient number of tastebuds to do their jobs outstandingly and you, perhaps, can easily outshine them. Many so-called wine tasters are complete frauds as experts and possess no greater expertise than that conferred by a good memory (which you must also cultivate).

10,000 is the maximum number of tastebuds it is possible to possess but many people, including, who knows, many wine tasters, may have less. They may not appreciate wine as deeply as they think they do. This explains why certain wine professionals simply don't spot faults like cork taint. With 10,000 tastebuds you are what Harvard University, which has done the research, calls a super taster. The average taster has between 5,000 and 10,000 tastebuds and so is a medium taster. Below 5,000 and you're a normal taster – yet perhaps working as a sommelier who simply can't understand when customers complain a wine smells and tastes funny.

This is why you should always ask yourself this question: who knows anything about taste except the person who experiences it? Taste is individual; translation nigh impossible. Your reaction, ergo, is equally personal and where one taster finds buttercups another taster will discern attar of roses.

Go forth, then, and taste. Above all, enjoy yourself without reservation. If you can't enjoy tasting, you'll never make a wine taster.

Lesson One: The Dark Side

Q: 'How many wine tasters does it take to change a light bulb?'
A: 'None. They work in the dark.'

Working in the dark gives the wine taster mystique. This in turn bequeaths to people like me (and you-in-the-future) enormous powers. This is because the wine buyer is in the dark too but imagines, believes indeed, that the taster knows her way around. This belief is based solely upon perception, not reality. The important point here is never to admit you are completely in the dark.

Lesson Two: Learning the Script

There are certain key metaphors. All Cabernets are 'peppery', all Merlots 'leathery', all Chardonnays 'melony' (or, better, 'Ogen melony'), and all Chenins 'wet-woolish'. Sauvignon Blancs reek of gooseberries, Viogniers (and Pinot Gris) of apricots, Sémillons of citrus, while Riesling has the tang of plasticine. Zinfandel is always spicy, Shiraz sweaty (though Syrah is earthy), and Gewürztraminer always offers lychees. With sparkling wines always search for the smell of fresh-baked bread. This is, technically, yeast autolysis, but offering up 'croissant' or 'Monsieur Poilaine's sourdough' will earn you more plaudits.

The list is not infinite since there are 4,000 or so grape varieties in use but less than 40 require metaphorical identification. Blends create a hurdle but this can be leapt with practice, always remembering that you can say anything about a wine and it will make sense to someone. Other flavours such as chocolate, pepper and toffee are commonly found in wines, and also have obvious power as metaphors which can be further embroidered.

But better than such metaphors for taste are the ones for texture. Fabrics are key here. Mundanities such as 'silky' and 'velvety' are okay but predictable. Cabernet as corduroy or Sauvignon Blanc likened to drip-dry cotton or Côtes du Rhône described as suede-like shows you really know your shmutter. The human body – hairy, fat, fleshy, thin, big-bodied – can also provide you with inspiration.

You may begin this lesson at home. Note down the essential flavour of all wines you sample and also what the texture suggests to you. Once you have mastered this, you are ready for the next lesson.

Lesson Three: Acting the Role

You must develop the knack of spotting corked wines and also faulty ones. Certain septuagenarian tasters do nothing else. There are, for example, a couple of old biddies who always make a nuisance of themselves at pro wine tastings, and who come just for the lunch, and, somewhere between the seventh and twentieth bottle, shout out they've found a corked one and thus they maintain their guru status. Only a rare wine merchant is capable of the chutzpah required to be defiant and call their bluff. That Loftus chap, up at Adnams, is one such, but then he wears an earring and looks like a trendy C of E vicar so he can get away with stuff denied the conventionally striped suited johnnies.

A corked wine is any wine which smells of cardboard, mushrooms or old library books. We all know these smells. We grew up with them.

The other three main faults are volatility, hydrogen sulphide, and oversulphuring. The first gives the wine a vinegary or sherry-like taste, not difficult to spot; the second the smell of rotten eggs; the third a burned rubbery aroma. This last is not to be confused with almost the same phenomenon with Pinotage, so practise on a few Pinotages and learn the difference. With Pinotage the rubberiness is more enmeshed with the sweet fruit whereas with sulphur there is a 'fireworky' and detached quality to the phenomenon.

Lesson Four: Smelling and Gargling the Part

You can easily master tasting technique. You pour out the wine sufficient to meet the depth of a thumbnail. You regard its colour. You sniff around it like a wise hound. You agitate the glass, a proper tasting glass or better, a big so-called Bordeaux or Burgundy glass, to release the esters of the perfume and so better to appreciate the aromas, the nuances of the bouquet. You inhale these odiferous pleasantries, or unpleasantries, through the chimney of the taste, the nostrils (the only access to the brain open to the air) and then you taste.

You swill the liquid around the mouth and breathe in air so that this liquid is aerated and experienced by your tastebuds. The tastebuds are arranged in sectors of differently orientated cohesion (one sensitive to salinity, another alkalinity, another sweetness and so on). They connect with the brain which in turn provides the sensory data, memory based, to form the taster's view of what s(he) is drinking. Some of the wine is permitted to contact the back of the throat, but only an incredibly tiny amount is allowed to proceed down the gullet, so that the finish of the wine can be studied. Then the wine is ejected and several seconds left to elapse whilst all these sensations are considered as the impression the wine has left is mulled over.

Lesson Five: Spitting the Part

It will help, of course, if you possess the appropriate physical appearance to expectorate. This will confer gravitas. Just as we cannot conceive of a premium division striker turning out on the pitch wearing designer sunglasses or a boxer clambering into the ring sporting a hearing aid, the wine taster must approach the business of wine tasting looking the business. Indeed, the wine taster can get away with both the accessories just mentioned; rather than being despised for a blind, deaf old fart, s(he) would be looked upon with reverence.

A cricketer approaching the crease with a bat in one hand and a walking stick in the other would be greeted somewhat derisively also, but for the wine taster this perambulatory aid would be seen merely as testament to gout (an eye patch is also arresting but by now I think you have grasped my point). If you can lay genetic claim to a toffee nose and offer the sociological proof of a plum in the mouth, in addition to all the qualities referred to above, you are home and dry.

A toffee nose and a plum in the mouth were, of course, once essential qualifications for a wine taster, but these days anything goes. However, style is important. Therefore, affect an air of utter disdain when tasting and keep the chin up. Et voilà! You have grown a toffee nose and to acquire the plummy vowels simply imitate Joanna Lumley.

Two observations must be made here. The first is that when the wine is ejected you must do this with passion and not incline the head, so losing the toffee nose you have so assiduously cultured. NEVER DRIBBLE OUT THE WINE WITH YOUR HEAD OVER THE SPITTOON. You must spit with your chin horizontal, aiming at the spittoon which is never nearer than eighteen inches. Suck in the cheeks and fire out the wine in one steady stream. Other tasters will note your technique and be overawed. You can practise it with water. Use the kitchen sink at home to get it dead right. If you have children, they will join in this game with enthusiasm and it'll keep them off drugs.

Lesson Six: Speaking the Part (technical)

The next trick to master is spoken command of the subject's technical arcana. Thus, a wine does not possess smell: it has a 'nose'. A wine's flavour is its 'palate' (further fragmented into mid-palate and back-palate). Any oaked wine you find unpalatable simply announce 'the phenolics of the wood are smothering the fruit' and you will be considered sage-like.

Curiously, 'terroir' enters into the picture here. Terroir is bullshit and manures all French vines. It merely means essence of place. If you are at a blind tasting it does not really matter if you guess all the wines incorrectly; what counts is being able to identify certain aromatic and taste factors which provide clues as to where the wine could have come from.

Thus a minty Cabernet is from Coonawarra. Or rather it might be. However, you achieve kudos merely by mentioning the fact (even if the wine turns out to be Moroccan). Any Pinot Noir, brick-dust red and smelling of shit, or Chardonnay from the new world, for example, can be described as being Burgundian and any leathery Merlot like Pomerol. Any red with a sweet after-taste can safely be categorised as Aussie, but if there is some tannin in it you will notch up brownie points if you narrow it down to Western Australia or McLaren Vale. There are, in fact (whatever the soi-disant experts will tell you), very few wines expressive of any terroir which is so distinct anyone can spot it. Two magnificent exceptions are Loire Cabernet Francs which have the tang of lead pencils and Moselle Rieslings which reek of slatey minerals.

The clue to a wine is in the soul of the wine maker not the soil of the vineyard (whatever the bullshitters may tell you), and so you may safely claim this when closely questioned.

Lesson Seven: Speaking the Part (fantasy)

The greatest book ever published on wine tasting (dwarfing even my own mould-breaking effort *The Sensational Liquid*) was written by Evelyn Waugh. In *Brideshead Revisited* one of the many things Charles Ryder discovers through his relationship with Sebastian Flyte is a 'serious acquaintance' with wine.

> We warmed the glass slightly at a candle, filled it a third high, swirled the wine round, nursed it in our hands, held it to the light, breathed it, sipped it, filled our mouths with it, and rolled it over the tongue, ringing it on the palate like a coin on a counter, tilted our heads back and let it trickle down the throat. . .
> '. . . it is a little, shy wine like a gazelle.'
> 'Like a leprechaun.'
> 'Dappled, in a tapestry window.'
> 'Like a flute by still water.'
> '. . . and this is a wise old wine.'
> 'A prophet in a cave.'
> '. . . And this is a necklace of pearls on a white neck.'
> 'Like a swan.'
> 'Like the last unicorn.'

What brilliance is here! What a lesson for us all! Who would not like to be so Wildean as spontaneously to describe a young Riesling as 'a necklace of pearls on a white neck'?

Better yet, who would not like to taste such a wine? Study the above closely.

Your rewards will come as you jostle with the crowd at an important tasting: Oz at one elbow, Gilly at the other, Charles Metcalfe burbling behind you. As they rabbit on about ugli fruit and sesame seeds and ginger root you trill out, 'It's like a necklace of pearls on a white neck' (this time, for a Kiwi Sauvignon Blanc) or 'It's like a flute by still water' (post-expectoration Monbazillac). The throng will fall quiet. Charles will fall at your feet. Gilly will kiss you on both cheeks. Oz will invite you down the pub (if your skirt's short enough).

What is the essential truth here? That you may make of a wine what you will. I once wrote that one particular Aussie Shiraz had the 'aroma of a sumo-wrestler's jock strap' and this so impressed Giles MacDonagh of the *Financial Times* that he's been writing me fan letters ever since.

Once you have mastered all of the above, you can call yourself a wine educator and apply to join the Circle of Wine Writers. This is a loose association of twats (one wit called it the Ellipse of Idiots), but you will find it useful in the beginning and although some members are PR reps or publishers or otherwise moonlight for the wine trade they are an amiable bunch of old soaks and not all are frauds. You will also, having mastered the above, be able to sail through the higher certificate examinations of the Wine Education Trust and you can contemplate going on to take the Master of Wine exams. This is a trade qualification solely (though this does not prevent certain masters of wine, some of whom wholly pretentiously insist on appending the initials MW after their names even when answering their telephones, from being incapable of finding decent wine for trade sale).

However, I would advise you, whatever the number of tastebuds it has, to take your tongue out of your cheek if you wish to notch up an MW. Members of its Institute take themselves very seriously indeed. My tongue, needless to remark, is always in my cheek and is not removed whether I am writing or tasting.

ALDI

Holly Lane,
Atherstone,
Warwickshire CV9 2SQ

Tel: (01827) 711800
Fax: (01827) 710899
Customer help-line: (08705) 134 262

Website: www.aldi.com

For Aldi wines 15.5 points and under visit
www.superplonk.com

16.5

Château Calbet Cabardes 2001

Here I am sitting in my little office, on Monday
afternoon, in front of my keyboard, wondering which
wines to choose for my weekly column, and a bloke
(looks like a psychotherapist down on his luck, you
know the sort) is walking, at a fair lick (wants to avoid
the next downpour), along my street carrying a very
full Aldi carrier bag in each hand. Is it an omen?
Where has he come from? The nearest store to me in
London NW3 is NW9. Can he have walked that far?
Now I appreciate a cynic might remark that he has
been hired to go and up and down my street with Aldi
carrier bags in the hope of catching my eye but I
really don't think this company goes in for that (or has
the imagination to even think of it) and in any case
how could they know an empty bottle of Aldi's
Château Calbet Cabardes 2001 is sitting beside my
iMac where it has been for a week since I downed its
contents? It is a remarkably couth yet characterful red
wine, gently rich and full of interest. It suggests
tobacco, chocolate, has a soft hint of licorice and there
are cherries on the finish. It's not a big fat wine or
clotted, it couldn't be for its absurdly reasonable price.
Cabardes, uniquely for a Languedoc appellation,
allows Bordeaux's Merlot and Cabernet grapes to be
grown and the wine features these in its blend along
with local favourites Syrah and Grenache. Aldi says
the wine has 28% Syrah in fact, though the wine's
back label claims 15%. More interestingly, the back
label also tells us the wine has not been fined or

filtered which means it has more character though it will have a little sediment. More worryingly (but that's Aldi for you), if you ring the store's help-line on 08705 134 262 you are told you can't ring individual stores because they are ex-directory but there is a website with stores' addresses at the address above. Let's hope that dodgy-looking psychotherapist made it home before the heavens opened.

16.5   RED £3.99

Le Brasset Grenache/Syrah 2001   FRANCE

A terrific blend of 60% Grenache and 40% Syrah of textured gamey ripeness and richness. Deliciously cultured softness yet really deep-finishing, characterful dryness. Sometimes out of stock, this wine cannot be ordered because Aldi doesn't go in for fancy retailing manoeuvres like that.

16   WHITE £3.49

Mayrah Estates Chardonnay NV   AUSTRALIA

Very rich thick, gooseberry, melon and citrus fruit, rated on its brilliantly compatibility with oriental fish and poultry dishes.

Only the most shallow individuals fail to judge by first appearances. Even the most experienced wine critic is swayed by his first glimpse of the words Château Lafite on a label. This is why if you eliminate labels from your dinner table's bottles, by using jugs, carafes or decanters, the first impression a wine makes is controlled by you.

16 WHITE DESSERT (50cl bottle) £2.99

St Amandus Beerenauslese 2001 GERMANY
Brilliant, value-for-money dessert wine with soft,
Greek honey and peach fruit.

16 RED £2.99

Chemin du Papes, Côtes du Rhône 2001 FRANCE
The perfect cheap house wine. Authentic earthy
berries, touch of tannins, hint of tar.

16 RED £3.99

Ransomes Vale NV AUSTRALIA
Delicious mouth-filling, tarry, gently floral fruit of
savouriness and class.

16 FORTIFIED £3.29

Fletchers Amontillado Sherry SPAIN
Bargain! Lovely baked apricot and molasses – rich
fruit which goes dry. A brilliant warm weather
aperitif.

16 FORTIFIED £3.29

Fletchers Cream Sherry SPAIN
Bargain cheap sweetness (edge of toffee and crème
brûlée) to have with ice-cream.

16 RED £2.99

Chilean Cabernet Sauvignon NV CHILE
Hugely attractive chocolate-undertoned berries with a
touch of grilled nut and firm racy tannins. Excellent
with cheese dishes, pasties, casseroles.

16

RED £4.99

FRANCE

Ile La Forge Cabernet Sauvignon, Vin de Pays d'Oc 2002

Vegetal, subtly peppery, very attractive tannins, well berried, smooth yet has some discrete suggestion of ruggedness underneath it all. Great value, great Cabernet quaffing.

ASDA

Head Office:
Asda House,
Southbank,
Great Wilson Street,
Leeds LS11 5AD

Tel: (0500) 100055 (230 branches nationwide)
Fax: (0113) 2417732

Website: www.asda.co.uk

For Asda wines of 15.5 points and under visit
www.superplonk.com

17.5
RED £7.78

Château Gigault, Premières Côtes de Blaye 1998 FRANCE
Terrific stuff! Real chocolate and cocoa undertone to
toasted blackberries and raspberries with frisky
tannins. Brilliant vintage from a desperately under-
rated appellation.

17
RED £8.48

Errazuriz Max Reserva Cabernet 2000 CHILE
It's like whacky Claret married to an eccentric Barolo,
cousin to McLaren Vale Cabernet who's slept with a
Crozes-Hermitage. Can you make sense of that? Okay.
Let's just say you get roasted berries with a touch of
wild strawberry, raunchy tannins and a finish which
makes you sit up and ask for another glass.

17
RED £4.96

Sagramosa Pasqua Valpolicella Superiore 1999 ITALY
This is an absolutely scrumptious performance from a
trio you may not have heard of before. These are (with
their constituent percentages in the wine) Corvina
70%, Rondinella 15%, Corvinone 15%. These grape
varieties present us with licorice, marzipan, a hint of
spice, roasted berries, and gripping but lithe tannins.
The wine is grown on the clay and limestone hills of
the valley of Illasi, a little way out of Verona – the
home town, need it be pointed out, of Shakespeare's
soppiest and most insufferably romantic couple
(which judgement can refer to Proteus and Valentine,
the two eponymous gentlemen of Verona, as much as
it does to randy Romeo and jittery Juliet). But there is

nothing soppy about this wine though it could be used as a romantic prop. It is aged for a year in oak barriques and this has bequeathed a backbone of seriousness to the wine which is belied by that price-tag. Wine maker Giancarlo Zanel, working for the three Pasqua brothers – Carlo, Umberto and Giorgio – has turned in a masterful wine. It is on sale at 125 Asda stores and to check if your local branch is one of them call Freephone (0500) 100055.

17 WHITE £6.01

Réserve du Baron de Turckheim Alsace FRANCE
Gewürztraminer 2000
Now this wine is in fact from a single vineyard, Herrenweg. And it is lovely. It has very dry spicy rose-petal fruit – hint of apricot here as well – and the class is outstanding for the money. It will, I feel, gain by cellaring for 2–4 years when it will get oilier and more sensual. This wine is superb with grilled spicy prawns.

17 FORTIFIED £6.98

Asda LBV Port 1996 PORTUGAL
Interesting aroma of fried tomatoes and some kind of herb. The fruit is raunchy and rich, uncluttered plum and sensual, and the tannins are tenacious to the point of rudeness – delicious!!!!

'Wine allows me to stay young and live forever. Every
time I open a bottle I'm reborn.' Agnes Champ

16.5

RED £5.48

Errazuriz Cabernet Sauvignon 2001 CHILE
Full of interest and provocative turns and twists. Has
cassis, chocolate and a hint of mint but it's the savoury
tannins and roasted plums which predominate.

16.5

WHITE (3 litre box) £13.09

35 South Chardonnay NV CHILE
A stunningly well-packed-with-goodies Chardonnay of
great class and elegance. Lovely smoky, oily fruit, great
melon, lychee and citrus (subtle but worth searching
for) and the texture and finish are exemplary. In 82
stores.

16.5

RED (3 litre box) £13.11

35 South Cabernet Sauvignon NV CHILE
Superbly muscular, deftly woven plums and berries
here, with touches of chocolate. Good firm tannins
and even an echo of coffee on the finish. In 82 stores.

16

WHITE £4.94

Brown Brothers Dry Muscat 2002 AUSTRALIA
Unusual dry spicy lychee and pear with touches of
Ogen melon – but it's all dry and very slightly spicy. A
wonderful aperitif tipple.
Also at Tesco.

16

RED £2.58

Asda Claret Red NV FRANCE
Are you good at lying? Are you plagued by wine
bores? These are not essential qualifications for

purchasing this wine but they can add immeasurably to the fun of it. When I noted its price ticket, my tastebuds veritably bristled with incredulity but then I poured the wine, looked at its plausible colour, noted the savoury aroma beneath my nostrils, and when the classy berries (Merlot, Cabernets Sauvignon and Franc) and accompanying tannins gallantly thumped the tastebuds the latter were bowled over. The wine is on sale at 107 Asda stores and you can enjoy it with anything from a cheese risotto to roast chicken and rare meats, but for the wickedest entertainment get together a decanter and a wine bore. You pour the wine into the former and then invite the latter to pour the wine into himself. Now invite the bore to guess which second-growth Médoc it is. When you reveal the truth he'll never darken your door, or your dinner-table cloth, again.

16

RED £2.97

Asda Corbières NV

FRANCE

Delicious strawberry and blackberry fruit with biscuity tannins. Real texture and class here. The price tag is absurdly easy to swallow but so is the wine (and these things do not always follow).

16

RED £4.98

Fitou Réserve La Montagne 2000

FRANCE

Firm chocolate richness here, clotted tannins which grip, and finesse to the finish.

16   RED £4.48

Rasteau Domaine de Wilfried, Côtes du   FRANCE
Rhone-Villages 2000
Delightfully forward wine with touches of burned
cocoa powder and leather and a hint of herbs (you
know the sort of thing, those aromatic Provençal
smelly things poking out of the scrub). The effect is
of lovely lashings of berries and tannins and though
the wine does bludgeon the throat it is a kindly
beating.

16   RED £5.48

Côtes du Rhône Belleruche Chapoutier 2000   FRANCE
Very classy and ripe with a delicious charred edge to
the berries.

16   RED £14.78

La Bernardine Châteauneuf du Pape 2000   FRANCE
Expensive Christmas treat this complex specimen. It
offers layers of blackberries and firm tannins, with
subtle interleavings of herbs and nuts. This is the
answer to the question: 'Look, doll, I must go and
spend fifteen quid at Asda on something sexy, so what
do I buy?'

16   WHITE SPARKLING £3.97

Asda Cava NV   SPAIN
Crisp, undertone of Ogen melon. Real class in a glass
and that price makes a mockery of more expensive
bubblies.

16

WHITE SPARKLING £6.49

Asda Vintage Cava 2000 SPAIN

The difference between this at £6.49, and its same
rating cousin at £3.97, is that you do get more texture
for your money and the wine, as a result, is more
luxurious and poles ahead of many champagnes at
twice and three times the price.

16

WHITE £5.98

Booarra Chenin Blanc 2001 AUSTRALIA

A crisply classic Chenin. Lovely touches of pineapple and
pear as an undertone. Classy texture provides elegance.

16

WHITE £2.96

Asda Chilean Sauvignon Blanc 2002 CHILE

One of the UK'S tastiest under three quid wines. It's
not, admittedly, hugely complex, but it has a rich yet
controlled texture and it performs diligently on the
palate without pretension or phoniness.

16

RED £4.87

Norton Malbec 2002 ARGENTINA

Dry, chewy plums, touch of savoury cherry. Good soft
grip to the fruit. Fits the tastebuds like a soft leather
Gucci loafer the feet – touch of luxury about it.

16

RED £2.96

Asda Chilean Merlot 2002 CHILE

Rich, gripping, faintly leathery plums and cherries. The
tannins are civilised and grip well but not raspingly.

Cork is a pain in the neck of every bottle of wine. It not
only contaminates a significant percentage of wine
(industry estimates are between 5 and 15%) but causes
bottles to vary in performance – dramatically so in
wine designed to be cellared for years.

16

RED £3.48
CHILE

35 South Cabernet/Merlot 2002
Excellent forthright berried richness and lip-
smackingly firm tannins. Hint of chocolate on the
finish.

16

RED £2.98
CHILE

Asda Chilean Cabernet Sauvignon 2001
Terrific turn of speed on the tongue, then goes dry
and lingering. Offers plum and cherries, brisk tannins
and dries to reveal a subtle catering-chocolate
undertone.

16

RED £3.48
SOUTH AFRICA

Dumisani Pinotage/Shiraz 2002
Exotic, funky, savoury, chewy, ripe, forward, young,
gauche – brilliant with spicy food.

16

RED £5.77
SOUTH AFRICA

Boekenhoutskloof The Wolf Trap 2002
This is one of those exuberant, brash, full frontal
fruity Cape reds which must make Europeans
despair. Lovely rubbery plums, spice and deep rich
jam. There is also some licorice in there. It is made

by one of the rising stars of the Cape wine scene, Marc Kent (in whose soft beard I saw no sign of larks or hens, owls or wrens, or anything remotely Leary, and I very much doubt any wolves let alone traps have been seen on the property in his lifetime). Also at Oddbins.

16
WHITE (3 litre box) £9.47
Asda French House Wine NV
FRANCE
An 80% Ugni Blanc, 20% Colombard, Rousanne and Marsanne blend which is crisp, clear, and superbly quaffable. The price works out at less than 40p a glass and so the occasional tippler, who overspends, perhaps, on three-legged race horses, will find the economy presented by this box to his advantage as he takes his everyday glass or two.

16
WHITE (3 litre box) £9.88
Asda Soave NV
ITALY
What lovely, crunchy gooseberriness, with a hint of grilled nut. Fresh and crisp of course, but has real classy edge to the fruit.

There was a time when the mark of a gentleman and a wine scholar was his knowledge of the dates of the great French and German vintages. Nowadays it is not years and châteaux the shrewd wine drinker needs to retain in his or her head, but which days of which months the supermarkets have their sales offers.

16

RED   (3 litre box) £11.12

Asda French Cabernet Sauvignon, Vin de Pays   FRANCE
d'Oc NV

What good, polished (yet faintly ruffled) rustic tippling
we have here. The fruit grips, charmingly, and it's
great with bangers and mash. In 82 stores.

16

RED £5.03

Fairview Goats du Roam 2002   SOUTH AFRICA

Tar and plums, roasted edge to the tannins, a finish of
morello cherry. Very bright fleshy plums, hint of
strawberries with a fine dusting of tannins. An excellent
casserole red.

Also at Booths, Morrison's, Oddbins, Sainsbury's,
Somerfield and Tesco.

BOOTHS

4–6 Fishergate,
Preston,
Lancashire PR1 3LJ

Tel: (01772) 251701
Fax: (01772) 255642

(Outlets throughout Cheshire,
Lancashire and Yorkshire)

E-mail: admin@booths-supermarkets.co.uk
Website: www.everywine.co.uk

For Booths' wines 15.5 points and under visit
www.superplonk.com

17.5

Wither Hills Chardonnay 2001   NEW ZEALAND

Screwcap. A wonderfully cheeky Chardonnay offering
a view of the grape which embraces Burgundian
vegetality and Australian richness. Huge class in a
glass. Like a refined Corton-Charlemagne so vegetal,
hay-edged, dry, toasted and. . . but this is to insult the
wine. No white Burgundy under £40 comes close.
Also at Oddbins.

17.5

RED £18.99

Amarone della Valpolicella Classico, Azienda   ITALY
Agricola Brigaldara 1999

A stunning treat and the ultimate Christmas
companion. The spiced berries and coffee-edged
tannins, sweet cherries and dry herbs would work to
overwhelming effect with that festive fowl or any
game dish with a fruity sauce.

17

RED £5.79

Château Pierrail, Bordeaux Supérieur 2001   FRANCE
A superbly well-collected claret offering the usual
berries – with a twist. The twist is chewy licorice
and chocolate, heavy and dark. The finish is
riveting.

17

WHITE £8.99

Clos d'Yvigne Cuvée Saint Nicholas, Bergerac   FRANCE
2000
Anyone who has ever dreamed of owning a patch of
vines in France and making wine should read Patricia

Atkinson's book *The Ripening Sun* (Century, £12.99). The title seems as banal as a cornflakes slogan but it refers to the author's own maturing as much as her grapes'. Ms Atkinson is an author of stout and manifold resources and she will doubtless inspire the dreamers because, against seemingly impossible odds (she didn't speak French, lousy marriage, knew nothing about oenology), she has conjured wines of great finesse from her hectares, Clos d'Yvigne in the Côtes de Bergerac. Three of the fruits of her devoted labours are now on sale in the UK. Cuvée Nicholas Bergerac is a blend of Sauvignon, Sémillon and Muscadelle grapes, fermented in French oak barrels and unfiltered. It has a gently oily texture, sinuous and sensual, and it offers crushed under-ripe Charentais melon, grapefruit, thyme, and a touch of lemon and orange peel on the finish. It is a seriously scrumptious white wine of considerable class and demeanour. *The Ripening Sun* is a more passionate tale than Anna Karenina's and all the more moving for being non-fiction and all the more incredible for never using the words romance, love or sex. This inspiring and delicate story (as delicate as the Atkinson wines) is one of the most attractively written and unpretentious stories of *la vrai vie rustique française* and surely the most striking since Peter Mayle's. Indeed, *mangez votre coeur dehors, Pete mon vieux, vous avez rencontrez votre allumette.*

Also at Waitrose.

17

RED £2.99

Domaine de la Bastide, Vin de Pays d'Hauterive FRANCE
2000

This vivacious red is amongst the highest rating
under-three-quid superplonks this book has ever
boasted. It has noteworthy tannins, layers of cherry,
strawberry and plum fruit, and a solid texture. It won't
age much above 6 months from purchase but then it
isn't designed to. Decant it an hour before drinking
and watch the wine snobs and bores compete to name
which Haut Médoc château it comes from (whilst you
sit there with a wicked smile on your face).

17

WHITE £6.99

Hermit Crab Marsanne Viognier, D'Arenberg AUSTRALIA
Vineyards 2002

Complex layer of very dry peach, apricot and Brazil
nut interleaved with a touch of tannin and white
chocolate (subtle).

17

WHITE £8.49

Jordan Estate Chardonnay 2002 SOUTH AFRICA

Offers some lovely subtle touches of grilled melon,
nuts and pineapple.
Also at Waitrose.

16.5

RED £7.99

Rasteau Cuvée Prestige, Domaine des Coteaux FRANCE
de Travers 2000

Coats the teeth, verily, with chocolate, prunes, coriander
and black olives. Enough of a feast for anyone.

Red wine is deeper and richer than white since it uses the skins of the grapes for colour and chemical extraction (most importantly the tannins), whereas white only flirts with the skins, but in spite of this I still regard Riesling as as great a grape as any red. White wine is more difficult to make as interesting as red wine because with the latter the skins are involved. With skins comes the colour, which is why red wine is red, as well as polyphenolic chemicals like tannins and other character-building elements. Red wine is generally more complex than white as a result. It is the reason why drinkable cheap reds are in more plentiful supply than cheap whites. There is more for the red wine wine maker to play with.

16.5

RED £8.99

Château Maris Cru La Livinière, Minervois 2000   FRANCE
Superb teeth-frightening thickness of raspberry and roasted cherries with thick tannins and balsamic intensity.

16.5

RED £5.99

Apaltagua Carmenere 2001   CHILE
Lush and lovely yet disciplined by scrumptious tannins. Delightful lingering finish.

16.5

WHITE £7.99

Montana Reserve Barrique Chardonnay 2002   NEW ZEALAND
If only white Burgundy would achieve this woody vegetality so classily and silkily.

16.5
RED £4.49

Beauvignac Préférence Merlot, Vin de Pays   FRANCE
d'Oc 2001
Stunningly complete and confident. Offers roasted
berries, chocolate and tobacco. All you need is a glass
(and a searching nose).

16.5
WHITE SPARKLING £18.99

Champagne Fleury Brut Biodynamic NV   FRANCE
Delicious, complex, dry, and very, very classy. Unites
teasing fruit and nuts.

16.5
RED £5.69

Mas Collet Celler de Capcanes, Montsant   SPAIN
2000
It flows over the tongue like apologetic lava: warm,
smouldering, and . . . well, tongue tingling.
Also in Waitrose.

16.5
WHITE £3.79

Château de Péranger Picpoul de Pinet, Cave   FRANCE
Co-op de Pomerols 2002
Gorgeous! Satin-textured at first then it goes chalky
and chewy. The fruit is mango, pineapple and citrus
(all subtle yet a sum of the parts).

16.5
RED £8.99

Clos d'Yvigne Le Petit Prince, Bergerac 2000   FRANCE
Three of the fruits of Patricia Atkinson's devoted
labours are now on sale in the UK and this specimen,
mostly Merlot with some Cabernet Franc, is a joy to

drink, offering globules of flavour which shift reluctantly throatwards. The savourily berried fruit is rugged yet smooth, handsome yet characterful, chewy yet fresh, and the tannins are balanced and teasing. For further details of the estate, see the entry for Clos d'Yvigne Saint Nicholas above.

16.5
WHITE £5.49

Peter Lehmann The Barossa Sémillon 2001　　AUSTRALIA
Really classy lemon, mineralised apricot, touch of nut, and very fine acids. Will age well for up to 8 years.

16.5
WHITE £6.49

Château Crabitan Bellevue, Ste-Croix du Mont 1999　　FRANCE
Yes, it's rich and sweet, but it has a glorious toffee-apple and pineapple richness which contrives to be dryish.

16
RED £5.99

Alamos Bonarda 2002　　ARGENTINA
Fruity but full of feeling, deep yet cheap, dry and ripe yet with a certain lingering delicacy. However, the theme is up-front richness and immediacy.

16
WHITE £7.49

Morgenhof 2001　　SOUTH AFRICA
Delicious pineapple, pear and melon richness. Very heartening and charming.
Also stocked at London Stores (Harrods) and Small Merchants (The Bristol Wine Co.).

16   RED SPARKLING £6.49

Concerto Lambrusco Reggiano Medici   ITALY
Ermete 2002
The real thing. A sparkling red tasting of raspberry
and roasted almonds.

16   WHITE SPARKLING £6.99

Chapel Down Brut NV   UK
An attractive, gently nutty bubbly. The most attractive
English sparkling wine I've tasted. Real character. No
bullshit.

16   WHITE SPARKLING £6.99

Sparkling Burgundy, Cave de Lugny Méthode   FRANCE
Traditionelle NV
Delicious dry citrus, very classy.

16   WHITE SPARKLING £11.99

Champagne Baron-Fuente NV   FRANCE
Most unusually dry, raspberry-edged bubbly. Classic
stuff.

16   WHITE SPARKLING £19.99

Bruno Paillard Première Cuvée NV   FRANCE
Easily one of the most stylish of twenty-quid
champagnes and more elegant than Bollinger, Krug
and Dom Pérignon.

16   WHITE £3.99

Château Lamôthe-Vincent, Bordeaux Sec 2002   FRANCE
Delicious crushed gooseberry, peach and citrus fruit.
Classy, amazingly cheap.

16

WHITE £4.29

Domaine Mont-Auriol Marsanne, Vin de Pays de FRANCE
Côtes de Thongue 2002
Delightfully melon, lime and dry apricot.

16

WHITE £4.99

Palacio de Bornos Rueda 2002 SPAIN
Fine lemon, peach, and lime-edged tangerine. A
superb aperitif whistle-whetter.

16

WHITE £4.99

Poema Sauvignon Blanc, Vino de la Tierra, SPAIN
Castilla y Leon 2002
Delicious dry grapefruit and pineapple.

16

WHITE £4.99

Casablanca White Label Chardonnay 2002 CHILE
Very calm fruit yet it impacts with melon, lemon and
white peach.

16

WHITE £4.99

Concha y Toro Casillero del Diablo Viognier 2002 CHILE
Very subtle lime and apricot fruit, a hint of tannin, a
touch of grilled citrus.

16

WHITE £4.99

Firefinch Colombar/Chardonnay 2002 SOUTH AFRICA
A superb whistle-wetter: dry, elegant yet fruitily
purposeful.

16

WHITE £5.79

Coteaux de Giennois, Jean Dumont 2002   FRANCE

Intense, grassy, made for oysters. Supremely good
with oysters. To the mollusc born.

16

WHITE £5.99

Château Tahbik Marsanne 2001   AUSTRALIA

The hint of subtle toffee (yeah, that's how subtle a hint
can get) is a touching delight to the fresh, keen wine.

16

WHITE £6.99

Gewürztraminer Aimé Stentz, Vin d'Alsace 2001   FRANCE

Rated as an accompaniment to rich oriental cuisine
only. The wine is hugely aromatic, rosy, spicy and
musky. It cannot be drunk unaccompanied.

16

WHITE £6.99

Springfield Estate Sauvignon Blanc,   SOUTH AFRICA
Life from Stone 2002

Very chewy with a ripe grapefruit edge to the
regulation gooseberry.

16

WHITE £6.99

Babich Vineyards Riesling 2002   NEW ZEALAND

Very complete performer now but will age gloriously
for the next 8–10 years. Offers complex pineapple,
lime and minerals.

If wine is the most sensual liquid on earth then isn't
this book the ultimate sex and shopping guide?

16

WHITE £6.99

Bonterra Chardonnay/Sauvignon Blanc/ CALIFORNIA, USA
Muscat Organic 2002

Interesting chewy edge to the pineapple and melon.

16

WHITE £7.99

Riesling Grand Cru Sommerberg Aimé Stentz, FRANCE
Vin d'Alsace 2000

Unusual nutty edge to this elegant yet thrusting white
wine, which offers unusually dry citrus, pineapple,
lemon and a hint of petrol.

16

WHITE £7.99

CV Unwooded Chardonnay, Capel Vale 2001 AUSTRALIA

Dry, untypically Euro-style Chardonnay with lovely
lingering toasted nuts and subtle tannic citrus.

16

WHITE £7.99

Dashwood Marlborough Sauvignon NEW ZEALAND
Blanc 2002

Limey, grapefruit, crushed gooseberry fruit. Very
classy and well textured.

16

WHITE £10.99

Brown Brothers Family Reserve Chardonnay AUSTRALIA
1997

Outstanding balance of wood and fruit really justifies
the outlay on barrels. A finely knitted blend of finesse
and flavour, subtlety and oomph.

16

ROSÉ £3.69

Nagyrede Estate Cabernet Rosé 2002 HUNGARY

One of the few rosés worthy of a glass in my house.
Good firm dry cherries.

16

RED £2.99

Viña Alarba Tinto Calatayud, Bodegas y Viñedos SPAIN
del Jalon 2000

Thundering good value for money. A tangy, berried
wine of licorice and lithe tannicity.

16

RED £4.99

Château Cluzan, Bordeaux 2000 FRANCE

Classy claret. Bargain price-ticket. Tannins and
blackberries in firm liaison.

16

RED £5.49

Alamos Bonarda 2001 ARGENTINA

Intense roasted plums and tobacco-edged tannins. Big
on flavour here.

16

RED £4.99

Château de Lascaux, Coteaux de Languedoc FRANCE
Classique 2001

Deliciously chewy and well roasted berries coated in
chocolate tannins.

16

RED £4.99

Château La Bastide, Corbières 2001 FRANCE

Lush but not OTT, the fruit proceeds stealthily to
reward the patient drinker with roasted almonds and
biscuity tannins.

16

RED £4.99

Fairview Goats du Roam 2002 SOUTH AFRICA

Tar and plums, roasted edge to the tannins, a finish of
morello cherry. Very bright fleshy plums, hint of
strawberries with a fine dusting of tannins. An
excellent casserole red.

Also at Asda, Morrisons, Oddbins, Sainsbury's,
Somerfield and Tesco.

16

RED £5.99

Firefinch What the Birds Left, SOUTH AFRICA
Ripe Red 2002

Very fresh and grippingly tannic undertone to ripe
cherries and pert berries. Has a brisk insouciance of
great charm. I visit many wine estates in a year and
talk to a good few producers. Springfield is one of the
most serious yet happiest I have encountered. It is
possible to be committed yet not fanatical, detached yet
not insular, wild without being whacky, and humane
without being sentimental – this is the remarkable
Springfield Estate run by Jeanette and her brother, the
wine maker, Abrie Bruwer.

16

RED £5.99

Viña Carmen Insigne Merlot 2001 CHILE

Very chocolatey wine. Very. You could pour it over ice-
cream.

16

RED £6.49

Ironstone Shiraz/Grenache 2001 AUSTRALIA

Unusually floral Grenache with delicious nuts, chocolate
and berries. Very dynamic approach to the grape.

What is an organic wine? There is no such thing, but
there is such a thing as wine made from organic
grapes. Such grapes are raised without the intrusion of
artificial fertilisers, pesticides, fungicides and
herbicides.
Will the absence of such repulsive adornments mean
you can drink and suffer no hangovers? No. Alcohol
causes hangovers, not infinitesimal residues of any of
the chemicals mentioned above. Organic wine
specialists who pretend that people who drink their
wines will avoid hangovers are liars.

16

RED £6.99

Guelbenzu Blue Label Ribera del Queiles 2001   SPAIN
Ripe plums coated with firm tannins. A very
controlled, polished performance.

16

RED £6.99

Domaine Combebelle Syrah/Grenache,   FRANCE
St Chinian 2000
Rustic richness with some modern touches.
Very herby and homely but knowing and all-
embracing.

16

RED £7.99

Poliziano Rosso di Montepulciano Azienda   ITALY
Agricola 2001
Very tobacco-ey and deep with a sense of lushness
not, deliciously, fully realised.

16

RED £8.99

Jordan Estate Cabernet Sauvignon 2000   SOUTH AFRICA
Deliciously complete and well kitted out with
chocolate and intense, lingering tannins.

16

RED £8.99

Spice Route Pinotage 2000   SOUTH AFRICA
One of the Cape's most perfect expressions of the
Pinotage grape.
Also available at Waitrose, where there are further
details of the wine maker and the estate.

16

RED £9.99

Peter Lehmann Futures Shiraz 2001   AUSTRALIA
A veritable fruit soup, savoury and thickly knitted and
full of interesting and nourishing bits and bobs.

16

RED (50cl bottle) £11.99

Pansal del Calas Celler de Capcanes, Montsant   USA
Vino de Licor 2000
Oh yes! A wine to drink with chocolate pudding.
Sheer heaven.

BUDGENS

**Stonefield Way,
Ruislip, Middlesex HA4 0JR**

Tel: (020) 8422 9511

Customer Services:
Tel: (0800) 526 002
Fax: (020) 8864 2800

E-mail: info@budgens.co.uk
Website: www.budgens.com

For Budgens' wines of 15.5 points and under visit
www.superplonk.com

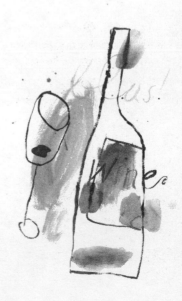

16.5

WHITE £8.49

Bonterra Chardonnay, Fetzer 2001 CALIFORNIA, USA

Organic grapes contribute a luxurious texture to this
spicily pear and peach wine (subtle spices note) with a
lovely creamy finish of style and concentration.
Also at Sainsbury's.

16.5

WHITE £4.99

Argento Chardonnay 2002 ARGENTINA

A very classy, superbly textured wine with touches of
grilled melon and gooseberry with fresh pear. Finishes
with a touch of cream and smoke. Really yummy stuff.

16.5

WHITE DESSERT (half bottle) £9.99

Brown Brothers Liqueur Muscat NV AUSTRALIA

Superbly balsamic-textured molasses, spiced peach
and plum and crème caramel. Excellent with desserts
as rich as they come. Especially good with Ferrero
Rocher chocolates, and the research undertaken to
confirm this idea has been long and arduous.

16.5

RED £4.99

La Baume Merlot, Vin de Pays d'Oc 2001 FRANCE

Superb roasted, savourily delicious berries with spicy
tannins and a hint of chocolate. A lovely warm, classy,
serious-yet-fun mouthful of outstanding Merlot for
your money.

16.5

RED £6.99

Durius Marqués de Griñon Tempranillo 2001 SPAIN

Gorgeous tannins to lovely brisk cherries and plums.
Shows just how civilised and polished (yet

characterful) the Tempranillo grape can become.
Beautiful plump, soft texture here.
Also at Morrison's, Majestic, Sainsbury's and Thresher.

16.5
RED £4.99

Argento Malbec 2002 ARGENTINA
Such a relaxed complete performance of guile and
style here. Lovely charmed berries with svelte tannins.
Also at Somerfield.

16
WHITE £4.99

James Herrick Chardonnay, Vin de Pays FRANCE
d'Oc 2001
A beautifully polished, gently opulent, melony, fruity
wine.

16
WHITE £5.99

Fetzer Chardonnay/Viognier 2001 CALIFORNIA, USA
Good peach, melon and apricot fruit, controlled and
decently textured.

16
WHITE DESSERT (half bottle) £6.65

Brown Brothers Orange and Muscat Flora 2001 AUSTRALIA
Rich, sweet, gently spiced lemon with a hint of
raspberry and lime. A superb match with lemon tart, I
have discovered.

16
RED £4.99

James Herrick Syrah, Vin de Pays d'Oc 2001 FRANCE
Has delicious blackberry charms, grilled tannins, and
a lingering finish of charm and chewiness.

16 RED £4.99

Osborne Tempranillo/Cabernet Sauvignon, SPAIN
Solaz 2000
Very chewy, richly textured, firmly compacted red of
substance and depth. Real grip – essential in a
successful fight with food.

16 RED £5.99

Palacio de la Vega Cabernet/Tempranillo SPAIN
Crianza 1999
Offers gobbets of rich plum, cherry and blackcurrant
fruitiness allied to a hint of chocolate to the tannins.

16 RED £4.99

Canaletto Nero d'Avola 2001 SICILY, ITALY
Brisk, flavoursome berries (hint of charred plum)
combine with meaty tannins to excellent, textured effect.

16 RED £3.99

Prahova Valley Reserve Pinot Noir 2000 ROMANIA
Terrific. Sweet, touch of tar, good, brisk tannins.
Richer and deeper than its cheaper cousin with the
same grape.
Also available at Sainsbury's.

16 RED £4.99

Peter Lehmann Wild Card Shiraz 2001 AUSTRALIA
Very fresh plums and berries with a lip-smacking
savoury edge. Has a burned undertone which is very
attractive.

16

RED £9.99

Leasingham Clare Valley Shiraz 1997   AUSTRALIA
Firm, yet soft, ripe yet dry to finish, mature yet
spritely. At its peak of drinkability and classy richness.
Very deep and delicious.

16

RED £9.99

Bonterra Merlot, Fetzer   2000   CALIFORNIA, USA
An organic red of real class and sumptuously berried
richness. Has lovely gripping tannins – they clench
softly rather than bite.

16

RED £4.99

Concha y Toro Casillero del Diablo Cabernet   CHILE
Sauvignon 2001
One of Chile's most agreeably under-priced yet
delightfully over-friendly Cabs: lithe, lush yet dry,
perfectly outfitted with savoury tannins to the polished
berries.

E-TAILERS

BARRELS AND BOTTLES

E-mail: sales@barrelsandbottles.co.uk
Website: www.barrelsandbottles.co.uk

Tel: (0114) 2556611
Fax: (0114) 2551010

CHATEAUONLINE.CO.UK

Website:www.ChateauOnline.co.uk

Tel: (0800) 1692736
Fax: 0033(0)38664237

EVERYWINE

E-mail: admin@everywine.co.uk
Website: www.everywine.co.uk

Tel: (01772) 329700
Fax: (01772) 329709

EUROPEAN WINE GROWERS' ASSOCIATION

E-mail: winetime@ewga.net
Website: www.winetime.ewga.net

Tel: (01524) 701723
Fax: (02524) 701189

LAITHWAITES

E-mail: orders@laithwaites.co.uk
Website: www.laithwaites.co.uk

Tel: (0870) 4448383
Fax: (0970) 4448282

THE WINE BARN

E-mail: iris@thewinebarn.co.uk
Website: www.thewinebarn.co.uk

Tel/fax: (01962) 774102

VINTAGE ROOTS (ORGANIC WINES)

E-mail: info@vintageroots.co.uk
Website: www.vintageroots.co.uk

Tel: (0118) 976 1999
Fax: (0118) 976 1998

VIRGIN WINES

E-mail: help@virginwines.com
Website: www.virginwines.com

Tel: (0870)1642034
Fax: (01603) 619277

For all E-tailers' wines 15.5 points
and under visit
www.superplonk.com

18.5

Ehrenfelser Iphofer Kalb Eiswein 1992   GERMANY

The Wine Barn

What a magically astonishing mouthful. This is the
first specimen I've tasted of a mature example of the
Ehrenfelser grape (a cross of Riesling and Silvaner
developed at the Geisenheim wine institute in the
1920s) and it is, I think, only the second time in all –
the first time was many years ago and made no
impression on me and I've lost my notes. On this
showing, it is surprising it hasn't found greater
favour. This is an extraordinary Eiswein – which is
to say a wine made from grapes picked very late in
the season when the temperature drops to ten below
and the water in the grapes freezes solid and the
fruit become highly concentrated and balsam-like
in texture when vinified. It has huge distinction
and distinctiveness, offering a magical texture,
clotted yet not cloying, and the flavours of raspberry,
lime, pineapple, apple, lychee and gooseberry with a
coating of balancing acids. It is a great wine to
drink now, for the sheer hedonistic pleasure of
grappling with such a layered, dizzily delicious
construct, but it will reach perfection in 6 years or
so and will carry on developing character for many
years more. How many? I can't really say. I'm not
much of an expert on Ehrenfelser. However, I'll stick
my neck out and reckon 15 years max for this
ambrosial bottle.

18

Casa Lapostolle Cuvée Alexandre Cabernet Sauvignon 1998
Everywine
Dry catering chocolate, toasted walnuts, rich cassis and plum, with touches of licorice – is this as good as this wine can get? It seems to be mature yet healthy, ripe yet far from sere, and fully in possession of that destiny of all great wine: itself (or rather that self which its maker has in mind for it). A magnificent wine for fresh Italian alpine cheeses and truffle omelette and risotto with wild mushrooms (plenty of Parmesan and a squizzle of green olive oil over it as it sits on the plate).
Also at London Stores (Selfridges) and Small Merchants (Berry Bros & Rudd).

17.5

RED £6.99
CHILE

Casa Lapostolle Cabernet Sauvignon 2000
ChateauOnline.co.uk, Virgin Wines
Dry chocolate, touch of bell pepper and black pepper, beautifully silky yet assertive tannins and a dry, cassis finish. Impressively textured and fruited, this has liveliness yet finesse. It went splendidly with coq au

At a recent supermarket refurbishment opening, I slurped expensive single-vineyard Alsatian Gewürztraminer and guzzled freshly prepared sushi passing on a small conveyor belt. How did Britain contrive to get itself into such a delicious state?

vin blanc I knocked up with shiitake mushrooms and baby turnips – the gaminess of the dish brought out the feral side of the wine.

Also at London Stores (Selfridges, Harrods) and Thresher.

17.5

WHITE £21.15

Ihringer Winklerberg Weissburgunder Spätlese GERMANY
Barrique Weingut Dr Heger 2001

The Wine Barn

Lovely, lightly grilled nutty fruit. Gorgeous structure, balance, texture and finish. Will improve if cellared. Each wine from the Dr Heger estate shows exemplary wine making, meticulous precision yet élan, so there is a real joy in the liquids as well as finesse and self expression. They are to be preferred to hundreds of famous estates in France, Italy and Spain and must be one of the greatest wine estates in the world. This is not wholly recognised by the prices, which though high in some cases still represent value because they are unique, complex, possess great integrity, very special, utterly delicious, and thought-provoking. They are not showy, pretentious, anxious wines. They are relaxed masterpieces, like Mozart piano sonatas. Note: Heger wines will develop excitingly and sensually in bottle for many years. They are all dry, elegantly dry in fact, whatever the label wording seems to imply (remember that Spätlese or Auslese refers to ripeness of grapes at harvest not at point of finished vinification).

17   RED £7.49–£8.49

Casa Lapostolle Merlot 2002   CHILE
ChateauOnline.co.uk, Everywine, European Wine
Growers' Association, Barrels and Bottles
Marvellously couth and civilised tippling here with
superbly soft tannins.
Also stocked at London Stores (Selfridges) and Small
Merchants (Hicks & Don, Charles Hennings Ltd,
Friarwood, Thos Peatling Fine Wines and Cambridge
Wine Merchants).

---

17   WHITE £26.35

Achkarrer Schlossberg Grauburgunder Auslese   GERMANY
Barrique Weingut Dr Heger 2001
The Wine Barn
That grilled nut again, superbly harnessed to slightly
softer minerals and acids. Will improve if cellared.

---

17   RED £14.99

Casa Lapostolle Cuvée Alexandre Merlot 2000   CHILE
Everywine, ChateauOnline.co.uk
Dry, jauntily craggy leather, damsons, and hints of
grilled nuts make this a classic Merlot capable of
accelerating within 14–18 months and putting on a
couple more points. The sheer ineffability of the
texture (is it velvet? satin? cashmere? something not
yet known to man or beast?) will begin to deepen and
show more complexity as it ages.
Also at London Stores (Harrods, Fortnum & Mason),
Majestic and Safeway.

16.5

Merdinger Buhl Spätburgunder Weingut Dr Heger 2001

RED £10.35   GERMANY

The Wine Barn

Red Burgundy lovers will find this has more sensual perfume and riveting complexities than many a fine Côtes de Beaune. It has superb dry cherry, gamey cassis touches, and such elongated, precisely tailored fruit it makes a hugely individual statement. Will improve if cellared.

16.5

Casa Lapostolle Chardonnay 2002

WHITE £6.49–£7.49   CHILE

Barrels and Bottles, ChateauOnline.co.uk, European Wine Growers' Association, Everywine

The secret of this estate's success, or should I say one of several secrets, is the ability to choose precisely the right time to pick its grape so that all the chemical elements in the berries co-operate to the maximum in producing a glorious sum of the parts. Here is a prime example of svelteness and balance to prove it.

Also stocked at London Stores (Selfridges) and Small Merchants (Partridges, Charles Hennings Ltd, Cambridge Wine Merchants and Thos Peatling Fine Wines).

16.5

Casa Lapostolle Cabernet Sauvignon 2001

RED £6.99–£7.99   CHILE

Barrels and Bottles, ChateauOnline.co.uk, European Wine Growers' Association, Everywine

What more can I add to the words I have expended on extolling the virtues of this estate's wines and their

popularity with my palate and pocket? This specimen is utterly smooth yet, paradoxically, rugged.
Also stocked at London Stores (Selfridges, Harrods), Thresher, and Small Merchants (Hicks & Don, Charles Hennings Ltd, Friarwood, Thos Peatling Fine Wines, Cambridge Wine Merchants).

16 (**18** by 2006)   WHITE £16.99
Ihringer Winklerberg Riesling Spätlese   GERMANY
Weingut Dr Heger 2001
The Wine Barn
Young but perfect balance. Seduces the palate by stealth.

16 (to **17** inside 3 years)   WHITE £9.40
Riesling Kabinett Weingut Dr Heger 2001   GERMANY
The Wine Barn
Long, dry, citrus, very young as yet, classy with great minerals and superb texture.

16   WHITE £5.15
Grand Gaillard Sauvignon Blanc/Sémillon,   FRANCE
Périgord Vin de Pays 2002
Laithwaites
Good oily fruit, very classily packaged and polished, under-ripe gooseberry and lime zest.

16   RED £7.19
Bila-Haut Côtes du Roussillon-Villages 2000   FRANCE
Laithwaites
Big juicy and generous but herby. The live tannins precisely counterpoint the vivid plum, cherries and

slightly tangy strawberry jam. Touch of svelte
strawberries on the finish.

16 (to **18.5** by 2007) WHITE £15.40
Ihringer Winklerberg Weissburgunder Spätlese GERMANY
Weingut Dr Heger 2001
The Wine Barn
Beautiful grapefruit-edged richness. A magnificent,
slow-to-evolve bookworm's wine.

16 (to **17.5** in 3 years) RED £31.20
Ihringer Winklerberg Spätburgunder Barrique GERMANY
Weingut Dr Heger 2000
The Wine Barn
Ouch! A lot of money but a lot of wine. Shows
delightful perfumed cherry fruit and soft, subtle
tannins. Give it a little time and. . . paradise will emerge.

16 RED £5.95

Novas Carmenere/Cabernet Sauvignon 2001 CHILE
Vintage Roots
Bitter chocolate, cherry liquor and licorice – quite a
load of flavour here from basically dry plums with
some berried earthiness (very subtle).

16 RED £5.95

Novas Cabernet Sauvignon 2001 CHILE
Vintage Roots
Rich, dry, mouth-puckering tannins (yet they become
soft and friendly after a few seconds). Good blackberry
and plum fruit, balanced, textured, firm.

16

WHITE £6.99
NEW ZEALAND

**Belmonte Marlborough Sauvignon
Blanc 2002**
Virgin Wines

The textbook is a dull tome at the best of times and
whilst this specimen does not exactly throw it out of
the window it does have its own translation – and this
is all to the good. Thus though we get gooseberry
(what Marlborough Sauvignon Blanc would be
complete without it) we find a touch of raspberry to
the citricity which gives it great appeal. I would serve
this wine with smoked fish or scallops with bacon
bits.
Also at Sainsbury's.

16

RED £9.99
FRANCE

**La Sauvageonne Pica Broca, Coteaux du
Languedoc 2001**
Virgin Wines

Rugged yet graceful, chocolatey yet not absurd,
rich yet full of spritely twists and turns. Lovely
compacted berries here with good, charcoal-edged
tannins.

16

WHITE £7.50
ARGENTINA

Don David Torrontes, Michel Torino 2002
Everywine

Unusually oily and rich, yet restrained elegant and
dry. Very lingering spicy fruit. Superb with scallops,
and minted pea purée. 18.5 (with such fare).

16

Wakefield Shiraz 2002

European Wine Growers' Association

Has interestingly characterful berries with subtle
coriander/paprika edging. This spicing is far from
OTT, almost genteel, certainly polite, and it's nicely
calmed by the savoury tannins. This vintage of this
wine is claimed to represent one of its best ever and
may, in the words of Mitchell Taylor, the managing
director of Wakefield, 'eclipse the previous great red
vintage of 1998'. Adam Eggins, the wine maker, is
silent on the matter (but then I did not ask him), but
his effort is claimed by the producer to offer 'aromas
of plum, cinnamon, liquorice [sic], and spice with
creamy nuances of vanilla oak, chocolate and coffee.' I
wasn't sure about the chocolate and failed to find the
coffee, and I did look hard, but perhaps readers
possessed of longer noses and more enquiring palates
than mine, would get in touch with their findings.
Also at Oddbins and Small Merchants (Stratford's,
Wiljay Wines, Wine Junction, Wright Wine Co.,
Raeburn Fine Wines, Hoults Wine Merchants, Big
Wines, Portland Wine Cellars, Paul Roberts,
Ballantynes of Cowbridge, Scathard, Nidderdale Fine
Wines, Bacchanalia, Wine in Cornwall, Terry Platt
Wine Merchants, Unwins).

LONDON STORES

FORTNUM & MASON

181 Piccadilly,
London WIA IER

Tel: (020) 7734 8040
Fax: (020) 7437 3278

E-mail: info@fortnumandmason.co.uk
Website: www.fortnumandmason.com

HARRODS

Brompton Road,
Knightsbridge,
London SWIX 7XL

Tel: (020) 7730 1234
Fax: (020) 7225 5823

E-mail: food.halls@harrods.com
Website: www.harrods.com

HARVEY NICHOLS

125 Knightsbridge,
London SWIX 7RJ

Tel: (020) 7201 8537
Fax: (020) 7 245 6561

E-mail: wineshop@harveynichols.com
Website: www.harveynichols.com

SELFRIDGES

400 Oxford Street,
London W1A 1AB

Tel: (020) 7318 3730
Fax: (020) 7318 3730

E-mail: wine.club@selfridges.co.uk
Website: www.selfridges.co.uk

For London Stores' wines 15.5 points and under visit .
www.superplonk.com

19   WHITE £10.99

Casa Lapostolle Cuvée Alexandre Chardonnay 2001   CHILE

Selfridges, Harrods

Simply wonderful from nose to throat. Stunning
texture (gripping yet elegant), complex, smoky fruit of
pear/melon/pineapple and a hint of lemon peel. What
is a perfect wine? One that cannot be bettered, surely.
And this cannot be bettered in so many respects that
though I dithered over whether I should award it the
penultimate accolade I felt not to do so would be
unjust. It is simply a staggeringly delicious
Chardonnay of supreme, world-class finesse and
potent delicacy (that crucial paradox!).
The wood here is a justified element (unintrusive and
sanely balanced) and as necessary to the wine scheme
of things as salt on a tomato. The vegetality, the youth
of the fruit, and the calm authority of its finish give
the wine cellaring potential of 2-3 years and doubtless
well beyond this (however, it will lose some energy if
laid down too long). Alas, there are few bottles left.
Also at Majestic and Safeway.

18.5 (2005–10) **14** (2003)   RED £45.00

Casa Lapostolle Clos Apalta 1999   CHILE

Selfridges, Harrods, Fortnum & Mason, Harvey Nichols

The price takes a lot of swallowing but then this is a
blend of Carmenere, Merlot, Cabernet Sauvignon and
Malbec from a single site and made to be a luxury item.
It has all of the fruit and nut (and chocolate elements)
alluded to in the metaphoric clothing given to its
brothers and sisters also rated here, but it is more

reluctant to release them. It has an excellent acidic structure which will take a few years to soften, and a freshness of tannicity which means the wine needs to be fully decanted 4–5 hours before drinking to achieve a modicum of amiability. However – trust me but it's true – it really needs 36 hours' whole decantation and breathing to be persuaded to get friendlier. Even so, and properly aged and cellared for half a decade or more, I cannot rate it higher than I do because £45 is a slightly fatuous valuation when there are brisker candidates for your dollars listed here. However, I would be grateful if game purchasers of this book possessed of cellars and capacious pockets would not mind putting down a couple of cases of this wine and inviting me to drink them – during the election the one after the next one (when perhaps sanity will return to the Labour Party, guts to the Tories, and chutzpah to the social democrats, the England cricket team will be composed of 8 Asian players who can wield a bat and spin a ball at speed, and the bellicose Bush has been replaced by the USA's first woman president). From this, as you may have already realised, any fool can pontificate about the future and as long as there are corks in wine bottles then cellaring such artefacts will be subject to chance and variation.

18.5   RED £7.49
Casa Lapostolle Merlot 2000   CHILE
Selfridges

Intense as the night sky over Manchester (not Marrakesh) during a blackout, this stunning wine is inspiring and exotic. The colour of opaque, bruised crimson, it gives off the perfume of leather, and the young yet complex fruit is enormously rich (alcoholic a touch too) and deep. It just might reach 20 points in 4–5 years . . . then again . . . is the gamble worth it when it's so gloriously chewy and invigorating now? I think not. This is a wine to eat as much as drink and open and decant many hours before consuming – with passion, with pals, with polished food. That's the good news. The bad news is that there are very few bottles left. Also at Majestic.

18.5

WHITE £5.49

GERMANY

Piesporter Goldtröpfchen Riesling Spätlese, Jacobus 1989

Selfridges

Dry yet full of mature, oily, paraffin-touched complexities. A wine of this maturity, and possible extinction from the shelves within days of this book's publication, tells us a great deal about the state of the German wine industry. Just a posh Liebfraumilch? By the same token Real Madrid are just a bunch of yobs who kick a football around on weekends. Also at Majestic.

18

RED £11.99

CHILE

Casa Lapostolle Cuvée Alexandre Cabernet Sauvignon 1998

Selfridges

Dry catering chocolate, toasted walnuts, rich cassis and plum, with touches of licorice – is this as good as this wine can get? It seems to be mature yet healthy, ripe yet far from sere, and fully in possession of that destiny of

all great wine: itself (or rather that self which its maker has in mind for it). A magnificent wine for fresh Italian alpine cheeses and truffle omelette and risotto with wild mushrooms (plenty of Parmesan and a squizzle of green olive oil over it as it sits on the plate).
Also at Small Merchants (Berry Bros & Rudd) and E-tailers (Everywine).

17.5   RED £6.99

Casa Lapostolle Cabernet Sauvignon 2000   CHILE
Selfridges, Harrods
Dry chocolate, touch of bell pepper and black pepper, beautifully silky yet assertive tannins and a dry, cassis finish. Impressively textured and fruited, this has liveliness yet finesse. It went splendidly with coq au vin blanc I knocked up with shiitake mushrooms and baby turnips – the gaminess of the dish brought out the feral side of the wine.
Also at Thresher and E-tailers (ChateauOnline.co.uk and Virgin Wines).

17.5   WHITE £19.90

Grosset Piccadilly Chardonnay 2001   AUSTRALIA
Fortnum & Mason, Harvey Nichols
Toasted citrus, vegetality-edged Ogen melon, and a rich texture of supreme class. Like a magical Montrachet, this wine comes even more alive with food – anything from roast fowl to mushroom risotto – but as a supreme treat to sip whilst reading a book it is superb.
Also at Small Merchants (Milton Sandford Wines, Veritas Wines, La Vigneronne, Philglas & Swiggot,

Turville Valley Wines, Vin du Vin, Bennets Fine Wines, Halifax Wine Company, D Byrne, Domain Direct).

17.5   RED £21.75

Grosset Gaia 2000   AUSTRALIA

Fortnum & Mason, Harvey Nichols

A Cabernet Sauvignon/Merlot/Cabernet Franc blend of wonderfully gently roasted soft berries and very calm tannins. It oozes class and finesse yet has that subdued power exciting wines have. It both invigorates and caresses the palate.

Also at Small Merchants (Milton Sandford Wines, Oz Wines, La Vigneronne, Philglas & Swiggot, Vin du Vin, Bennets Fine Wines, Halifax Wine Company, D Byrne, Robersons Wine Merchants, Domain Direct).

17   RED £14.99

Casa Lapostolle Cuvée Alexandre Merlot 2000   CHILE

Harrods, Fortnum & Mason

Dry, jauntily craggy leather, damsons, and hints of grilled nuts make this a classic Merlot capable of accelerating within 14–18 months and putting on a couple more points. The sheer ineffability of the texture (is it velvet? satin? cashmere? something not yet known to man or beast?) will begin to deepen and show more complexity as it ages (and indeed may well rate 18 by the summer of 2004).

Also at Majestic, Safeway and E-tailers (Everywine, ChateauOnline.co.uk).

17   RED £7.49–£8.49

Casa Lapostolle Merlot 2002   CHILE
Selfridges

Marvellously couth and civilised tippling here with
superbly soft tannins.

Also available at Small Merchants (Hicks & Don,
Charles Hennings Ltd, Friarwood, Thos Peatling Fine
Wines, Cambridge Wine Merchants) and E-tailers
(ChateauOnline.co.uk, Everywine, European Wine
Growers' Association and Barrels and Bottles).

16.5   WHITE £6.49–£7.49

Casa Lapostolle Chardonnay 2002   CHILE
Selfridges

The secret of this estate's success, or should I say one
of several secrets, is the ability to choose precisely the
right time to pick its grape so that all the chemical
elements in the berries co-operate to the maximum in
producing a glorious sum of the parts. Here is a
prime example of svelteness and balance to prove it.
Also available at Small Merchants (Partridges, Charles
Hennings Ltd, Cambridge Wine Merchants, Thos
Peatling Fine Wines) and E-tailers (Barrels and
Bottles, ChateauOnline.co.uk, European Wine
Growers' Assocation and Everywine).

16.5   RED £6.99–£7.99

Casa Lapostolle Cabernet Sauvignon 2001   CHILE
Selfridges, Harrods

What more can I add to the words I have expended on
extolling the virtues of this estate's wines and their

popularity with my palate and pocket? This specimen
is utterly smooth yet, paradoxically, rugged.
Also available at Thresher, Small Merchants
(Friarwood, Cambridge Wine Merchants, Hicks &
Don, Thos Peatling Fine Wines, Charles Hennings
Ltd) and E-tailers (Barrels and Bottles,
ChateauOnline.co.uk, European Wine Growers'
Association, Everywine).

16.5 (18.5 in 3–4 years) — WHITE £12.99–£13.99

Grosset Watervale Riesling 2002 — AUSTRALIA

Fortnum & Mason, Harvey Nichols

See entry for Grosset Polish Hill Riesling in Small
Merchants for more on this estate.

This is screwcapped and so will age without hindrance
from its cork. It is young but it bursts with potential. It
shows great concentration of dry peach and citrus with
fine acids and I would expect the texture to develop
greater finesse with time. Exactly how good will it get?
See my reactions to this wine of various vintages tasted
in July 2003 in the Small Merchants section.

Also at Small Merchants (Milton Sandford Wines, Oz
Wines, La Vigneronne, Philglas & Swiggot, Turville Valley
Wines, Vin du Vin, Robersons, Bennets Fine Wines,
Halifax Wine Company, D Byrne, Berry Bros & Rudd).

16 — WHITE £6.49

Casa Lapostolle Sauvignon Blanc 2002 — CHILE

Selfridges

Unusual, gently oily rendition of a grape which many
wine makers consider the height of tediousness and

easy-to-make-ness. There is, then, no regulation gooseberry here, rather bitter orange and lemon and under-ripe Ogen melon. It is a first-class shellfish wine and, best of all, rather tasty with Thai-influenced marine dishes like grilled prawns with chillies and mussels with lemongrass.

16

WHITE £6.49

Casa Lapostolle Chardonnay 2001   CHILE
Selfridges

Calm, beautifully controlled, dry melon fruit, with nuttiness and a charmingly dry, elegant finish. It insists on being itself in spite of the comparison which can be made between it and Californian specimens and southern France. It has neither the exuberance of many an Aussie Chardonnay nor the fleshiness of say, a Cape specimen, and therefore foods for it have be subtle rather than spicy. I think a watercress and smoked eel salad would be perfect (which doesn't sound subtle because of the pepperiness of the cress but the fruit in the wine melds perfectly with such greenery).
Also at Majestic.

16

WHITE £7.49

Morgenhof 2001   SOUTH AFRICA
Harrods

Delicious pineapple, pear and melon richness. Very heartening and charming.
Also at Booths and Small Merchants (The Bristol Wine Company).

16 **(18.5** in 3-5 years) WHITE £14.99–£15.99
Grosset Polish Hill Riesling 2002 AUSTRALIA

Fortnum & Mason, Harvey Nichols

Mr Grosset makes Australasia's most complex and incisive Rieslings which age with huge distinction, charm and calm. He is a great enthusiast for screwcaps and this only adds to the guarantee that he provides of excitement to come – as with this young specimen. It can be cellared with confidence, though its melon, citrus and dry white peach edge can be enjoyed now (otherwise that 16 rating is a mockery). I drank it several times last year in Australia and thought it wonderful, but it went through a quiet phase in the summer of 2003 but will pick up by late 2003. This wine has a great, great future and it is wise to consign that future to the certainty of a screwcap rather than the gamble of a cork. How it might develop is shown by the tasting notes of previous vintages, in July 2003, in the Small Merchants section, along with more information about the estate. Also at Small Merchants (Milton Sandford Wines Limited, Oz Wines, La Vigneronne, Philglas & Swiggot, Turville Valley Wines, Vin du Vin, Robersons, Bennets Fine Wines, D Byrne, Halifax Wine Company).

The ugliest wine I have ever tasted in my entire life was Cretan red retsina. It was highly oxidised and redolent of creosote, and it came complete with a verbal warning from the maker's daughter which unwisely I chose to ignore.

16

WHITE £13.55

Grosset Sémillon/Sauvignon Blanc 2002   AUSTRALIA

Harvey Nichols

Yet another healthy, screwcapped liquid from Mr
Grosset. Lovely lashings of under-ripe gooseberry and
mineralised melon make this a classic blend to my
mind and it will age, and put on points, with great
ease over the next few years and at 6 or 7 years of age
will be sublime.

Also at Small Merchants (Milton Sandford Wines, Oz
Wines, La Vigneronne, Philglas & Swiggot, Turville
Valley Wines, Vin du Vin, Robersons, Bennets Fine
Wines, Halifax Wine Company, D Byrne, Berry Bros &
Rudd).

16

RED £10.45

Willow Bridge Shiraz, Winemaker's Reserve   AUSTRALIA
2001

Fortnum & Mason, Harvey Nichols

Expensive but impressively complete, gently spicy,
very firmly berried and classy.

Also at Small Merchants (Stevens Garnier).

MAJESTIC

Head Office:
Majestic House,
Otterspool Way,
Watford, Hertfordshire WD25 8WW

Tel:(01923) 298200
Fax:(01923) 819105

E-mail: info@majestic.co.uk
Website: www.majestic.co.uk

For all Majestic wines of 15.5 points and under visit
www.superplonk.com

19

Casa Lapostolle Cuvée Alexandre Chardonnay 2001 CHILE

Simply wonderful from nose to throat. Stunning
texture (gripping yet elegant), complex, smoky fruit
of pear/melon/pineapple and a hint of lemon peel.
What is a perfect wine? One that cannot be bettered,
surely. And this cannot be bettered in so many
respects that though I dithered over whether I should
award it the penultimate accolade I felt not to do so
would be unjust. It is simply a staggeringly delicious
Chardonnay of supreme, world-class finesse and
potent delicacy (that crucial paradox!).

The wood here is a justified element (unintrusive
and sanely balanced) and as necessary to the wine
scheme of things as salt on a tomato. The vegetality,
the youth of the fruit, and the calm authority of its
finish give the wine cellaring potential of 2–3 years
and doubtless well beyond this (however, it will lose
some energy if laid down too long). Alas, there are
few bottles left.

Also at Safeway and London Stores (Selfridges and
Harrods).

18.5

Piesporter Goldtröpfchen Riesling Spätlese, GERMANY
Jacobus 1989

Dry yet full of mature, oily, paraffin-touched
complexities. A wine of this maturity, and possible
extinction from the shelves within days of this book's
publication, tells us a great deal about the state of the
German wine industry. Just a posh Liebfraumilch? By

the same token Real Madrid are just a bunch of yobs who kick a football around on weekends.
Also at London Stores (Selfridges).

18.5

RED £7.49
CHILE

Casa Lapostolle Merlot 2000

Intense as the night sky over Manchester (not Marrakesh) during a blackout, this stunning wine is inspiring and exotic. The colour of opaque, bruised crimson, it gives off the perfume of leather, and the young yet complex fruit is enormously rich (alcoholic a touch too) and deep. It just might reach 20 points in 4–5 years. . .then again . . . is the gamble worth it when it's so gloriously chewy and invigorating now? I think not. This is a wine to eat as much as drink and open and decant many hours before consuming – with passion, with pals, with polished food. That's the good news. The bad news is that there are very few bottles left.
Also at London Stores (Selfridges).

18

RED £14.99
FRANCE

La Réserve de Léoville-Barton 1998

So richly knitted and thick it can be worn as an overcoat. The tannins are as oily and coagulated as axle grease. The fruit, uncowed, releases berries of very roasted aroma, hue and flavour.

18

WHITE £19.99
FRANCE

Sancerre 'Les Romains' 2000

The most complex, oaky Sauvignon Blanc, the most complete of its kind I've tasted. Lovely dry

apricot, under-ripe gooseberry, nuts and a leafy
richness pervade this unusual specimen.

18

WHITE £5.49

Erdener Treppchen Riesling Spätlese, Jacobus GERMANY
1989
Stunning petroleum-tinged fruit of peach, gooseberry
and citrus. Great acids keep it balanced.

17.5

WHITE £5.49

Zeltinger Sonnenuhr Riesling Spätlese, GERMANY
Jacobus 1990
Still young and capable of development in bottle. A
wonderfully minerally lime-zest and dry pineapple
beauty.

17.5

RED £6.99

Lirac, Château d'Aquéria 2000 FRANCE
Intense clotted berries, beautifully toasty and herby,
with soft, palate-enveloping tannins which grip but
never bruise.

White wine, a passionate wine lover once remarked
to me, can aspire only to the level of Gilbert and
Sullivan. It lacks the complexity to be Wagner.
However, I think one can enjoy many performances
of *The Pirates of Penzance* and endure only very
few of *Parsifal*.

17.5   RED £5.99

FRANCE

Mas de Guiot Cabernet/Syrah, Vin de Pays du Gard 2001

A Cab/Syrah marriage of perfect harmony between roasted berries and rich tannins.

17   RED £10.99

FRANCE

Moulin de la Lagune, Haut Médoc 1999

What gracious stealth this lovely claret exudes as it proceeds demurely from nose, to end rousingly in the throat.

17   WHITE £6.99

FRANCE

Montagny Vieilles Vignes Cuvée Spéciale 2000

Delicious apricot, melon, citrus and a hint of tannin. Real class here.

17   WHITE £7.99

SPAIN

Albarino Martin Codax Rias Baixas 2002

Ripe, dry, peachy fruit with a nutty finish. Miguel Torres, the great Catalan wine maker, entrepreneur, linguist and tennis player, told me he reckons the Albarino grape is related to the Riesling vines left behind by pilgrims centuries ago on the road to Santiago di Compostela. He may be right. This specimen seems more like Tokay-Pinot Gris than Riesling, but so what? It's Albarino, from the wettest part of Spain.

17   RED £6.99

Minervois La Livinière, Domaine des Aires   FRANCE
Hautes 2000
Concentrated blackberries with twigs, leaves and a
hint of catering chocolate.

---

17   RED £4.99

Château Guiot, Costières de Nîmes 2001   FRANCE
A great Syrah blended superbly, with textured leafy
berries.

---

17   RED £7.99

Château de Gaudou Cuvée Renaissance,   FRANCE
Cahors 2000
Stunningly dry and tannins as old boots. But what
character!

---

17   WHITE £5.99

Montes Sauvignon Blanc, Casablanca 2002   CHILE
This is one of the most gripping of new world
Sauvignons with the usual gooseberry fruit but with
graceful mineralised acids and a textured, tangy
finish which hints at the salinity of breathing fresh
littoral air.

---

17   RED £11.99

Montes Alpha Syrah, Colchagua 2000/2001   CHILE
Both vintages of this wine are, unusually, rated
similarly though there are differences too subtle to
remark at this point in time (it requires opening a few
hours for the differences to become apparent – the '01

has fresher and plummier fruit). The wine is gently
spicy with classy damson fruit and shows the house
style of tannicity with finesse.

The '00, though, has several oddities (freshness,
eagerness, lack of pretension) but one overriding
virtue. It is gorgeous! All over! I would rather this
Syrah than many of the Aussies' much-vaunted
legends (like Grange or Hill of Grace), for it is not
only massively cheaper but massively sexier.
Available at Morrison's, Sainsbury's (not the 2001)
and Waitrose.

17
WHITE £8.99
Penfolds Thomas Hyland Chardonnay 2002 AUSTRALIA
Minerals, honey, peaches and acids – this has weight
and class to it, and for further details see the Tesco
entry.
Also at Tesco.

17
WHITE £4.49
Domaine Plantade Chardonnay/Viognier, FRANCE
Vin de Pays d'Oc 2001
Delicious maturity with elegant urban chic. Has
peach, apricot, gooseberry and lime.

17
RED £3.99
Grange du Midi Merlot 2002 FRANCE
Stunning mouth-filling strawberries and raspberries
with the thorns included, so we get character, guile,
point and urgent deliciousness.

17

Casa Lapostolle Cuvée Alexandre Merlot 2000   CHILE

Dry, jauntily craggy leather, damsons, and hints
of grilled nuts make this a classic Merlot capable
of accelerating within 14–18 months and putting
on a couple more points. The sheer ineffability
of the texture (is it velvet? satin? cashmere?
something not yet known to man or beast?) will
begin to deepen and show more complexity as it
ages (and may well rate 18 by summer of 2004).
Also at London Stores (Harrods, Fortnum & Mason),
Safeway and E-tailers (Everywine, ChateauOnline.
co.uk).

16.5

WHITE £4.69

Concha y Toro Casillero del Diablo Chardonnay   CHILE
2002

Lovely, quite lovely, baked melon, smokily deep and
oily. Top-class texture here.
Also at Waitrose.

16.5

RED £4.99

Concha y Toro Casillero del Diablo Malbec 2001   CHILE

Biscuity richness and cocoa-edged tannins coat
berries of great aplomb and luxuriousness.

16.5

RED £4.69

Cono Sur Merlot 2002   CHILE

It's all of a piece you see, that's what makes it so lovely,
from nose to throat, and such astounding value.
Spreads like some amazing brand of juice (dry) on the

tongue and the actual berry has yet to be classified
(strawb and black is more or less about right).
Also at Tesco.

16.5   RED £7.49

Barbera d'Alba Sucule 2000   ITALY

Shows a delicious turn of speed as it goes from baked
cherry to roasted blackcurrant.

16.5   RED £4.49

Les Fontanelles Merlot 2002   FRANCE

Hint of charred leather to rich, dark plums. Terrific
pace here.

16.5   WHITE £3.99

Neblina Sauvignon Blanc 2002   CHILE

Bargain gooseberry fruit which is surprisingly classy
and concentrated.

16.5   WHITE £4.69

Concha y Toro Casillero del Diablo Sauvignon CHILE
Blanc 2002

Superb class of gooseberry here with a white peach
undertone. Great texture. Supremely sure of itself with all
manner of fish dishes from oysters to pan-fried scallops
and, natch, fish and chips.
Also at Thresher.

16.5   WHITE £7.99

Muscat d'Alsace Riquewihr 2000   FRANCE

What a stunning aperitif this wine makes.
Whomsoever serves this grapey dryness to his/her

guests will be elevated and find friends for life. It is,
then, wise to consider which neighbours will be on
the receiving end of your largesse and select carefully,
otherwise you may find yourself besieged.

16.5

WHITE £7.99
FRANCE

Gewürztraminer 2001
Delicate yet thick and peachy with spicy lychee
undertones. Lovely ripeness yet gracious subtle layers.

16.5

WHITE £9.99
NEW ZEALAND

Villa Maria Reserve Sauvignon Blanc 2002
Screwcapped and wonderfully gripping, this
gooseberry and peach wine will age brilliantly, with its
exceptional texture, for many years.

16.5

WHITE £8.99
FRANCE

Menetou-Salon Pierre Jacolin 2002
Gorgeous peachy edge to the gooseberry which then
goes thick and rich before bringing in elegant citrus.

16.5

RED £8.99
AUSTRALIA

Pirramimma Petit Verdot 1999
Delicious, serious, big-berried and bustling, this is a
terrifically aromatic and toasted berried artefact with
great style.

16.5

RED £4.49
FRANCE

Corbières Domaine Madelon 2001
So smooth and civilised. It's got such polished berries.

16.5

RED £4.99

Abadia Real Vino de la Tierra, Castilla y Leon 2000 SPAIN
Unabashed chocolate with crunchy tannins which fail
to disturb the luxury of the fruit one whit.

16.5

RED £6.99

Durius Marqués de Griñon Tempranillo 2001 SPAIN
Gorgeous tannins to lovely brisk cherries and plums. A hint
of chocolate to the rich berries. Shows just how civilised
and polished (yet characterful) the Tempranillo grape can
become. Beautiful plump, soft texture here. Flashy, rich,
textured, gripping and, for the price, a steal.
Also at Budgens, Morrison's, Sainsbury's and
Thresher.

16.5

RED £6.99

Château Flaugergues, Coteaux du Languedoc FRANCE
2000
Very ripe berries, touch of cocoa, grilled edge to the
tannins.

16.5

WHITE £9.99

Penley Estate Chardonnay, Coonawarra 2001 AUSTRALIA
Very elegant Ogen melon (under-ripe) with toasted nuts.

16.5

WHITE £5.99

Domaine Lafage, Côtes du Roussillon Blanc FRANCE
2001
Superb chilled melon, hint of lemon and herbs,
fantastic quality of fruit.

How long should a wine breathe? The number of readers who have asked this question is so numerous that to list them would exhaust the pages of this book. I have come to the conclusion that for many people the question has about it something slightly louche, something secret, as though in asking it an accompanying wink or nudge wouldn't be out of place. Rather as if I was being pumped to provide the name of the dead-cert winner of the 3.30 at Aintree.

Yet there is only a gamble about letting air get to a wine when the bottle is ancient (or the cork is faulty). As when an acquaintance recently and excitedly revealed that she had been present when a bottle of La Tâche 1943, the legendary wine from Domaine de la Romanée-Conti, had been opened. Alas, it went raisiny and sere within minutes of being in the glass. La Tâche, like any wine, is anxious to hasten to its inevitable end, which is vinegar (from the French *vin aigre* or 'sour wine'). The older the wine the quicker it will reach this condition. Air is then the great enemy of wine but also its great ally. I use it constantly, most especially when I am serving wine at home. It is not enough, though, merely to remove the cork of a wine. This is not letting the wine breathe much beyond the top few centimetres of liquid. Wine, all wine but in particular red wine, should always be given the chance totally to interact with air. This is achieved most dramatically, yet simply and unpretentiously, by using large (three- or four-bottle size) glass jugs into which one or several bottles can be poured – after first having ascertained the wines' perfect state of health (no cork taint or a variation in quality so as to render a single bottle unfit for marriage).

Whether a red wine is young or old, I invariably jug it. Most wine, whatever soi-disant experts may say, is the better for being aerated, even white. With white wine, decanted into plastic water jugs which fit into the fridge, the acids will develop and a more exciting wine emerge. With red, the tannins will soften with the acids and greater perfume and texture emerge.

There is one other interesting side-effect of jugging wine. No dinner guest, invariably male, can pick up a bottle and pontificate over the label for ten minutes when conversation on more compelling themes is required. Jugs add an air of mystery and excitement – and indeed great confidence – to any dinner table. Your standing in the community will be greatly enhanced.

16.5 RED £9.99

Montes Alpha Merlot, Santa Cruz 1999 CHILE
An elegant yet emphatic wine, the fruit becoming
more cassis-like as it nears the throat. One of the
most convincing of Merlots from the new world (and,
for that matter, from the old).

16.5 RED £5.99

Côtes du Rhône-Villages Sablet 2000 FRANCE
Strict, disciplined tannins coat vivid plums.

16.5 RED £4.99

Château Guiot 2002 FRANCE
Meaty, well-roasted berries combine with healthy
lashings of tannin.

16.5 RED £19.99

Côte Rôtie Domaine André François 2000 FRANCE
Rustic masterpiece. Takes me back 40 years! Classic
Rhône richness, chewy as coal, deep as a mine-shaft,
and very, very dark.

16.5 RED £4.69

Concha y Toro Casillero del Diablo Merlot 2001 CHILE
One of Chile's most delicious Merlots, finely textured,
tannicly classy, and ripe, and the finish is gripping
and lengthy.

16.5 RED £11.99

Penfolds Bin 407 Cabernet Sauvignon 2000 AUSTRALIA
Delicious minty, leafy touches to soft berries with adult
tannins and characterfully deep-finishing finesse.
Also at Safeway and Oddbins.

16

Casa Lapostolle Chardonnay 2001

Calm, beautifully controlled, dry melon fruit, with
nuttiness and a charmingly dry, elegant finish. It insists
on being itself in spite of the comparison which can be
made between it and Californian specimens and
southern France. It has neither the exuberance of many
an Aussie Chardonnay nor the fleshiness of say, a Cape
specimen, and therefore foods for it have be subtle
rather than spicy. I think a watercress and smoked eel
salad would be perfect (which doesn't sound subtle
because of the pepperiness of the cress but the fruit in
the wine melds perfectly with such greenery).
Also at London Stores (Selfridges).

16

Pouilly-Fumé Les Griottes, Jean-Pierre Bailly 2001   FRANCE

A touch more ripeness (and a hint, just the tiniest
hint, of peach) and not as dry and austerely unfriendly
as other specimens of this appellation have struck me
over recent years.

16

**Montes Alpha Cabernet Sauvignon, Santa Cruz
1999**

This shows sweet – I'm tempted to say sentimental –
berries with a fine dusting of tannins. However, this
suggests simplicity when, within 2 or 3 hours of
whole decantation, some biting Cabernet fruit
emerges. Not a lot of spice or pepperiness, but
beautifully polished cohesive fruit and tannins.
Also at Oddbins.

16

RED £8.99

Bonterra Vineyards Zinfandel 2000   CALIFORNIA, USA
Delightfully chewy, gently grilled berries with touches
of cinnamon. Has a joyously rich and devil-may-care
fruitiness which, thrown in the face of decades of
European po-facedness from old-world wines which
might try to compete (Rhône, Rioja, Chianti), makes an
eloquent case for this wine's inclusion in any
candidate's list for must-drink-wines with first-class,
elegant Indian, Pakistani and Bangladeshi food without
clumsy spicing. Not a cheap wine but then it isn't a
cheap wine: it doesn't warble or trill, it richly roars.
Also available at Oddbins, Safeway, Sainsbury's and
Waitrose.

16

WHITE £7.99

Villa Maria Private Bin Sauvignon Blanc,   NEW ZEALAND
Marlborough 2002
Tangy and very forwardly gooseberryish, but better
tasted in a year, and then in the years to come, as its
screwcap permits such slow delicate maturation.
(Indeed, it will age interestingly for 3 decades but not
everyone will find the interest uplifting by then.)
Also at Tesco.

16

WHITE £6.99

Villa Maria Private Bin Riesling,   NEW ZEALAND
Marlborough 2002
Screwcap. To really appreciate this wine at its rating,
do not unscrew its cap for 18 months to 2 years. The
citrus brilliance of the wine will develop beautifully.

16

WHITE £9.99
FRANCE

Chablis 1er Cru Beauregard, Cave Co-op La Chablisienne 1998

Classic Chablis offering demure hay-edged melon, citrus and a mineral undertone. Really at its peak of seductiveness and charm.

16

WHITE £5.99
GERMANY

Dorsheimer Pittermännchen Riesling Auslese 1989

Delicious textured toffee and citrus, cream and peach. Not sweet at all. Wonderful with spicy asparagus dishes.

16

RED £10.99
SOUTH AFRICA

The Ridge Syrah, Graham Beck, Robertson 2000

Can Syrah of this uncompromising solidity and exotic sunny richness compete with Australia? Oh yes!!! Convincingly rich and jammy (in a relaxed, new world way) but has chocolate and tannins to give it serious textured richness. The Graham Beck vineyard in Robertson is one of the neatest, tightest-managed, most commercially astute yet quality-driven operations of its kind in the Cape: 500 acres of vines, 3,000 tons of grapes, 250,000 cases of wine (with the 2003 harvest), and able to go from the bottom end of the market to the top with ease and finesse.

16

RED £8.99
AUSTRALIA

Penfolds Thomas Hyland Shiraz 2001

Very elegant assured berries with a hint of chocolate. Good tannins. Dry, classy, very confident.

16

RED £4.99
FRANCE

Château de Gaudou Cuvée Tradition, Cahors 2000

Delicious serenity and lovely, leafy, very dry fluid.

16

WHITE £8.99
FRANCE

Sancerre La Duchesse Vieilles Vignes, Co-op de Sancerre 2001

Minerally rich and gooseberryish.

16

WHITE £4.99
FRANCE

Domaine Caillaubert Sauvignon, Vin de Pays des Côtes de Gascogne 2001

Superb, elegant and crunchy concentration.

16

WHITE £8.49
FRANCE

Chablis Vieilles Vignes Vocoret 2001
A gorgeous lean Chablis with touches of slightly charred cobnut.

16

WHITE £8.49
ITALY

Gavi di Gavi Raccolto Tardivo Villa Lanata 2001
Individual, different, hint of cream custard to crisp dry citrus.

One of the problems of communicating about wine is the ineffability of the subject. Metaphors help but what you regard as sweet I may think of as half-dry and what you infer as being peachy in a wine I may conclude is more like kumquat. These are some of the reasons why I have a scoring system, points out of 20.

16   RED £4.99

Terra Vitis Corbières 2001   FRANCE
Warm, chewy fruit which has a touch of charred chocolate.

16   RED £14.99

Château Gontey St-Emilion Grand Cru 2000   FRANCE
Still young, 2–3 years away from its peak, but the
tannins are joyous now.

16   RED £3.79

Coldridge Estate Merlot 2002   AUSTRALIA
A bargain of serious plummy/berried richness, plus
excellent, thick toasty, almost burned, tannins.

16   WHITE £6.49

Soave Ca' de Napa, Cantina di Negrar 2002   ITALY
Superb blend of 75% Gargenega, 20% Chardonnay, 5%
Trebbiano di Soave which manages to be classy and fun
at one and the same time. Terrific apricot-edged fruit.

16   WHITE £6.99

Soave Classico Ca' Visco Superiore, Coffele 2002   ITALY
Ripe peach tempered by pineapple.

16   WHITE £5.99

Pinot Grigio Bidoli 2002   ITALY
Lovely dry peach and citrus fruit.

16   WHITE £7.99

Pinot Grigio San Angelo Vineyard, Banfi 2002   ITALY
Superb clumps of apricot and peach.

16   WHITE £4.99

Sauvignon Fournier Père et Fils 2002   FRANCE
So much more convincingly unpretentiously
gooseberryish (and much cheaper) than scores of
Sancerres (but not all).

16   WHITE £6.99

Quincy, Domaine Martin 2002   FRANCE
Gorgeous citrus richness which turns almondy and
dry.

16   WHITE £6.99

Reuilly, Henri Beurdin 2001   FRANCE
Terrific texture to the minerals which tinge the tangy
fruit.

16   WHITE £7.99

Menetou-Salon Domaine Fournier 2000   FRANCE
Dry gooseberry with a hint of lemon peel. Terrific fish
wine.

16   WHITE £7.99

Sancerre 'Les Chanvrières' 2001   FRANCE
Well, it's classic Sancerre – crushed gooseberries with
minerals.

16   WHITE £8.49

Sancerre 'Chavignol' 2002   FRANCE
Another classic, this time with the gooseberries
having a nutty edge.

16 WHITE £8.99

Sancerre 'Les Boucauds' 2002 FRANCE
Ah! The 2002 vintage is on song here.

16 WHITE £6.49

St Véran La Solitude 2000 FRANCE
Delicious! A delicate, lemony, melony, dry white wine,
subtle and nutty.

16 WHITE £4.99

Duque de Viseu Branco Dão 2001 PORTUGAL
Very finely tailored fruit, a marriage of Encruzado,
Assario and Cerceal grapes provide individuality and
dry peachiness.

16 WHITE £3.99

Esperanza Sauvignon Blanc 2002 ARGENTINA
Sticky, rich, melon/gooseberry fruit with the ability to
handle tandoori fish and Thai fishcakes.

16 (in 18 months) WHITE £5.99
Cono Sur Viognier 2002 CHILE
Very rich and very thickly knitted apricot jam fruit.
Brilliant with oriental food.
Also at Morrisons.

16 WHITE £6.99

Santa Rita Reserva Chardonnay 2001 CHILE
Very rich and oily, almost clotted, but the citrus saves
it on the finish.

16

WHITE £7.99

Beringer Appellation Collection Fumé CALIFORNIA, USA
Blanc 2001

Spicy, tangy, rich, ripe – and essential with Chinese
food.

16

WHITE £9.99

Beringer Appellation Collection CALIFORNIA, USA
Chardonnay 1999

Intense, brilliantly oriental-food rich fruit. Thick and
oily, gripping and complete.

16

WHITE £9.99

Vasse Felix Chardonnay 2001 AUSTRALIA

Subtle, classy, gripping and beautifully textured. Never
loses concentration. A complex, though very delicate,
experience.

I know Majestic are a pain for insisting on flogging
wine by the case or the mixed case, but what can we
do about it? I get letters and e-mails beefing about this
retailer's trading peculiarities, but all I can say is that
it's fun to put together a mixed dozen, and I really do
think that even the most curmudgeonly of *Superplonk*
readers is missing something if he/she
passes up on these wines just because Majestic has
its funny little ways.
The staff are invariably charming and helpful.

16   RED £5.99

Chinon Les Garous 2001   FRANCE
Typical earthy (and wild) raspberry. Utterly delicious, convincing, stylish.

16   RED £3.19

Cuvée des Amandiers Rouge 2002   FRANCE
A thrillingly serious bargain: tannins, herbs, structure, texture and a gently roasted berry finish.

16   RED £3.99

Grange du Midi Grenache 2002   FRANCE
Big, rich tenacious berries, broad bottomed and dry, give this wine real appeal. Fantastic value for money.

16   RED £4.49

Les Fontanelles Syrah 2002   FRANCE
Superb roasted cherries with cherry tomatoes.

16   RED £4.49

Les Fontanelles Cabernet Sauvignon 2002   FRANCE
Jammy, baked, great tannic shroud keeps it serious (and fun).

16   RED £5.99

Château de Panéry La Marquise 2001   FRANCE
Faint touch of plum to grilled blackberries, hint of thyme and olive.

16

RED £6.99

Château de Blaignan 1998   FRANCE
Convincing claret of depth and gently chocolate
firmness (before it melts in the mouth).

16

RED £14.99

Château Gontey 2000   FRANCE
The essence of claret as produced by Merlot and
Cabernet Franc – a lovely, lively textured red to
heighten all the senses.

16

RED £22.99

Gianni Brunelli, Brunello di Montalcino 1997   ITALY
Delicate in spite of its ferocious tannin onslaught on
the finish. Mature and very ready. Expensive but
impressive.

16

RED £7.99

Alentejo Reserva 2000   PORTUGAL
Rich, ready, very full of itself (but can handle it).

16

RED £3.99

Esperanza Merlot 2002   ARGENTINA
Simply delicious from the roasted raspberry bouquet
to the grilled strawberry finish.

16

RED £3.99

Neblina Merlot 2002   CHILE
Delicious plums, touch of sweet peach, then a serious
finish of tannins.

16   RED £4.69
CHILE

Cono Sur Syrah 2002
So ripe and ready, so deep and delicious (I love the
touch of cocoa and cream as it dries in the throat) that
the drinker feels blessed.

16   RED £6.99
CHILE

Santa Rita Reserva Merlot 2001
Joyous berries sing and dance on the tongue like
chocolate-coated blackberries.

16   RED £6.99
CHILE

Santa Rita Reserva Cabernet Sauvignon 2001
Offensively edgy, readily accessible to anyone who
loves blackberries and herbs, and gripping on the
finish – genteel yet firm.

16   RED £9.99
CHILE

Montes Alpha Merlot 2000
Firm yet fleshy, ripe yet classy, dry yet full of layered
berries.

16   RED £5.99
SOUTH AFRICA

Antony's Yard, Graham Beck 2001
A Cabernet Sauvignon, Merlot and Cabernet Franc
mélange of immediacy and instant richness (on nose,
tongue and throat).

16   RED £6.99
SOUTH AFRICA

Landskroon Shiraz 2001
The berries, lightly aromatic, are thickly applied to the
roasted tannins and ready for anything.

16

RED £3.99
AUSTRALIA

Tatachilla Grenache/Mataro 2000
What a bonny bargain! Shows deep layers of
plum and blackcurrant with burned tannins on
the finish.

16

RED £3.99
AUSTRALIA

Tatachilla Cabernet/Malbec 2000
Juicy, but oh so brilliantly curry friendly.

16

RED £9.99
AUSTRALIA

**Vasse Felix Cabernet/Merlot, Margaret
River 2000**
Creamy and rich, jammy yet serious, this has a
generous berried richness of appeal and charm.

16

RED £9.99
AUSTRALIA

Tim Adams, The Fergus 1999
Jam but classy jam. Spread it on live tongue with a
mushroom casserole on hand and wallow.

Australia is a wonderful country and, literally, it's
teeming with Australians. The younger ones are
remorselessly cheerful, healthy, good looking, bright,
enthusiastic, multi-talented and increasingly
multi-cultural, and it is enough to make any old
European feel uneasy and outpaced. Australia is the
future of the planet and once they get shot of old Betty
in Buck House and embrace their Far-Eastern destiny,
then there will be no stopping them.

16 WHITE £5.99

Alamos Chardonnay 2002 ARGENTINA
Spicier than previous vintages, creamier and funkier.

16 RED £9.99

Penfolds Bin 28 Kalimna Shiraz 2000 AUSTRALIA
One of Penfolds' most harmonious, savoury blends
of fruit and tannins. It opens out well after a couple
of hours of breathing (full decantation) to reveal
genteel spice and smooth berries and those lively
tannins.
Also at Oddbins, Sainsbury's, Safeway, Somerfield,
Tesco, Thresher and Small Merchants (Unwins).

16 RED £18.99

Petaluma Coonawarra Cabernet Sauvignon/ AUSTRALIA
Merlot 1999
Intense, very dry (almost like ashes in the mouth as it
quits the throat), but very elegant, classy and compact.
It is expensive but its concentrated, very subtle
tobacco-leaf edge is impressive.
Also at Oddbins and Sainsbury's.

MARKS & SPENCER

Michael House,
57 Baker Street,
London w1u 8ep

Tel: (020) 7268 1234
Fax: (020) 7268 2380

E-mail: customer.services@marks-and-spencer.com
Website: www.marksandspencer.com

For Marks & Spencer wines 15.5 points and under visit
www.superplonk.com

17.5

RED £6.99
FRANCE

Château Gallais Bellevue Cru Bourgeois, Médoc 2000

What a terrific clash of cultures here! We get the mustiness of old-fashioned claret with the feistiness of ripe new world plumminess. The two cohere beautifully on the finish in fine style. Remarkable price for such firmly elegant delivery from the Médoc.

17.5

RED £6.50

Pirque Estate Cabernet Sauvignon, Brougham 2001   CHILE

Has a label like a coach company's business card (or somewhat mannered undertaker's), but this stiffness is not apparent in the juice that flows freely and deeply, offering chocolate, licorice, roasted berries and commanding tannins. A sensational wine.

17

RED £5.99
FRANCE

Gold Label Barrel Aged Syrah, Domaine Virginies 2000

Superb!!! Aussies, watch out. This has stunning plum and raspberry fruit with very raunchy, chewy tannins.

17

RED £9.99

Canale Merlot Reserva, Patagonia 2001   ARGENTINA

A big treat to drink with a spicily stuffed fowl as a seasonal treat. Very rich, chocolatey fruit with gripping tannins of depth and chutzpah. The wine went brilliantly with a Peking-style roast duck with a sweet sauce.

17   WHITE £7.99

Shepherds Ridge Chardonnay 2001   NEW ZEALAND
Superbly insouciant, dry fruit of complex melon,
herbs, citrus and a fair touch of cream milk – odd?
Not when it's toasted (lightly).

16.5   RED £6.99

Chinon Domaine René Couly 1999   FRANCE
Serve lightly chilled to enhance the dry cassis, herby fruit
which has lithe tannins in full, though gentle, support.

16.5   RED £4.99

Casa Leona Merlot La Rosa 2002   CHILE
Ooooh . . . just gorgeous! Chocolate, tannins, roasted
berries, touch of leather and cocoa on the tannins as
they clog the throat.

16.5   WHITE £5.50

Domaine du Boulas, Côtes du Rhône 2002   FRANCE
Superb! And so much more sensual and layered than
whites costing twice and three times as much. The dry
hay-edged fruit goes nutty and titillating and develops
peach and apricot (very subtle). So much better than
anything from Burgundy at the same price.

16.5   RED £6.99

Villa dei Furesi Primitivo di Puglia 2000   ITALY
Delicious! Delicious! Delicious! No, not an
overstatement of the obvious. For it has chocolate,
burned berries and, to finish a trio of treats,
burnished tannins. A big thick liquid sensation.

16.5

Kaituna Hills East Coast Chardonnay Reserve 2001

NEW ZEALAND

A very lovely wine. It achieves that apotheosis of paradoxicality: dryness with sensual fruitiness. The stern, hard and soft fruits are buttered and there are elegant acids with a hint of minerality.

16.5

WHITE £5.99

Torresoto White Rioja 2001

SPAIN

A sensationally oily Rioja Blanco of great individuality and textured richness. More exciting and sensually perfumed and flavoured than, say, a lot of white Burgundies.

16.5

RED £4.99

Rustica Primitivo Salento, Mondo del Vino 2001

ITALY

Rustic my backside! This is urbane, complex, cosmopolitan and hugely entertaining.

16.5

RED £6.99

Torre Scalza Montepulciano d'Abruzzo, Mondo del Vino 2001

ITALY

Touch of sweet nut chocolate, strawberries and cherries. But the tannins are tremendous and make the wine spry, sly and very dry.

16

RED £7.99

Rasteau Côtes du Rhône-Villages 2001

FRANCE

Manages the delicious trick of being meaty and rich yet dry and delicate. Lovely toasty tannins offset heavy berries of great depth.

16   WHITE £5.99

Darting Estate Riesling Durkheimer   GERMANY
Michelsberg 2002
Such delicate, yet decisive touches! Nuts, dry peach,
citrus – and it's so young. Cellar for 3, 4 or 5 years and
it'll pile on points (as it increases in concentration).

16 (in 18 months)   WHITE £7.99

Georg Breuer Estate Rauenthal Riesling 2001   GERMANY
So put it away in a dark, cool cupboard and wait for its
minerals and citrussy fruit to learn to crawl (and then,
after 8 years, to stride into the world with confidence).

Long ago I worked out the recycling programme for
everything I receive in the way of wine. The empties are
collected by the Council, as is all the waste paper
generated by PR companies. The cardboard, which the
Green men won't collect, is cycled off, when I'm feeling
virtuous, to the appropriate bank but there is only so
much cardboard you can get on a bike. The used stamps
from all the envelopes my daughter's school takes. The
annual influx of calendars, diaries and unreviewable
books find their way to the Oxfam shop (as do many
gifts, though I know the day will come when a vinous
object I have donated to a charity shop is given back to
me as a Christmas present). The polystyrene containers
have been used as flower holders by a florist and War
Hammer model shops for the building of fortifications.
The corks (until recently) went to an infants' school to
be turned into pinboards and saucepan mats and little
log cabins. The wine itself? That goes down my throat,
and that of my neighbours.

16

Pinot Grigio Podere La Prendina Estate 2002   ITALY

Lovely opulent touches of plump apricot sprinkled
amongst crisp citrus and minerals. An excitingly
textured, rich yet dry Pinot Grigio, it has a lovely nutty
finish (but it is unexpectedly forward and ripe too).

16

Old Vines Grenache Noir 2001   FRANCE

Delicious berries with a touch of sweet chocolates
disciplined by wily, dry, lingering tannins.

16

Tupungato Chardonnay 2001   ARGENTINA

Very lively, dry, toasty melon fruit with firm intrusive
citrus. Good oily texture. Good grip for food.

16

Vacqueyras Cuvée des Vieilles Vignes 2001   FRANCE

The earthy herbs and chocolate tannins are wholly
integrated here with the rich berries. No separation.
No divide. Complete cohesion.

16

Wickham Estate Chardonnay 1995   AUSTRALIA

A treat of mature grouchiness and oily individuality.
At its peak now, and will decline rapidly hereafter, for
its butteriness and vegetal fruit are perfect now. A
superb food wine – and luxurious food at that (grilled
lobster, poached chicken with truffles).

16

WHITE £2.99

Vin de Pays du Gers Plaimont 2002   FRANCE

A lovely soft peachy wine with a tang of pineapple
and citrus on the finish. It's elegant and very easy to
drink.

16

WHITE £4.99

Gold Label Sauvignon Blanc, Domaine   FRANCE
Virginies 2002

Delicious, controlled, under-ripe and with great
finesse as it finishes. Well textured, gently rich and
very stylish.

16

WHITE £4.99

Gold Label Chardonnay, Domaine Virginies 2002   FRANCE

What a satisfyingly rich yet demure Chardonnay!
Delicious gently toasty melon and citrus – faint touch
of wood.

16

RED £4.99

Padronale Syrah, Mondo del Vino 2001   SICILY, ITALY

Interesting chewy chocolate, firm plums and
blackberries.

16

WHITE £11.99

Domaine des Sénéchaux, Châteauneuf-du-Pape   FRANCE
2002

A superb, classic Rhône blanc of chalky richness and
brilliant acidic balance.

16

RED £3.99
FRANCE

Saumur Réserve Jules Peron, Caves des Vignerons de Saumur 2002
Rated as drunk well chilled with rare salmon or tuna steaks. The wine is divine so partnered.

16

WHITE £3.99
SPAIN

Moscatel de Valencia 2002
A sweet wine of great aplomb and utility. Has honey and orange peel, very subtle marmalade edge on the finish.

16

RED £5.99
SPAIN

Castillo de Madax Monastrell/Cabernet Sauvignon Jumilla Finca Luzon 2002
So very couth, civilised and polished of manner. It is of a piece. Deliciously whole and expressive.

16

WHITE £6.99
CALIFORNIA, USA

Canterbury Chardonnay, Ehlers Grove 2001
Not the full-on richness of some Californian Chardonnays, but demure melon, peach and gooseberry, subtle, controlled, classy.

16

WHITE £7.49
AUSTRALIA

Bush View Margaret River Chardonnay 2002
Most unusually European style richness (melon, herbs, touch of citrus), which by the finish has become firmly un-Australian and fine.

16

RED £7.99

Kaituna Hills Reserve Cabernet/Merlot   NEW ZEALAND
2000
Very dry, very calm, very elegant. Slow-to-evolve
tannins provide a fine touch of finesse to cassis and
herbs. Very roasted feel to the finish.

16

WHITE £5.50

Sierra Los Andes Gewürztraminer, Carmen Estate   CHILE
2002
Very restrained grapefruit and dry citrus with the
spicy, rosy qualities of this grape à l'Alsacienne very
much in the background. A marvellous aperitif.

16

RED £4.99

Casa Leona Cabernet Sauvignon La Rosa 2002   CHILE
Delicious chocolate berries with full-throttle tannins.
Real personality, poise and purpose here.

MORRISON'S

Hillmore House,
Thornton Road,
Bradford,
West Yorkshire BD8 9AX

Tel: (01274) 494166
Fax: (01274) 494831

Website: www.morereasons.co.uk

For Morrison's wines 15.5 points and under visit
www.superplonk.com

17   RED £11.99

Montes Alpha Syrah, Colchagua 2000/2001   CHILE

Both vintages of this wine are, unusually, rated
similarly though there are differences too subtle to
remark at this point in time (it requires opening for a
few hours for the differences to become apparent –
the '01 has fresher and plummier fruit). The wine is
gently spicy with classy damson fruit and shows the
house style of tannicity with finesse.
The '00, though, has several oddities (freshness,
eagerness, lack of pretension) but one overriding
virtue. It is gorgeous! All over! I would rather this
Syrah than many of the Aussies' much-vaunted
legends (like Grange or Hill of Grace), for it is not
only massively cheaper but massively sexier.
Also available from Majestic, Sainsbury's (not the
2001) and Waitrose.

17   WHITE £6.99

Villa Maria Riesling 2002   NEW ZEALAND

Screwcapped deliciousness of great style and subtlety.
A lovely balanced, dry, melon/lemon wine with a
restrained undertone of gooseberry.
Also at Sainsbury's and Thresher.

16.5   RED £5.99

Castillo de Molina Reserva Shiraz 2001   CHILE

Perfectly roasted, coffee-edged berries (not burnt) with
lovely lithe tannins. Has real character yet beautifully
mannered charms.

16.5
RED £4.99

Stephan & Philippe Cabernet Franc, Vin de Pays FRANCE
d'Oc, Maurel Vedeau 2000
Immensely civilised and polished, with grilled berries,
discrete tannins, and a hint of tobacco.

16.5
WHITE £5.99

Castillo de Molina Reserva Chardonnay 2002 CHILE
A lovely roasted-nut finish with apricot concludes the
peachy/citrus opening.

16.5
RED £6.99

Durius Marqués de Griñon Tempranillo 2001 SPAIN
Gorgeous tannins to lovely brisk cherries and plums.
A hint of chocolate to the rich berries. Shows just how
civilised and polished (yet characterful) the
Tempranillo grape can become. Beautiful plump, soft
texture here. Fleshy, rich, textured, gripping and, for
the price, a steal.
Also at Budgens, Majestic, Sainsbury's and Thresher.

16
RED £4.99

Fairview Goats du Roam 2002 SOUTH AFRICA
Tar and plums, roasted edge to the tannins, a finish of
morello cherry. Very bright fleshy plums, hint of
strawberries with a fine dusting of tannins. An
excellent casserole red.
Also at Asda, Tesco, Booths, Oddbins, Sainsbury's and
Somerfield.

16   RED £4.49

Santa Julia Bonarda/Sangiovese 2002   ARGENTINA
The tension between the blackberries and the spicy
tannins (and hint of cocoa) provides great
entertainment on the tongue. Wonderful brisk
tannins with roasted plums. Bargain tippling here
(and great with cheese dishes and cold meats).

16   WHITE £5.99

Gewürztraminer Preiss Zimmer 2001   FRANCE
Soft, dry, not too sweet, needs Chinese food.

16   WHITE £4.99

Kiwi Cuvée Chardonnay/Viognier, Vin de Pays   FRANCE
d'Oc 2001
Soft apricot, a touch of pineapple, an elegant, gently
rich finish. A really elegant specimen.

16   WHITE £3.99

Wild Pig Chardonnay, Vin de Pays d'Oc 2002   FRANCE
Bargain melon, hint of soft pear, good balanced finish.

16   WHITE £4.99

Domaine de Pellehaut Symphonie, Vin de Pays   FRANCE
des Côtes de Gascogne 2001
Delicious melon and slight toffee-pineapple fruit.
Excellent with oriental food and occidental mood.

16   WHITE £4.49

Noble House Riesling, Ewald Pfeiffer 2001   GERMANY
Terrific, honeyed richness totally balanced by limey
acids. Lovely aperitif style.

The Co-op (although not included in this book) has
become one of the most adventurous wine retailers on
the high street in one important respect: on its own-
label bottles it provides, in defiance of European
regulations, a full list of ingredients even though most
leave no residue in the finished wine. No other retailer
goes to these lengths. Now you may say 'But surely
wine is just made from grapes and yeast?', but the
French routinely add beet sugar to wines from their
less solar-charged climates like Bordeaux and
Burgundy. In Australia, South Africa and such clement
places tartaric acid may be thrown in (sugar addition
being unnecessary because of sufficient sun and in
certain countries, like Australia, prohibited). Enzymes
may be used to clarify the juice, prior to ferment, but
they can be added after, and the result is a fruitier
wine. Lactic bacteria may be also used. They encourage
the secondary ferment where sharp malic acids are
transformed into soft lactic acids. The fining agents
used to clear fully fermented wine such as egg white,
milk or gelatine obviously are not present in the
finished wine but nevertheless offend vegetarians and
vegans. Bentonite clay is widely used for white wines
and offends no-one (except the proteins and the larger
bacteria it may snare and cause to be deprived of their
environment). Polyvinylpolypyrrolidone sounds a
repulsive mouthful but after it has been used to take
out tannins it leaves no mouthful whatsoever, not even
a trace of itself. Sulphur is added as an essential
preservative to almost all wine, in very low levels, and
I've never tasted a wine without it which hadn't gone
sour or oxidised in some way.

16   WHITE £3.99

Montblanc 362 Viura Chardonnay 2002   SPAIN
A triumph of dry peach and walnuts. Great balance,
effortless style, relaxed fruitiness, and real elegance on
the finish. The price is miraculous.

16   WHITE £4.99

Marqués de Alella Parxet 2002   SPAIN
Not everyday you taste a 100% Pansa Blanca grape
variety wine. Try it. You'll like it.

16   WHITE £4.99

Terramar Chardonnay de Muller, Tarragona 2001   SPAIN
Has a luxurious, slightly roasted, caramel-edged
finish. Excellent with poultry dishes.

16   WHITE £4.99

Rapitala Cateratto/Chardonnay 2001   ITALY
Very elegant, polished, under-ripe fruit with a finish
faintly echoic of nuts.

16   WHITE £5.99

Accademia del Sole Familia Plaia Cateratto/   ITALY
Viognier 2001
Interesting dry, almost fuzzy-skinned peachiness.

16   WHITE £3.99

Riverview Chardonnay/Pinot Grigio 2002   HUNGARY
Very exotic-tasting, dryish mango fruit with a
suggestion of satsuma. Dry apricot, hint of
gooseberry. High-class texture.
Also at Safeway.

16

WHITE £4.99

Three Choirs Willowbrook 2001 ENGLISH
I'm feeling charitable. There should be at least one
English wine in this book and this is the most
deserving. It tastes of grapes, forsooth!

16

WHITE £4.45

Woolpunda Chardonnay, Thomson 2001 AUSTRALIA
Has pleasant layers of rich melon, then peach then
toffee, then. . . it relaxes – as does the drinker.

16

WHITE £4.99

Yellow Tail Chardonnay 2002 AUSTRALIA
Nice touches of roasted pineapple, peach and custard
on the finish.

16

WHITE £6.99

Wolf Blass Chardonnay 2002 AUSTRALIA
Thrusting but delicate, rich but not OTT, forward yet
doesn't outstay its welcome. Perhaps Wolf Blass's
most civilised, least angst-ridden tipple.

16

WHITE £4.99

Yellow Tail Verdelho 2002 AUSTRALIA
Something different, the Verdelho grape: musky, ripe,
peachy, hint of cream.

16

WHITE £4.99

Peter Lehmann Riesling 2001 AUSTRALIA
Screwcapped and all the better for it. A rich yet not
ungainly Riesling of depth and balance, it has a soft
citrussy style. In 2012 it will rate 18.5 points.

16

WHITE £6.99

Rosemount Estate Riesling 2001   AUSTRALIA
Good chewy mineral-tinged, lime/melon fruit. Will
cellar well until 2008/9.
Also in Tesco.

16

WHITE £4.99

Seventh Moon Chardonnay 2001   CALIFORNIA, USA
Dry, unhurried, slightly baked-cream melon with a
touch of dry tarte tatin.

16

WHITE £4.99

Leaping Horse Chardonnay 2001   USA
Well textured, rich and clinging. Good melon and
paw-paw fruit.

16 **(in 18 months)**

WHITE £4.99

Cono Sur Viognier 2002   CHILE
Good now but given some time to develop, from its
peachy base, it'll develop more funkiness and richness.
Also in Majestic.

16

WHITE £6.49

Casablanca Santa Isabel Gewürztraminer 2002   CHILE
An immensely delicate ready-now Gewürztraminer
with dry pear and rose-petal fruit – very dry, very
subtle, very elegant. The result is exciting.

16

WHITE £3.99

Danie de Wet Chardonnay Sur Lie 2002   SOUTH AFRICA
A delightfully delicate peach/gooseberry design.

16   RED £3.99

Château Le Pin, Bordeaux 2001   FRANCE
Dry, chocolatey thick and hugely rare-meat friendly.
The tannins shape deliciously.

16   RED £9.99

Château Caronne Ste-Gemme, Haut-Médoc 1997   FRANCE
A handsome, rugged, roasted-berried claret of
uncompromising richness and elegance. Has real
character.

16   RED £4.99

La Chasse du Pape Réserve, Côtes du Rhône 2001   FRANCE
Delicious plums and cherries with earthy tannins.
Will age well for 2–3 years and improve.

16   RED £4.99

Les Planels Minervois, Domaine des Comtes 1999   FRANCE
Good tannins, finely roasted berries with a hint of
coffee.

16   RED £3.99

Wild Pig Syrah, Vin de Pays d'Oc 2001   FRANCE
I love the gripping earthy tannins. And, boy, do they
linger.

16   RED £4.99

Stephan & Philippe Malbec, Vin de Pays d'Oc,   FRANCE
Maurel Vedeau 2000
Chocolate and roasted berries – a winning recipe.

16

RED £6.49

La Cuvée Mythique, Vin de Pays d'Oc 2000   FRANCE
Smooth yet characterful, fruity yet subtle, rich yet has
finesse with flavour. Delicious warmth here with firm
berries and chocolate-edged tannins.
Also at Waitrose and Safeway.

16

RED £4.99

Yellow Tail Shiraz 2002   AUSTRALIA
Chewy, rich, ripe and enthusiastic, but the tannins
give it such charm without spoiling its berried
immediacy. Perfect for spicy casseroles.

16

RED £4.99

Misiónes de Rengo Carmenere 2002   CHILE
Nicely berried and roasted – with a slow-moving,
creamy chocolate finish.

16

WHITE SPARKLING £3.99

Cristalino Cava NV   SPAIN
Dry and tangy, good nutty finish.

16

WHITE SPARKLING £5.49

MÔ Vintage Cava Agusti Torello 1999   SPAIN
Very rich style of bubbly but it does turn crisp on the
finish.

16

RED SPARKLING £7.99

Banrock Station Sparkling Shiraz NV   AUSTRALIA
Still a great wine – a red bubbly no less – to have with the
Christmas bird.
Also at Sainsbury's, Waitrose and Somerfield.

16

WHITE DESSERT (half bottle) £4.99
Cranswick Estate Botrytis 2001   AUSTRALIA
Brilliant with sushi. It's the acidity, you see (not the
honey). It does work with the ginger and green mustard.

16

RED £5.52
Torres Sangre de Toro 2001   SPAIN
Brisk tannins, delicious smoky berries. A good vintage
of this established brand.

16

RED £3.99
Inycon Merlot 2001   SICILY, ITALY
I like very much the touch of tobacco leaf to the
berries, which are boosted by tangy tannins.

16

RED £5.02
Cono Sur Pinot Noir 2002   CHILE
Tobacco, tannins, chocolate, herbs and . . . some
gaminess to remind you it is actually Pinot.

16

WHITE £2.99
Zimmermann Riesling 2002   GERMANY
Good balance between ripe melon with a hint of
honey and crisp compensating acids. Excellent with
spicy fish dishes.
Also at Sainsbury's

You can buy wine by clicking on a mouse, but what do
you do if it tastes of rats' tails? Ensure that any e-wine
merchant you deal with has an immediate no-hassle
refund policy.

16

Franz Reh Spätlese 2001
GERMANY

Very sweet and unctuous, and perfect with ice-creams
and Greek-style pastry desserts.

16

Inycon Chardonnay 2001
SICILY, ITALY

Lovely oily apricot, pineapple, toasty melon and soft
acids (if acids can be termed soft). The texture and
that oil are the exciting things here. Deliciously rich
yet not OTT, this is one of the smartest white wines
(modern) to come out of Sicily. Lifts a bad mood, and
lifts good food (fish, poultry, risottos, pasta).
Also at Tesco.

16

Jindalee Chardonnay 2000
AUSTRALIA

Good, rich, mature, buttery richness with the
vegetality still civilised. Drink it by Christmas 2003.

16

Durius Marqués de Griñon Rioja 2001
SPAIN

Always one of the smoothest, most elegant, satisfying
and civilised of Riojas – and certainly the most
elegant. Has character as well as class.
Also at Thresher.

ODDBINS

31–33 Weir Road,
Wimbledon,
London SW19 8UG

Tel: (020) 8944 4400
Fax: (020) 8944 4411

E-mail: customer.service@oddbinsmail.com
Website: www.oddbins.com

For Oddbins' wines 15.5 points and under visit
www.superplonk.com

18

RED £10.99

Fairview SMV 2001   SOUTH AFRICA

A marvellous blend of Shiraz, Mourvèdre and Viognier,
which is both electrifyingly safe yet fine and brisk.

18

WHITE £7.29

Pinot Blanc Auxerrois, Albert Mann 2001   FRANCE

'Auxerrois' is Alsatian for Chardonnay, but this
stupendous specimen is nothing like any Chardonnay
you've ever tasted with its apricot, citrus and
pineapple dexterity.

17.5

RED £12.99

Katnook Estate Cabernet Sauvignon 1999   AUSTRALIA

This is one of Australia's smoothest, most polished
Cabs, classic Coonawarra Cabernet. That is to say
minty, crisp and yet soft, energetic yet demure, rich
yet subtle. You travel in plushly upholstered comfort,
catching the whiff of mint and crushed blackberries.
Drink with a pea risotto – wonderful!!!
Also available at Waitrose and The Wine Society.

17.5

WHITE £8.99

Wither Hills Chardonnay 2001   NEW ZEALAND

Screwcap. A wonderful cheeky Chardonnay offering a
view of the grape which embraces Burgundian
vegetality and Australian richness. Huge class in a
glass. Like a refined Corton-Charlemagne so vegetal,
hay-edged, dry, toasted and. . . but this is to insult the
wine. No white Burgundy under £40 comes close.
Also at Booths.

17.5

WHITE £9.99

Columbia Crest Chardonnay 2000 USA

I love the sheer chutzpah of this wine, with its oily sensuality. I like its smoothness yet ability to ruffle the palate. It offers dry melons, apricot, a hint of buttered citrus, and a joyous finish which seems to induce a sigh of delight in even the most jaded of palates.

17

WHITE £9.99

Raats Chenin Blanc 2002 SOUTH AFRICA

Very individual, incisive dry fruit with 'touches' of gooseberry and dry peach.

17

WHITE £12.99

Hamilton Russell Chardonnay 2001 SOUTH AFRICA

A major reason to abandon £45 a bottle white Burgundy.

17

WHITE £13.49

Boekenhoutskloof Sémillon 2001 SOUTH AFRICA

A stunningly complex, layered yet joyous wine.

17

RED £6.99

Goat d'Afrique Indigenous Red 2002 SOUTH AFRICA

Wonderful chewy plums, biscuits (jam-centred) and huge tannins.

17

RED £10.99

Fairview Mourvèdre 2001 SOUTH AFRICA

Sweet berries, herbs, touch of lavender, hint of thyme – get the 'picture'? It's Provence.

On my first visit to an Oddbins shop, the year the England football team was managed by a bald man in a macintosh, I paid 24 shillings for three half bottles of Château Smith-Haut-Lafite 1933. I wasted my money and didn't get any of it back (one bottle oxidised, one bottle corked, one bottle boring). Oddbins has come on a lot since then.

17
WHITE £9.49

Buitenverwachting Chardonnay 2001   SOUTH AFRICA
One of the classiest on the block. A master class in wood/fruit balance.

17
WHITE £6.99

Etoile Filante Chardonnay, Vin de Pays d'Oc 2001   FRANCE
Better than many a much vaunted Burgundy with its creamy vegetality and classy texture.

17
WHITE £8.99

Muscat Albert Mann 2001
FRANCE
A wonderful grapey aperitif wine of wit and gentle spicy richness. Superb with flash-fried scallops.

17
WHITE £8.99

Errazuriz Wild Ferment Chardonnay, Casablanca 1998
CHILE
There are several things about this white wine which will set on edge the pocket and palate of the so-called connoisseur. Let us deal first with the most banal: the price tag. It is £8.99. Not obscene, but comfortingly heading in the right direction towards a tenner. Then

there is the country of origin: Chile. Good things have
been said about Chile. Now things get really
tantalising. The wine comes not just from Chile but
from a specific vineyard area called Casablanca. Our
connoisseur's eyes light up. Casablanca is getting a
reputation; acquiring status as one of the 'in' vineyard
regions like Marlborough in New Zealand or Napa in
California. Finally, and perhaps what clinches the deal,
is the fact that the wine announces itself as a 'wild
ferment' specimen. This means that the juice is not
inoculated with a commercial yeast as the majority of
the world's wines are, but left to ferment – that is to
say the yeast goes through the process of turning the
sugar into alcohol – via whatever native yeast strains
are already present on the skins of the grapes and
inhabit the winery (which cannot be wholly and purely
wild as they will have been influenced by the stronger
commercial yeasts in use elsewhere in the winery).
All of this information is readily inferable from the
name on the label. What is not is that it has a
beautiful flaxen plastic object guaranteeing that no
bottle will be tainted (or 'corked' as parlance has it).
What is also not conclusive until the liquid is in the
glass is that our connoisseur, for once, has been
absolutely right and has acquired a gorgeous golden
wine representing great value for money (unless he
has cellared it for a few years which is inadvisable
with wine sealed with a plastic cork because it may
leak and let in air). The wine now demonstrates that it
has the dazzlingly improbable effect of smelling and
tasting like a vivacious Meursault made in Alsace in
conditions they only get in Provence. If our

connoisseur, poor plonker that he is, comes to this seemingly crazy conclusion then he can only be a wine correspondent and thus you may say, well, what do you expect, he's barking.

17

WHITE £4.99

Terre dei Messapi Chardonnay, Salentino 2000   ITALY
Not your usual dollop of melon by any stretch of the imagination. This has a stunning turn of pace, almost creamy in its richness, as it cascades over the tastebuds, and there is tremendous individuality and character to the wine which is in no way forced or manufactured. It is absolutely delicious.

17

WHITE £9.99

Petaluma Riesling 2001   AUSTRALIA
Gorgeous waxy, chewy pear/pineapple, minerally. Citrus fruit with precocious acids and an already haughty demeanour. Will rate 20 points in 10–12 years. Screwcap.

17

RED £6.99

Porcupine Ridge Pinotage 2001   SOUTH AFRICA
Classic Cape Pinotage offering perfume, punchy berries, spice and tannins.

17

WHITE £9.99

Catena Chardonnay, Mendoza 2001   ARGENTINA
Lovely creamy richness, toasty and gripping, with a hint of caramel and citrus. And it lingers in the throat like nectar.
Also at Sainsbury's.

17   RED £23.99

Boekenhoutskloof Syrah 2000   SOUTH AFRICA
Syrah as chocolate. Remarkably complete. Superb toffee-
edged fruit of cassis and brilliantly tailored tannins. One
of the new world's greatest expressions of this grape (see
entry for Porcupine Ridge Syrah in Waitrose for further
remarks about the maker of this wine and the winery).
Also at Waitrose.

16.5   WHITE £11.99

Glen Carlou Chardonnay Reserve 2001   SOUTH AFRICA
Gorgeous vegetal richness, remarkable.

16.5   RED £6.99

Boekenhoutskloof Porcupine Ridge   SOUTH AFRICA
Merlot 2001
Such bonny, brisk tannins! Thick as axle grease and
almost as difficult to shift – it lingers with roast
berries and chocolate.

16.5   RED £8.49

Vinum Cabernet Sauvignon 2001   SOUTH AFRICA
Monster of berried, bustling fruit and good tannins.

16.5   RED £9.69

Radford Dale Merlot 2001   SOUTH AFRICA
Highly civilised and smooth yet raunchy and
characterful.

16.5   RED £9.99

Goat-Roti 2001   SOUTH AFRICA
Oh, northern Rhône, weep! What a delicious wine.

16.5
RED £5.59

Labeye Grenache/Syrah, Vin de Pays d'Oc 2001 FRANCE
Superb deep blackberries and grilled nutty plums with
herbs and rippling tannins of great wit.

16.5
WHITE £8.99

Villa Maria Cellar Selection Riesling 2000 NEW ZEALAND
Superb oily richness, hint of petrol developing, great
texture, superb poise and finishing. Will rate 18–19 in
3–4 years, cork permitting.

16.5
RED £11.99

D'Arenberg 'The Galvo Garage' Cabernet/ AUSTRALIA
Merlot/Cabernet Franc 2001
Convincing cohesive blend of berries, vibrant
tannins and rich acids. Huge personality, great
entertainer.

16.5
WHITE £6.99

Etoile Filante Viognier, Vin de Pays d'Oc 2001 FRANCE
Dry, peachy (but subtle here) with a touch of grilled
seediness (in the nicer sense of that word).

16.5
RED £4.99

Terre dei Messapi Salice, Salentino 2000 ITALY
A most unusual pepper, cinnamon and anise-seed
spiced red which manages to have some elegance with
this individuality of approach. The wine is superbly
balanced and has great acids, making it superb with
spicy, particularly Indian-style, food.

16.5

RED £5.49

Terre dei Messapi Primitivo, Salentino 2000   ITALY

Not unlike its cousin above, it has a touch of cigar-leaf
and more tannins. It is a very virile red wine.

16.5

RED £11.99

Penfolds Bin 407 Cabernet Sauvignon 2000   AUSTRALIA

Delicious minty, leafy touches to soft berries with adult
tannins and characterfully deep-finishing finesse.
Also at Safeway and Majestic.

16

WHITE £8.99

Geoff Weaver Riesling 2001   AUSTRALIA

Dry, grapefruit/gooseberry/citrus, but very young –
will cellar for 8–12 years and may then reach 18.5
points. Screwcap.

16

WHITE £6.99

Knappstein Hand-Picked Riesling 2001   AUSTRALIA

Lovely, slow to evolve waxy pineapple/pear/petroleum-
tinged fruit. Will reach 20 points in 6–8 years.
Screwcap.

16

RED £9.99

Penfolds Bin 28 Kalimna Shiraz 2000   AUSTRALIA

One of Penfolds' most harmonious, savoury blends of
fruit and tannins. It opens out well after a couple of
hours of breathing (full decantation) to reveal genteel
spice and smooth berries and those lively tannins.
This is one of those wines which wrote its own 16-
point rating, no second thoughts: just the afterthought

that how perfect such a red would be to drink with
spicy food (excellent, therefore, for a BYOB treat).
Also at Sainsbury's, Safeway, Somerfield, Thresher,
Majestic, Tesco and Small Merchants (Unwins).

16   RED   (3 litre box) £15.99 (bottle) £3.99

El Calchorro 2001   CHILE

Unusual individuality and bite, class and clout in a
boxed wine. The blend of Cabernet Sauvignon, Merlot
and Carmenere produces a fresh, keen, flashy red
with supple plums and charred berries with soft
crumbly tannins. Immensely easy to quaff and
versatile with food (light poultry dishes to fish).

16   RED   £9.99

Montes Alpha Cabernet Sauvignon, Santa Cruz 1999   CHILE
This shows sweet – I'm tempted to say sentimental –
berries with a fine dusting of tannins. However, this
suggests simplicity when, within 2 or 3 hours of
whole decantation, some biting Cabernet fruit
emerges. Not a lot of spice or pepperiness, but
beautifully polished cohesive fruit and tannins.
Also at Majestic.

16   RED   £8.99

Bonterra Vineyards Zinfandel 2000   CALIFORNIA, USA
Delightfully chewy, gently grilled berries with touches
of cinnamon. Has a joyously rich and devil-may-care
fruitiness which, thrown in the face of decades of
European po-facedness from old-world wines which
might try to compete (Rhône, Rioja, Chianti), makes an

eloquent case for this wine's inclusion in any
candidate's list for must-drink-wines with first-class,
elegant Indian, Pakistani and Bangladeshi food without
clumsy spicing. Not a cheap wine but then it isn't a
cheep wine: it doesn't warble or trill, it richly roars.
Also at Waitrose, Majestic, Safeway and Sainsbury's.

16

ROSÉ £5.99
FRANCE

**Vignes des Deux Soleils 'Les Romains', Vin de
Pays d'Oc 2001**
The most succinct expression of the metaphysical
essence of rosiness I have tasted in years.

16

WHITE £5.59
FRANCE

**Labeye Viognier/Chardonnay, Vin de Pays
d'Oc 2001**
Delicious rich apricot fruit on various levels.

16

RED £5.59
FRANCE

Mosaïque Syrah, Vin de Pays d'Oc 2001
Delicious roasted, deeply charred indeed, berries, with
excellent firm tannins.

Ah, Oddbins! Or should that now be La Oddbins? I
have heard no intelligence to suggest that this
retailer's new French masters, the owners of the
Nicolas wine-shop chain, have any plans to change the
name and they would be mad to try. How would it
translate? Les Casiers Bizarres? Les Coffres Drôles? Les
Poubelles Curieuses is my favourite.

16

RED £5.59

Labeye Cuvée Gauthier, Minervois 2001 FRANCE

Chocolate and dry tannins persuasively gripping and
rich!

16

RED £6.99

Etoile Filante Cabernet Sauvignon, Vin de Pays FRANCE
d'Oc 2001 £6.99

Juicy but rampantly tannic and unconcentrated.

16

WHITE £6.49

Clos Petite Bellane, Côtes du Rhône 2002 FRANCE

The perfect dry white (though the adjective is relative)
for trout and salmon fishcakes.

16

WHITE £9.99

St Véran 'Les Chailloux', Domaine des Deux FRANCE
Roches 2001

Very calm, collected, warm, yet dry white Burgundy of
deftly woven fruit and acids.

16

RED £4.99

Aradon Rioja 2002 SPAIN

Interesting coal-black tannins, intense and chewy,
with roasted berries. Most assertive and gripping.

16

WHITE £9.99

Raats Chenin (Oaked) 2002 SOUTH AFRICA

Lovely example of this under-rated grape. Has dry
apricot/peach hint of oil, touch of roasted walnut.

16

RED £6.99
CHILE

Equus Cabernet Sauvignon, Maipo 2001
Fat tannins which coat the teeth like lacquer – and the
berries are sticky too.

16

RED £6.99
CHILE

Top Dog Syrah, Colchagua 2001
Juicy but disciplined by brisk, roasted tannins.

16

WHITE £7.49
AUSTRALIA

Annie's Lane Riesling 2002
Screwcap. Delicious tonic to the palate! Wakes it up
with citrus and melon and a hint of passionfruit.

16

WHITE £8.49
AUSTRALIA

Nepenthe Lenswood Sauvignon Blanc 2001
Deliriously well-poised crisp acids and firm fleshy fruit
(melon and paw-paw).
The 2002 is available at Waitrose.

16

WHITE £9.49
AUSTRALIA

Nepenthe Lenswood Riesling 2001
Screwcapped. Rich but capable of interesting development
in bottle (9 years) to reach 18 points.
The 2002 is available at Waitrose.

16

RED £18.99
AUSTRALIA

**Petaluma Coonawarra Cabernet Sauvignon/
Merlot 1999**
Intense, very dry (almost like ashes in the mouth as it
quits the throat), but very elegant, classy and compact.

It is expensive but its concentrated, very subtle tobacco-leaf edge is impressive.
Also at Majestic and Sainsbury's.

16

WHITE £3.99
SOUTH AFRICA

Forrester's Petit Chenin 2002
Gorgeous elderflower/mineral richness.

16

WHITE £4.99
SOUTH AFRICA

New World Sémillon/Chardonnay 2001
Has a lovely vegetal undertone to crisp, fresh, mineral-tinged fruit.

16

WHITE £8.99
SOUTH AFRICA

Green on Green Sémillon 2001
Delicious, dry, soft, rich, classy, very elegant.

16

WHITE £8.99
SOUTH AFRICA

Radford Dale Chardonnay 2001
Has soft apricot richness, very charming.

16

WHITE £7.99

Fairview Terroir Trial Sauvignon Blanc 2002 SOUTH AFRICA
Classic!

16

WHITE £9.99
SOUTH AFRICA

The Berrio Sauvignon Blanc 2002
Gorgeous balance of acid, fruit and chutzpah.

16

RED £4.99
SOUTH AFRICA

Oracle Pinotage 2001
Delicious rich tannins.

16   RED £4.99

Oracle Shiraz 2001   SOUTH AFRICA
Biscuity, rich, berried and nicely textured.

16   RED £4.99

Fairview Goats du Roam 2002   SOUTH AFRICA
Tar and plums, roasted edge to the tannins, a finish of
morello cherry. Very bright fleshy plums, hint of
strawberries with a fine dusting of tannins. An
excellent casserole red. Better than any Côtes du
Rhône at the same price (under a fiver).
Also at Asda, Booths, Morrison's, Sainsbury's,
Somerfield and Tesco.

16   RED £5.99

New World Shiraz 2002   SOUTH AFRICA
A nice touch of Marmite to the fruit.

16   RED £5.99

Boekenhoutskloof The Wolf Trap 2002   SOUTH AFRICA
Stunningly rich and meaty. A real bargain. Superb
tannins.
Also at Asda.

16   RED £6.99

Fleur du Cap Unfiltered Merlot 2000   SOUTH AFRICA
No leather but soft cherry/plum fruit with crushed
tannins.

16   RED £8.99

Post House Cabernet Sauvignon 2000   SOUTH AFRICA
Brilliant chewy, charcoal-edged berries and tannins.

16

RED £9.99

Flagstone Writers Block Pinotage 2001 SOUTH AFRICA

Terrific – and it works. Suddenly I feel free to flow. . .!

16

RED £9.99

Flagstone Dragon Tree Cabernet Sauvignon/Pinotage 2000 SOUTH AFRICA

Has a delicious fresh, flashy edge to rich berries.

16

RED £9.99

Radford Dale Shiraz 2001 SOUTH AFRICA

What a brisk, rich wine of weight and wit.

16

RED £9.99

Southern Right Pinotage 2000 SOUTH AFRICA

A beginner's entry point. How seductive the grape can be?

16

RED £19.99

Boekenhoutskloof Cabernet Sauvignon 2000 SOUTH AFRICA

Very fresh apple-skin edge to some superb tannins.

Wine is alone amongst alcohols in being so beautifully olfactorily striking (stronger distilled alcohols are merely fiercer), and it is unique amongst liquids in being able to so express its odiferous personality whilst unheated.

16

Wakefield Shiraz 2002 AUSTRALIA

Has interestingly characterful berries with subtle
coriander/paprika edging. This spicing is far from
OTT, almost genteel, certainly polite, and it's nicely
calmed by the savoury tannins. This vintage of this
wine is claimed to represent one of its best ever and
may, in the words of Mitchell Taylor, the managing
director of Wakefield, 'eclipse the previous great red
vintage of 1998'. Adam Eggins, the wine maker, is
silent on the matter (but then I did not ask him), but
his effort is claimed by the producer to offer 'aromas
of plum, cinnamon, liquorice [sic], and spice with
creamy nuances of vanilla oak, chocolate and coffee.'
I wasn't sure about the chocolate and failed to find the
coffee, and I did look hard, but perhaps readers
possessed of longer noses and more enquiring palates
than mine, would get in touch with their findings.
Also at Small Merchants (Stratford's, Wiljay Wines,
Wine Junction, Wright Wine Co., Raeburn Fine
Wines, Hoults Wine Merchants, Big Wines, Portland
Wine Cellars, Paul Roberts, Ballantynes of Cowbridge,
Scathard, Nidderdale Fine Wines, Bacchanalia, Wine
in Cornwall, Terry Platt Wine Merchants, Unwins)
and E-tailers (European Wine Growers' Association).

16

Columbia Crest Cabernet Sauvignon 2000 USA

A very full-on, plump, rich and ripe red as soft as
pillow on the palate.

16

RED £9.99

Columbia Crest Merlot 1999　　　　　　　　USA

Good mature berries, touch of cocoa, hint of roast
lamb. Soft and very charming.

16

RED £14.99

Château Ste-Michelle Indian Wells Merlot 1999　　USA

Has a very engaging sense of humour, this sly red. It
seems as if it'll engulf the palate with ripe plums and
then soft-fruit flavours cruise in and jostle for
attention and the result, whilst expensive to acquire, is
certainly deliciously attention-getting.

SAFEWAY

Safeway House,
6 Millington Road,
Hayes,
Middlesex UB3 4AY

Tel: (020) 8848 8744
Fax: (020) 8573 1865

E-mail: safewaypressoffice@btclick.com
Website: www.safeway.co.uk

For Safeway wines 15.5 points and under visit
www.superplonk.com

19

Casa Lapostolle Cuvée Alexandre Chardonnay 2001   CHILE

Simply wonderful from nose to throat. Stunning texture (gripping yet elegant), complex, smoky fruit of pear/melon/pineapple and a hint of lemon peel. What is a perfect wine? One that cannot be bettered, surely. And this cannot be bettered in so many respects that though I dithered over whether I should award it the penultimate accolade I felt not to do so would be unjust. It is simply a staggeringly delicious Chardonnay of supreme, world-class finesse and potent delicacy (that crucial paradox!).

The wood here is a justified element (unintrusive and sanely balanced) and as necessary to the wine scheme of things as salt on a tomato. The vegetality, the youth of the fruit, and the calm authority of its finish give the wine cellaring potential of 2–3 years and doubtless well beyond this (however, it will lose some energy if laid down too long). Alas, there are few bottles left. Available in 70 stores. Also at Majestic and London Stores (Selfridges, Harrods).

18.5

Montes Alpha Chardonnay 2001   CHILE

Gorgeous texture, like velvet with satin trimmings. Lovely creamy, vegetal richness. Like a magical Meursault (the much vaunted white Burgundy which is rarely this toothsome and certainly not this good under a tenner).

Available in 70 stores.

> Now that Chardonnay manifests itself in so many
> boring, and indeed many beautiful, ways, its eponym,
> the village in Burgundy, must rue the fact that it never
> internationally trademarked its name.

18.5   RED £29.99

Peter Lehmann Stonewall Shiraz 1996   AUSTRALIA
Baked-cream edge to berries so big and clotted they
clog the throat. An immense wine of sensational
liquidity and thrills. Utterly mature and won't get
any better than this. A lot of dosh, true, but a helluva
lot of posh.
Available in 15 stores.

18.5   WHITE £9.99

Pewsey Vale Museum Reserve The Contours   AUSTRALIA
Riesling 1997
When Mr Fort, my food and drink editor at the
Guardian, invited me to lunch at a new BYOB
restaurant, I felt that he had taken to heart my tirade
against restaurant pricing on wines and its espousing
of the BYOB – Bring Your Own Bottle – restaurant
cause. However, he would admit only to a need to
review the place. The restaurant is in the most
unlikeliest of places for a BYOB, just down the road
from Harrods. It is called Chez Max. Its extant
eponym has run BYOBs for years in and around town
and so I was duly excited as I pedalled off to
Knightsbridge with two bottles of Australian wine in
my saddlebag, nabbed from the tasting of such wines

I had enjoyed that morning. Alas, en route, whipping
along Jermyn Street, a dark-windowed silver Bentley
ungraciously pulled out and my diversionary tactics in
avoiding death caused the delicious bramble-fruited
Peter Lehmann Barossa Valley Shiraz 2000 to fall
off and smash. However, made of sterner stuff was
the wine under review here. It hit the road with a
solid thump but did not break and I was able,
triumphantly, to bear it to Mr Fort's table when I
arrived with only a tiny dent visible in its delightful
screwcap. It was still cold enough to drink (evidence
of the speed, though not the care, with which it had
been transported from Australia House in the Strand
to west London).

The Contours is stunning: a sinously oily, already-
tending-to-petroleum-edged Riesling with fruit which
the screwcap's neutrality and integrity enhance for it
will permit more exciting complexities to develop as it
ages (for the next 15 years). It is thrillingly citrussy,
minerally and classic and has the texture and bite to
not only refresh the bookworm but to inspire the
gourmet as s(he) chews through a plateau des fruits
de mer or merely a ham sandwich or, as in Chez Max,
first a dish of boudin, then one of fried whiting, then
a hearty saucisse artisanale. The wine is both
gloriously subtle and emphatically full of personality
and at ten quid it is a steal. Max, to whom I offered a
glass, very generously charged no corkage for the
bottle when the bill came ('It hasn't got a cork, so how
can I?' he joked) and you might be inclined to
respond 'big deal' to this until you learn that the

corkage at his restaurant is £15 a bottle. This is of course outrageous but then Max says his customers often bring in such grand bottles that he must place a disincentive in their way in order to encourage them to plunder the restaurant's excellent wine list rather than their own cellars.

This wine is available in 5 stores. It is also stocked in certain branches of Sainsbury's.

18.5 WHITE £9.99

Yalumba Eden Valley Viognier 2001 AUSTRALIA

Wonderful texture – like balsam. Rich and very charming apricot fruit. Very classy, great finesse. Available in 20 stores. Also at Waitrose.

18 RED £9.99

Errazuriz Max Reserva Syrah 2000 CHILE

Superb smooth berries and tannins of such finesse it takes one's breath away. A wonderful wine.

17.5 RED £14.99

Errazuriz Single Vineyard Syrah 2001 CHILE

Intense charred berries of exquisite balance and richness. Tannins like velvet with ruffled corduroy edges.

17 RED £4.99

Bella Fonte Touriga Franca & Tinta Roriz 2001 PORTUGAL

What a bonny performer! Offers lush cherries and berries with disciplined, chocolate tannins.

17   RED £9.99

Norton Privada 2000   ARGENTINA

Chocolatey, rich, so intense! Delicious class of berry
here, striking tannins, and real depth of fruit to make
Bordeaux go greener than it is already.
Also at Waitrose.

17   RED £6.99

Norton Barrel Select Malbec 2000   ARGENTINA

Wonderful relaxed, roasted berries with smoky tannins,
hint of cigar, touch of cocoa. Terrific class and style.
Also at Sainsbury's and Waitrose.

17   RED £14.99

Casa Lapostolle Cuvée Alexandre Merlot 2000   CHILE

Dry, jauntily craggy leather, damsons, and hints of
grilled nuts combine to make this a classic Merlot
capable of accelerating within 14–18 months and
putting on a couple more points. The sheer ineffability
of the texture (is it velvet? satin? cashmere? something
not yet known to man or beast?) will begin to deepen
and show more complexity as it ages over the coming
year and beyond to 2006.
Also at Majestic, London Stores (Harrods, Fortnum &
Mason), and E-tailers (Everywine,
ChateauOnline.co.uk).

16.5   WHITE £16.99

Pernand Vergelesses Caradeaux ler Cru 1999   FRANCE

Very classy and authentically dry, tannic on the finish.
Modern and modish.

16.5   RED £4.99

Santa Julia Malbec 2002   ARGENTINA

A marvel of an under-a-fiver red, with urgent, grilled
tannins in attendance on rich, deep berries. High
class from nose to throat.

16.5   RED £11.99

Penfolds Bin 407 Cabernet Sauvignon 2000   AUSTRALIA

Delicious minty, leafy touches to soft berries with adult
tannins and characterfully deep-finishing finesse.
Also at Oddbins and Majestic.

I am a great fan of wines with excruciatingly dull
labels. When I see egregious typography, a cack-
handed illustration or an unenticing name on a bottle,
my antennae go out before I bring a glass of the wine
to my nose. Of course in many instances the wine
within the bottle may be in keeping with its outward
appearance and so I concern myself no more with
either. Sometimes, however, the liquid is something
special and it is then that I regard the label anew, not
now with disdain, but with delight.

Why? Because a bottle which looks as though it
cannot possibly contain an exciting wine will be judged
as such, it will befuddle so-called experts. This, then, is
why I treasure the off-putting label. It makes the wine
an even greater prize. It keeps the price down. It
means readers of this book will have more
opportunities to strike a bargain.

16.5   WHITE £4.99

Grand'Arte Alvarinho 2001   ARGENTINA

Very unusual pear-thick texture which floods the
mouth with flavour. Fat but very fit.
Available in 65 stores.

16.5   WHITE DESSERT £3.75

Safeway Moscatel de Valencia 2002   SPAIN

Screwcapped, as always, this wonderful bargain
dessert wine is a sheer honey and marmalade delight.

16.5   RED £9.99

Rupert & Rothschild Classique 2000   SOUTH AFRICA

More gripping than many a premier cru Médoc. I
know comparisons are odorous but I cannot help
making them and in this case it is much ado about
something.
Available in 76 stores.

16.5   RED £4.99

Anciennes Vignes Carigan, Vin de Pays de   FRANCE
l'Aude 2001

Terrific class of berry you meet here – with gripping
tannins. A complex specimen.

16.5   WHITE £7.99

Sileni Cellar Selection Chardonnay 2001   NEW ZEALAND

Has delicious, gently toasted, nutty Ogen-melon fruit
with a vague, but nicely judged, citrussy quality. There
is, though, nothing vague about its classy finish. It is a
handsome, firm wine of great wit and weight. It

would be wonderful with smoked fish, mild poultry dishes, scallops, crab cakes (touch of chilli here is fine) and anything marine if it is not too saline (like oysters).

16.5   RED £4.99

Primi Rioja 2001   SPAIN

A very deep Rioja of pleasing classiness and wit. It is brilliantly priced and it offers none of the usual flabby fruit or vanillary woodiness. Instead we get sturdy berries, a touch roasted, fine tannins, and a very thickly knitted texture.

16.5   RED £4.99

La Paz Old Vines Tempranillo 2000   SPAIN

Beats most Riojas, not just penny for penny but berry for berry.

Available in 78 stores. Also at Sainsbury's.

16   RED £4.99

Quinta de Cabriz, Dão 2001   PORTUGAL

Very fresh, slightly charred fruit. Splendid quaffing red.

16   WHITE £4.99

Jindalee Chardonnay 2002   AUSTRALIA

Great fun: individual, smoky melon/pear/gooseberry fruit of striking richness yet deftness.

16   WHITE £5.99

Simon Gilbert Chardonnay 2001   AUSTRALIA

Very, very elegant and daringly un-Australian.

16

WHITE SPARKLING £18.99

Fernand Thill Grand Cru NV FRANCE

A real classy, small grower's champagne to shame
many a big marque at twice the price. Very classy,
classic, controlled, dry.

Available in 70 stores.

16

WHITE £3.99

Riverview Chardonnay/Pinot Grigio 2002 HUNGARY

Very exotic-tasting, dryish mango fruit with a
suggestion of satsuma. Dry apricot, hint of
gooseberry. High-class texture.

Also at Morrison's.

16

RED £8.99

Bonterra Vineyards Zinfandel 2000 CALIFORNIA, USA

Delightfully chewy, gently grilled berries with touches
of cinnamon. Has a joyously rich and devil-may-care
fruitiness which, thrown in the face of decades of
European po-facedness from old-world wines which
might try to compete (Rhône, Rioja, Chianti), makes an
eloquent case for this wine's inclusion in any
candidate's list for must-drink-wines with first-class,
elegant Indian, Pakistani and Bangladeshi food without
clumsy spicing. Not a cheap wine but then it isn't a
cheap wine: it doesn't warble or trill, it richly roars.

Also at Waitrose, Majestic, Oddbins and Sainsbury's.

16

WHITE £2.99

Safeway Irsai Oliver 2002 HUNGARY

Superb dry spice and melon. Lovely aperitif, quite lovely.

16

Riverview Sauvignon Blanc 2002 HUNGARY
Delicious, very dry, marvellously chewy gooseberries
and hints of spice and rhubarb.
Also at Waitrose.

16

WHITE £4.99

La Mouline Viognier 2002 FRANCE
Dry peach, gooseberry and melon. Superb mineral
balance. Elegant, textured, classy.

16

WHITE £6.99

Vire Clesse Vieilles Vignes 2001 FRANCE
A deliciously textured, very classy fruit. An exceptional
white Burgundy for the money. More like this, please,
Burgundians!

My quondam publisher, Faber & Faber, once received a
letter from a provincial wine merchant who wished to
kill me. This charitable fellow was exercised by the
plight of his shop, occasioned, so he said, by the
intrusion of a large supermarket in his area which had
proved fulsomely attractive to his customers and thus
fatally detractive to his income. He reckoned that were
it not for this book no-one would have given the
supermarket's wine aisles a second glance. I pointed
out in my reply to this aggrieved dinosaur that readers
were well able to make up their own minds and if they
found value and fascination at his shop they would
continue to patronise it. He went out of business and
is rumoured now to be a wine adviser at the very
supermarket which so upset his applecart.

16

WHITE £3.99
SPAIN

Espiral Macabeo/Chardonnay 2000
Big apple and pear aroma, curious woody edge, fresh
citrus finish.

16

WHITE £3.99
SPAIN

Alteza Viura 2002
Crushed melon in texture and taste, a hint of
gooseberry on the finish.
Available in 100 stores.

16

WHITE £4.49
SOUTH AFRICA

Danie de Wet Chardonnay 2002
Makes a delicious change from the usual Chardonnay
recipe. Dry yet impishly plump (well, why not? can't
you imagine a plump imp?).

16

WHITE £5.99
AUSTRALIA

Yalumba Riesling 2002
Engagingly rich and of huge cellar potential. 18–19
points in 7–8 years.

16

WHITE £8.99
AUSTRALIA

Jim Barry The Lodge Hill Riesling 2002
Dry melon/gooseberry fruit but the screwcap will
allow it to develop very excitingly and flow with
greater feeling over the next decade.
Available in 30 stores.

16

WHITE £7.99
AUSTRALIA

Alkoomi Riesling 2002
Delicious tangily ripe fruit which though young is well on

the way to being a complete wine. It will age well for half
a decade before a plateau is reached and then become
hugely individualistic some 5 years after that which, cork
permitting, it will attain with great distinction.
Available in 83 stores.

16

WHITE £7.99

Cono Sur Riesling Vision 2002   CHILE

Screwcapped and all the better for it. Needs time to
reach 18 points. Very dry, very elegant, restrained style
but in 3–6 years, with that screwcap, it'll be even
more sensual, more complex, more seductive.

16

RED £4.89

Nero d'Avola Palmento 2001   ITALY

Hugely palate-engaging berries with earthy yet soft
tannins.

16

RED £4.99

Château Montbrun de Gautherius, Corbières   FRANCE
2001

Very intense herby, grilled berries with lipsmackingly
tasty tannins.

16

RED £8.99

Domaine La Prade Mari Chant de l'Olivier 2000   FRANCE

Fed up with acid, pricey, poncy Bordeaux reds? Here
is the answer.
Available in 70 stores.

16

RED £11.99

Château Rozier St-Emilion Grand Cru 2000 FRANCE
Chunky berries of great tannic richness. This is one
non-acidic, non-pricey, unponcy Bordeaux of great
finesse and style.

16

RED £5.99

DFJ Touriga Nacional/Touriga Franca 2001 PORTUGAL
Tannins like crumbled digestive biscuits! Way to go,
brothers and sisters! A wine with which to celebrate
life!

16

RED £7.99

Smith and Hooper Wrattonbully Cabernet AUSTRALIA
Sauvignon/Merlot 2001
Delicious class act here. The grapes sing and touch
the high notes.

16

RED £4.99

Argento Bonarda 2002 ARGENTINA
Jammy but, as always with this estate, elegant and
rich with real class to the texture.

> Women make better smellers and tasters of wine
> than men as a rule because they are biologically
> predispositioned to appreciate perfumes and flavours
> better. We men have to learn to do it. Women are
> born to it.

16 RED £9.99

Zuccardi 'Q' Malbec 2000 ARGENTINA
Sheer velvet berries. This is a remarkably couth yet
characterful wine which manages to be fantastic value
at a tenner.

16 RED £7.49

Mont Gras Syrah Limited Edition 2001 CHILE
Oddly spicy berries – but very delicious. Brilliant with
robust meat and vegetable dishes.

16 RED £9.99

Montes Alpha Cabernet Sauvignon 2000 CHILE
Very dry but immensely chocolatey and spicy, rich and
classy. I have a sneaking suspicion that within 18
months of this book's publication I will look at its
rating and wonder if I shouldn't have tacked on at
least 2 more points.

16 RED £15.99

Concha y Toro, Don Melchor 1999 CHILE
Very classy – and an object lesson in Cabernet making from
Chile (for Bordeaux to marvel at and copy).
Available in 75 stores.

16 WHITE DESSERT (half bottle) £4.99

Dom Brial Muscat de Riversaltes 2001 FRANCE
Gorgeous spicy peach and honey pudding wine.

16 RED £22.99

Château Branaire Ducru, St-Julien 1977 FRANCE
A classy blend of the usual red varieties (including

Petit Verdot) which manages, even at £23, to be easy to
swallow (in spite of cocoa-tinged, heavy tannins which
lie heavy and delicious on the back of the throat).
Available in 10 stores.

16

WHITE £4.99

Norton Sauvignon Blanc 2002   ARGENTINA
Bargain gooseberry richness and a gentle mineral
undertone.

16

RED £19.99

Gerard Bertrand 'La Forge', Corbières 1999   FRANCE
Classy melange of 50% Syrah and 50% Carignan
which contrives catering chocolate, herbs and fruit,
with racy tannins.
Available in 15 stores.

16

RED £11.99

Koltz The Carbine Shiraz/Cabernet 2001   AUSTRALIA
A jammy marriage which offers disciplined tannins
and some real class on the finish.
Available in 15 stores.

16

RED £29.99

Penfolds St Henri Shiraz 1998   AUSTRALIA
Says it's Shiraz but Cabernet plays a part too, and the
result is very classy, bold, rich, complex and very
excitingly textured. Really it's like a great mad claret/
Rhône marriage of unlikely yet very toothsome
succulence.
Available in 30 stores.

16

RED £4.99

Santa Julia Shiraz 2002 ARGENTINA

Grip, polish, savouriness and dash. A real competitor
to Aussie specimens but has more chocolate and
greater depth to the tannins (for that risible price tag).

16

RED £9.99

Penfolds Bin 28 Kalimna Shiraz 2000 AUSTRALIA

One of Penfolds' most harmonious, savoury blends of
fruit and tannins. It opens out well after a couple of
hours of breathing (full decantation) to reveal genteel
spice and smooth berries and those lively tannins.
This is one of those wines which wrote its own 16-
point rating, no second thoughts: just the afterthought
that how perfect such a red would be to drink with
spicy food (excellent, therefore, for a BYOB treat).
Also at Sainsbury's, Somerfield, Thresher, Oddbins,
Majestic, Tesco and Small Merchants (Unwins).

16

RED £6.49

La Cuvée Mythique, Vin de Pays d'Oc 2000 FRANCE

Smooth yet characterful, fruity yet subtle, rich yet has
finesse with flavour. Delicious warmth here with firm
berries and chocolate-edged tannins.
Also at Waitrose and Morrison's.

16

WHITE £5.99

Domaine Schlumberger Le 'S' d'Alsace NV FRANCE

A blend of Pinot Blanc, Riesling and Gewürztraminer
from one of Alsace's greatest producers. The wine has
an acquired smell (grassy, under-ripe vegetality) but I

like its austere richness which suggests vague apricots. It is uncompromisingly individual and entertaining.

16   WHITE £7.99

Handpicked Chardonnay 2001   AUSTRALIA

Delicious fatness of peach and melon, little compensating acidity (but it still gets there). A terrific accompaniment to roast chicken and if done in the Persian style, so a little spicy, this is all to the good. The wine comes from a newish area in Australia called Orange. Orange is a region I was keen to visit since it is representative of the burgeoning confidence and strength of the Aussie wine industry which has seen it destroy the hegemony of Europe. Orange is 150 miles west of Sydney (whose most famous region is the Hunter Valley) and is between 600 and 1050 metres above sea level. It is, then, what is known as a cool climate region (though after my visit I would disagree and say it occupies a nebulous area between cool and warm).

The Reynolds winery makes this wine and its range, also sold under the Little Boomey label, has been making itself known recently to some effect. It is a new company yet has captured a remarkably prompt and cheeky share of the UK market. It is something of a rapid commercial success story and must surely be held up in Australia as an example: to demonstrate that the gold-rush mentality is still alive and, incredibly, paying off handsomely. Reynolds is so new as to make a German or a French wine producer, still

struggling after 300 years, froth at the mouth. The
company was set up in 1994 as a grape producer
supplying Penfolds. With its 2300 acres of vineyards
in the discretely unfashionable Orange region it was
nothing more glamorous than a large-scale orchard
owner or farmer. But now it has a new winery and is
listed on the Sydney stock market (under the name
Cabonne). It has been exporting only since July 2001
and will be selling around a quarter of a million cases
this year. The company has managed to so impress
hard-nosed UK retail wine buyers that it has achieved
listing at top supermarkets many other Aussie
companies have been trying for a decade to achieve.
The only worrying thing, however, is that word
'Handpicked' on this wine's label. Does it not suggest
that this refers to the grapes? The grapes, however,
were picked by machine. The wine maker insists that
'Handpicked' can only mean 'specially selected', as he
bases the fruit choice on his best parcels of grapes. I
put this to the wine maker himself when I met him.
His name is Jon Reynolds. ('Always mistrust a man
who drops his aitches,' my mother warned, though
she offered no evidence as to why this might be so –
besides, maybe Jon was so named and sent aitchless
into life by his adoring parents.) As it happens, Jon is
the antithesis of untrustworthy in any context,
including his involvement in the motivation for
choosing the name 'Handpicked'.

'To us,' he explains, 'it merely means specially
selected, because that's what it is. The grapes are hand
selected from the best regions of Australia. I wanted a

premium range of complexity and superior fruit.' This may be so but the niggle remains that this range is misleading. However, I have an open mind. If I receive sufficient evidence to tell me that the majority of UK consumers do not consider a range called 'Handpicked' to refer to hand harvesting, I will keep my mouth shut.

In Jon's tasting room, of course, I kept it open, with great pleasure. Jon Reynolds' presence was palpable, both in the room and in the wines. When terroir is discussed the most crucial element is always left out by romantics. They insist that a wine is made by its vines and given its personality by its soil and climate. The missing element is the individual or individuals who make it. Jon Reynolds is a part of the terroir of Reynolds Orange vineyards and he cannot be discounted. Wines this provocative don't make themselves. You might as well assert that a coq au vin owes everything to the corn fed to the chicken and the wine you use to boil the fowl in. These ingredients are vital but the chef is the person who must take the most credit. And so it is with Jon's 'Handpicked' wines (however dubious that name).

SAINSBURY'S

Head Office:
33 High Holborn,
London ECIN 2HT

Tel: (020) 7695 6000
Fax: (020) 7695 7610

Customer Careline: (0800) 636262

Website: www.sainsburys.co.uk.

For Sainsbury's wines 15.5 points and under visit
www.superplonk.com

20

DESSERT WHITE (half bottle) £99.00

Château d'Yquem Sauternes 1997 1er Grand   FRANCE
Cru Classé

Simply a perfect wine. Complex, vivid, provocative yet
caressing, it is a statement of humankind's creative
genius (but that is not to say this wine has anything to
do with artistic expression). The liquid is not mono-
dimensionally sweet but full of myriad butterscotch,
soft and hard fruit flavours and combines delicacy
with magnificently textured, satiny richness yet
subtlety. It is of course young and can be laid down
for many years (as few as 5, as many as 20 and
more) but when I drank it, sipping a small glass
with some fruit and soft goat's cheese, I was ravished
by its pertinacity, and its youth was beguiling, not
gauche.

Available at the Kings Road and Cromwell Road
branches only (and at two branches of Waitrose).

20

FORTIFIED £49.99

Blandy's Madeira Malmsey 1978   PORTUGAL

Purists will protest this is hardly a superplonk. I
agree. But once you smell and taste this wine you
can forgive anyone anything. True, this style of
fortified wine is as out of fashion as monocles for
men and whalebone stays for women but it insisted
on selection and I can resist everything where beauty
is concerned except insistence. It has an utterly
perfect aroma of toasted nuts and finely roasted
tomatoes and plums. 'Another Madeira, m'dear?'
is a redundant supplication with such a bouquet, for

the bottle will, mysteriously, empty itself. The fruit plays sweet and dry, is bold and definitive, and it can represent the planet as a wine, so utterly delicious and remarkable is it. It offers a totally sensational experience from nose to throat and once opened the bottle will last months and so to those purists who grumble further that fifty quid buys a case of wine I respond that this specimen, opened, will outlast twelve bottles any month. Madeira may simply mean wood in Portuguese (and Malmsey is just the Malvasia grape variety), but this is a hugely complex and exciting wine and the Duke of Clarence when he chose death by drowning in it was a shrewder fellow than his executioner knew.

Available in 19 stores.

 18

RED £8.99

Canale Black River Reserva Malbec 2001   ARGENTINA

Marks & Spencer has a Merlot from this estate and it is not dissimilar to this Malbec, though there are even crunchier tannins here and a full rip-roaring richness on the finish which is even more unabashed, luxurious, hedonistic, and characterful. If young men do still prepare 'getting-to-know-you' dinners for their fiancée's parents, then this is a wine to avoid at all costs for it will give the impression that its server has a wicked, louche disposition which will make the daughter deliriously happy but the parents most disturbed.

18

Argento Chardonnay Reserva 2001   ARGENTINA

Around the top of the list of the world's under-seven-quid-Chardonnays-which-make-Montrachets-at-seven-times-the-price-seem-like-gnat's-piss. It has a beautiful texture, warmth, dryness yet fruit, and its delicacy is utterly captivating.

What is a classic wine? Certain grape varieties have become known as 'classics': Cabernet Sauvignon, Merlot, Pinot Noir, Syrah, Riesling, Chardonnay, Sauvignon Blanc, Chenin Blanc and Sémillon. It is a nonsense. The Piedmontese would certainly add Nebbiolo to this list, the Spaniards Tempranillo, the Alsatians Tokay Pinot-Gris and Gewürztraminer, the Tuscans Sangiovese, the Uruguayans Tannat, the Hungarians Furmint, the Californians Zinfandel and. . . I could go on.

Then there is the subject of what constitutes a classic wine area. Bordeaux? Tokaj-Hegyalja? Burgundy? Barolo? Champagne? Coonawarra? Franschhoek? Maipo? Yes, in each case – and there are hundreds more.

A classical wine, however, is not open to argument. It can only refer to the Falernian of the Romans, the antique wines of the Myceneans and Spartans, and to the Iliadic vinifications of the Thracians (now Bulgarians). This usage apart, we should be wary of the term 'classic' or 'classical'.

18

Pewsey Vale Museum Reserve The Contours   AUSTRALIA
Riesling 1997

When Mr Fort, my food and drink editor at the
Guardian, invited me to lunch at a new BYOB
restaurant, I felt that he had taken to heart my tirade
against restaurant pricing on wines and its espousing
of the BYOB – Bring Your Own Bottle – restaurant
cause. However, he would admit only to a need to
review the place. The restaurant is in the most
unlikeliest of places for a BYOB, just down the road
from Harrods. It is called Chez Max. Its extant
eponym has run BYOBs for years in and around town
and so I was duly excited as I pedalled off to
Knightsbridge with two bottles of Australian wine in
my saddlebag, nabbed from the tasting of such wines
I had enjoyed that morning. Alas, en route, whipping
along Jermyn Street, a dark-windowed silver Bentley
ungraciously pulled out and my diversionary tactics in
avoiding death caused the delicious bramble-fruited
Peter Lehmann Barossa Valley Shiraz 2000 (16 points
out of 20, Oddbins, Waitrose, Sainsbury's and
Safeway) to fall off and smash. However, made of
sterner stuff was the wine under review here. It hit
the road with a solid thump but did not break and I
was able, triumphantly, to bear it to Mr Fort's table
when I arrived with only a tiny dent visible in its
delightful screwcap. It was still cold enough to drink
(evidence of the speed, though not the care, with
which it had been transported from Australia House
in the Strand to west London).

The Contours is stunning: a sinously oily, already-tending-to-petroleum-edged Riesling with fruit which the screwcap's neutrality and integrity enhance for it will permit more exciting complexities to develop as it ages (for the next 15 years). It is thrillingly citrussy, minerally and classic and has the texture and bite to not only refresh the bookworm but to inspire the gourmet as s(he) chews through a plateau des fruits de mer or merely a ham sandwich or, as in Chez Max, first a dish of boudin, then one of fried whiting, then a hearty saucisse artisanale. The wine is both gloriously subtle and emphatically full of personality and at ten quid it is a steal. Max, to whom I offered a glass, very generously charged no corkage for the bottle when the bill came ('It hasn't got a cork, so how can I?' he joked) and you might be inclined to respond 'big deal' to this until you learn that the corkage at his restaurant is £15 a bottle. This is of course outrageous but then Max says his customers often bring in such grand bottles that he must place a disincentive in their way in order to encourage them to plunder the restaurant's excellent wine list rather than their own cellars.

Sainsbury's stock it in the Kings Road and Cromwell Road branches only. Available in 5 Safeway stores.

17.5   SPARKLING WHITE £7.99

Cava Vendrell Reserva, Albet i Noya, Organic NV   SPAIN

Is it really better than Krug? Indisputably. The fruit is rich yet classy, flavoursome yet with toasty finesse, there are tannins to give grip and guidance to the acidity, and the whole construction is a joy. The Catalans are geniuses, aren't they? Not only is the fruit organic, and the wine making exemplary but the packaging is superb, elegant, high class. It really should rate 20 points.

17.5   RED £7.99

Château de la Gard, Bordeaux Supérieur 1999   FRANCE

Why can't more clarets be like this? Totally authentic, dry, mysteriously rich yet shy, full of craggy tannins playing footie with fine fruit of berries, herbs and a touch of licorice. A fantastic claret for the money.

17.5   FORTIFIED £21.49

Graham's Malvedos Vintage Port 1995   PORTUGAL

This is one of those fortified reds, still young though and capable of much further developments, which manages to persuade people who say 'ugh!' to port to change their tunes the moment a glass of the glorious, tarry stuff is under their noses.

17.5   WHITE £8.03

Villa Maria Sauvignon Blanc 2002   NEW ZEALAND

Screwcapped master-work. This is a brilliant Sauvignon Blanc for it has superior tufted texture yet refreshing crispness. The fruit is multi-layered yet delicate, and shows finesse yet purposefulness from nose to throat.
Also at Thresher.

17.5 RED £6.99

La Chasse du Pape Grande Réserve 2001 FRANCE
Gorgeous! Striking tobacco and chocolate, hint of
sage, great warm yet soft tannins. Terrific texture.

17 RED £6.99

Montgras Carmenere Reserva 2001 CHILE
It fills the mouth, nose, and throat to bursting, with
aromatic, roasted berries, herbs, chocolate and nutty
tannins.

17 RED £13.99

Château La Vieille Cure, Fronsac 1999 FRANCE
Intense tobacco aroma of high class leads to superb
chocolate-tinged berries and concentrated tannins. A
very delicious claret deservedly expensive (but still
great value).

17 WHITE £6.99

Delegats Oyster Bay Sauvignon Blanc 2002 NEW ZEALAND
Superb, one of the Kiwis' most delicious Sauvignon
Blancs. It has exhilarating minerals and tangy
gooseberry, under-ripe Ogen melon/fruit/pineapple
acids, and a superb texture.

17 WHITE £10.03

La Crema Chardonnay 2000 USA
Superb lushness yet finesse here and as such a
paradoxical artifact, classic Californian Chardonnay.
Creamy, slightly spicy, hugely palate engaging.
Available in 54 stores.

17

WHITE SPARKLING £11.99

Cloudy Bay Pelorus NV   NEW ZEALAND

One of the world's greatest sparkling wine bargains:
dry, classically mature yet crisp, beautiful complex
toasty fruit (hint of strawberry and melon) and a firm
elegant finish.
Available in 17 stores.

17

RED £6.99

Norton Barrel Select Malbec 2000   ARGENTINA

Wonderful relaxed, roasted berries with smoky tannins,
hint of cigar, touch of cocoa. Terrific class and style.
Also at Safeway and Waitrose.

17

WHITE £7.03

Villa Maria Riesling 2002   NEW ZEALAND

Screwcapped and all the better for it – it's fresh,
vibrant, minerally full of complex citrus and melon,
and it'll age for years and years and years.
Also at Morrison's and Thresher.

17

WHITE £5.99

Graham Beck Chardonnay 2002   SOUTH AFRICA

Superb Burgundian-style vegetality but with
creaminess and sensuality as it finishes. The touches
of wood are perfectly poised and the texture is superb.

17

RED £4.99

Concha y Toro Casillero del Diablo Shiraz 2001   CHILE

This has the most gorgeous silky texture with patches
of denim. It parades spicy plums and berries, with a

hint of softening cassis as it nears the throat. There is a light under-layer of chocolate, tinged with tannins. I must admit that the ratatouille niçoise I prepared for it was fine except I threw in some strong Toulouse sausages – and this blunted the edge of the wine. On this evidence, the wine is best drunk young, for it is delicate and the tannins will not, in the absence of a screwcap, last.

17

RED £5.49

Sainsbury's Reserve Selection South African Shiraz 2001

SOUTH AFRICA

Great label, great personality inside the bottle too. The fruit is exuberantly berried, thick yet comely and lissom.

17

RED £11.99

Montes Alpha Syrah, Colchagua 2000

CHILE

The berries here are high class and complex and they come with a stunning undertone of black olive. More like Provence than Chile.

Also available from Majestic, Morrisons and Waitrose, along with the 2001.

17

WHITE £9.99

Catena Chardonnay, Mendoza 2001

ARGENTINA

Lovely creamy richness, toasty and gripping, with a hint of caramel and citrus. And it lingers in the throat like nectar.

Also at Oddbins.

17

Yalumba Y Series Viognier 2002   AUSTRALIA

Not as crunchy or concentrated as the previous
vintage but still a well-tailored specimen. Gorgeous
apricot fruit-cake of a wine leavened with a hint of fig
and fine citrussy acids, scrumptious citrus, mango
and pineapple with apricot on the finish. Classy and
complete.

Also at Tesco and Waitrose.

16.5

RED £4.99   CHILE

**Concha y Toro Casillero del Diablo Cabernet
Sauvignon 2002**

One of the world's most elegant Cabs under a fiver.
Takes you from nose to throat in superior upholstered
comfort. It's the chewiness of the tannins I love –
they will not be shifted and are almost protean as they
shift and shape and linger. Superb edge to the chewy
tannins gives the wine breadth and depth. Terrific
tension between the tannins and the berries, which
lingers lushly, yet responsibly.

Also at Thresher and Waitrose.

16.5

WHITE £6.99   SOUTH AFRICA

**Springfield Estate Special Cuvée
Sauvignon Blanc 2002**

Superb Sancerre frightener for it offers squashed
gooseberry and citrus, minerals, and a hint of grass
and peach (whereas many a Sancerre gives up once it
gets to the gooseberry).

The healthiness of wine has never been so newsworthy a subject since 74% of Britons now quaff it regularly. Yet the health benefits of wine drinking were known to the ancient Greeks who suspected it had a role in strengthening the heart. Even during Prohibition in America it was possible for angina sufferers to get red wine from pharmacies upon presentation of a doctor's prescription.

16.5
WHITE £6.03

Bert Simon Serrig Wurtzberg Riesling   GERMANY
Kabinett, Mosel-Saar-Ruwer 1997
Superb (nicely aged) and with a hint of spicy grapefruit, but it's fine and crisp, a petrol-edged minerality developing. The honey is suppressed under dry peach and there's a terrific ruffled texture.

16.5
WHITE £7.49

Querbach Oestricher Lenchen Riesling Spätlese   GERMANY
Halbtrocken, Rheingau 1993
Ten-year-old Riesling? At this price? Superb bargain! The wine is classy and textured with very dry citrus and under-ripe gooseberry, a hint of aniseed, and it develops gloriously, lingeringly in the throat.

16.5
WHITE £5.99

Shingle Peak Sauvignon Blanc 2002   NEW ZEALAND
Very classy, rich (but subtle), finely textured, tangy yet layered and firm, and gooseberries and lemons in cahoots as it finishes.

16.5

WHITE £5.03

Inycon Fiano 2002 SICILY, ITALY

A very interesting wine. Fiano is a Neapolitan grape
here transported to Sicily and the result is riper and
plumper. The fruit is decidedly more Rubenesque
than Lowryesque and 3 hours' whole decantation
helps enormously.

16.5

FORTIFIED £3.99

Sainsbury's Rich Cream Sherry SPAIN

Delicious! One of the best dessert wine bargains
around (and no-one realises it!). It's composed of
crème brûlée and honey yet it's not too sweet or
cloying. Pour it over ice-cream.

16.5

RED £6.99

Petaluma Bridgewater Mill Shiraz 1999 AUSTRALIA

Benchmark Aussie Shiraz at under seven quid. Has
elegance and yet bite to it, caress yet character, richness
yet finesse. Has firm berried fruit, fine gripping
tannins and a lovely roasted finished classy fruit.

16.5

WHITE £5.99

Villa Wolf Pinot Gris, Pfalz 2001 GERMANY

Gorgeous demure citrus, nuts and apricot.
Concentrated yet delicate, very classy and delicious.

16.5

RED £5.79

Sainsbury's Reserve Selection Chilean Merlot 2001 CHILE

Has superb biscuity tannins, juicy plums and a touch
of chocolate on the finish.

16.5   RED £4.99

La Paz Old Vines Tempranillo 2000   SPAIN

This is an extremely toothsome red from Quixote country,
La Mancha in Spain. The windmills it tips at are, I
suppose, those of Rioja. The grape is the same,
Tempranillo, but it beats most Riojas not just penny for
penny but berry for berry. The wine comes from the Co-
operativa Nuestra Señora de la Paz, in Corral de Almaguer
in the Province of Toledo, and it is made by Señora Teresa
Ameztoy (who is from Rioja) with the active involvement
of Aussie flying wine maker Peter Bright. This co-op is a
modern set-up with 680 members farming 12,500 acres
mostly under white vines. This red, then, is an exception,
coming from vines 30-40 years old planted on red-brown
sandy clay (plenty of limestone and chalk) and what an
exception it proves to be. The grapes are late picked with
high levels of ripeness and alcohol (14%) and the result is
a stupendously rich and gripping Tempranillo bursting
with cherries, plums and strawberries with crisp, toasted
tannins. Great with spicy food or benevolent mood, it is a
terrific summer wine for barbecues (and you can chill it,
to advantage, in humid weather). Wholly decanted 2
hours beforehand also gives it a boost, via aeration, and
makes it less rustic, more luxurious.
Also at Safeway.

16.5   RED £5.03

Inycon Shiraz 2002   SICILY, ITALY

The texture is magnificent and it releases its fruit by
degrees so the palate gets toasty berries, herbs and then
flowing, molten tannins. And they grip wonderfully.

16.5

WHITE £7.99

Fetzer Vineyards Barrel Select Chardonnay 2001   USA

Very vigorous and exotic fruit showing dry mango and
lime, pineapple and paw-paw, a hint of custard and
creamy woodiness lingering in the throat. Fine texture
here!

16.5

RED £6.99

Durius Marqués de Griñon Tempranillo 2001   SPAIN

Gorgeous tannins to lovely brisk cherries and plums.
A hint of chocolate to the rich berries. Shows just how
civilised and polished (yet characterful) the
Tempranillo grape can become. Beautiful plump, soft
texture here. Flashy, rich, textured, gripping and, for
the price, a steal.
Also at Morrison's, Budgens, Majestic and Thresher.

16.5

WHITE £8.49

Bonterra Chardonnay, Fetzer 2001   CALIFORNIA, USA

The texture is high class and gripping and, as it dives
in the throat, shows lemon and fine creamy peach.
Delicious arrangement of fruit and acid. Made from
organically grown grapes.
Also at Budgens.

16

RED £7.03

Grand'Arte Tourig Franca, Estremadura 2001   PORTUGAL

Wonderful colour, this wine. It quickens the blood just
looking at it and races the pulse as the fruit,
composed of genteel, spicy plums, caresses the palate.

16 RED £7.99

Amativo 2000 ITALY

A wonderfully invigorating, rich and raunchy red
offering roasted plums and spicy berries. Brilliant
cheese and casserole red.

16 RED £3.99

Santerra Tempranillo Utiel Requena 2001 SPAIN

Bargain richness and generosity. Offers cream and
berries and a touch of chocolate.

16 RED £9.99

Penfolds Bin 28 Kalimna Shiraz 2000 AUSTRALIA

One of Penfolds' most harmonious, savoury blends
of fruit and tannins. It opens out well after a couple
of hours of breathing (full decantation) to reveal
genteel spice and smooth berries and those lively
tannins. This is one of those wines which wrote its
own 16-point rating, no second thoughts: just the
afterthought that how perfect such a red would be to
drink with spicy food (excellent, therefore, for a
BYOB treat).

Also at Safeway, Somerfield, Thresher, Oddbins,
Majestic, Tesco and Small Merchants (Unwins).

16 WHITE £4.03

Réserve St Marc Sauvignon Blanc, Vin de Pays FRANCE
d'Oc 2002

I always think this stands up very well, at half the
price, to Sancerre. The resemblance is uncanny.

One of the early complaints laid against the *Superplonk* column and indeed the book was the absence of romance. Reviewers (far more than readers) beefed that the hard-headed rating of wines at points out of 20, on a strict value for money basis, left no room for wine's soft side. What these critics meant was wine's bullshit side.

Wine writers, you see, are of two sorts. And what sort of wine writer you are depends on which end of the bottle you start from. There are those, the great majority, who begin at the bottom: on the lees, amongst the microscopic bits and bobs of the grapes left over from the wine making. Such writers focus on the minutiae of the wine, the vineyard, the terroir, the variety of the grapes, the philosophy – the words 'style' and 'approach' are insufficient to do justice to the depth of feeling considered appropriate here - of the wine grower. Such writers on wine are social animals before anything else. They are fabulists with a great many friends in the world of wine.

These bottom-enders are almost invariably besotted by the legends which surround a wine and they cannot divorce this from the reality of tasting the liquid itself. Once, in the cellar of Château Lafite (autumn 1978, I think it was), the cellar-master with great ceremony extracted some young wine from a barrel and solemnly filled three glasses. He handed a glass to my French companion, one to me, and one he took himself. What followed then, as the wine was reverentially sipped, was a neo-religious ritual from which only I dissented since the wine was simply 'quite nice'. It wasn't marvellous nor would it have become so.

The writer who starts from the business end of the bottle must have no illusions and no friends. In a perfect world, as

he knows in his heart, he would have no friends who grow
and make wine just as no film critic worthy of the status
could hardly boast of an abundance of friendships amongst
directors and stars since he will have cause regularly to see
and to comment upon their performances perhaps
unflatteringly.

It is much harder, lonelier work being a wine critic rather
than being a mere wine commentator. As part of a working
week, a critic like me may taste hundreds of wines and write
up copious notes describing each wine, perhaps rating each
wine, and also providing ideas as to how each wine will
perform with food. It is extremely concentrated analysis
since it requires the taster, in arriving at a rating, rapidly to
run through similar performing wines at all price levels and
thus arrive at a sensible value-for-money judgement.

Such a critic pays no heed to the religion of the wine
maker, the location of the grapes, the colour of the skins of
the grapes, and what fabulous stories may be attached to the
vineyard's or the wine grower's reputation. These things
may be taken into account after the wine has hit the
spittoon and indeed will have to be if the wine is a
reputed colossus with an appropriate price-tag since
such a wine will have had to have hit those thousands
of tastebuds with some impact and complexity if
this reputation is a worthy one and not simply a
fable – as, so often, it is.

In splendid Lilliputian fashion, then, we wine writers are
either top-enders or bottom-enders. Take note which end of
the bottle your wine writer writes from. Sensibly, of course,
not caring whether a wine writer is off her top or out of his
bottom, you may decide the devil can take the lot of us.

16
WHITE £4.53

Sainsbury's Cuvée Prestige Sauvignon Blanc,   FRANCE
Vin de Pays d'Oc 2002
Nice toasty undertone to some far-from-routine
gooseberry richness which is leavened by citrus.

16
WHITE £3.33

Sainsbury's Chardonnay, Vin de Pays d'Oc NV   FRANCE
Lovely warm, almost apricot (Pinot Gris-style) richness
and a nutty dryness to finish.

16 (in 3 years)
WHITE £5.03

Vouvray La Couronne des Plantagenets,   FRANCE
Chapelle de Cray 2002
Good dry honied fruit (ignore the demi-sec on the
label) reveals as-yet-young but well balanced acids and
gooseberry, under-ripe melon fruit. Cellar it for a
happier future.

16
WHITE £7.03

Sainsbury's Classic Selection Albarino 2001   SPAIN
Something different, something surprisingly complex,
something unexpected. Elegant, cool, white wine from
Spain's rainiest region! Pear, citrus, pineapple and
lychee here.

16
WHITE £4.99

Eaglehawk Chardonnay, Wolf Blass 2002   AUSTRALIA
A restrained, elegant, citrussy (but not sharp)
Chardonnay of charm and precision.

16
Little Boomey Chardonnay 2001   AUSTRALIA
Creamy, touch of satsuma and apple, interesting fresh
edge. Great value for money.

16
WHITE £6.99
Capel Vale Sauvignon Blanc/Sémillon 2001   AUSTRALIA
Most unusual ripe gooseberry/melon/lychee and
chalky-mineral finish. Terrific with Thai fishcakes
et al.

16
WHITE £5.99
The Sanctuary Sauvignon Blanc 2002   NEW ZEALAND
Lovely herbacious richness, not crude or OTT. Elegant
under-ripe gooseberry, demure melon and citrus, and
firm textured on the finish.

16
WHITE SPARKLING £7.99
Graham Beck Sparkling NV   SOUTH AFRICA
Finely compacted under-ripe melon with good,
refreshing acids. One of the Cape's crispest
champagne competition contenders.

16
RED SPARKLING £7.99
Banrock Station Sparkling Shiraz NV   AUSTRALIA
Still a great wine – a red bubbly no less – to have with
the Christmas bird.
Also available at Somerfield, Waitrose and
Morrisons.

16

WHITE £7.99
SPAIN

Codorniu Cuvée Raventos NV
The toasty richness is delicately done and there are
some tannins on the finish. A very fine, classy tipple.

16

WHITE £5.99
FRANCE

Sainsbury's Classic Selection Vouvray 2002
Delicious vintage for this wine and it makes a
wonderful refreshing change from Chardonnay. It has
a hint of spice and mango to the citrus. Very elegant.

16

WHITE £8.53
FRANCE

**Sainsbury's Classic Selection Pouilly-Fumé
Fouassier 2002**
Very elegant, classy, subtle, demure, restrained – these
are not synonymous for a lack of fruit but the wine is
old world and quintessentially delicious today.

16

WHITE SPARKLING £2.99
ITALY

Araldica Moscato Spumante NV
I can hear the sniggers now. You can't hide them, can
you? A frivolous air-head of a wine like this rating 16
points? A barely-bubbly wine reeking of Muscat-
grapiness and cheap to boot? But consider. Consider
coming home from work, knackered, and being able
to lay into something cool, chilled, aromatic and
pétillant, offering joyous melon fruit with a hint of
custard along with a crisp, fresh citrussy edge to make
you demand a second glass and then a third. This
wine is surely one of the great pre-prandial whistle
whetters. It is grown on the Monferrato hills in the

province of Asti, in Piemonte, on limestone-clay soil.
The fruit was hand harvested from 8th to 20th
September, fermented in a pressure tank under
temperature control, and the natural gently spicy
sweetness was retained by stopping the fermentation
via chilling. The wine was, then, born chilled and it
has to be drunk chilled.

And if your local branch isn't one of the 100 lucky
ones then go down the road and visit Tesco. This
retailer has a very similar wine called Villa Jolanda
Moscato d'Asti (16 points, £3.25) and it, too, reeks and
tastes of grapes – which, curiously, few wines do.
Available at 100 stores.

16

FORTIFIED £6.99

Sainsbury's Finest Reserve Port   PORTUGAL

A thundering bargain! Lovely sweet, roasted plums
with superb tannins. A terrific port for blue cheese
and even mild desserts.

One of the most exciting aspects of my trip to
Argentina was not dancing at midnight with a beautiful
young local wine maker under a vivid half-moon in the
middle of a Mendoza vineyard within sight of the
snow-capped Andes but the revelation, by José Alberto
Zuccardi of La Agricola vineyards, that within five years
he wanted all his considerable acres of vines to be
wholly organic. Indeed, I see nothing to prevent
Argentina becoming the leading organic wine producer
in the world.

16

WHITE £5.99

Leopards Leap Sémillon/Chardonnay 2002   SOUTH AFRICA
This has a most agreeable level of fruit, showing some
finesse, but this leanness is not to be confused with
meanness. There is a suggestion of a straining towards
exuberance with the lemon and pineapple but overall
the wine finishes elegantly and properly. Excellent with
grilled prawns and fish and with mild Thai dishes.

16

FORTIFIED (half bottle) £14.99

Dow's Vintage Port 1983   PORTUGAL
What it does for fifteen quid that JS Finest Reserve
Port can't do for seven is permit the mature, luxurious
fruit to spread like sweet, warm gravy to every muscle
in the body.

16

WHITE DESSERT (half bottle) £3.83

Sainsbury's Muscat de St Jean de Minervois NV   FRANCE
Stunningly well textured and honied, with undertones
of ripe apricot and sweet pear. Great dessert wine for
fruit tarts and tarty fruits.

16

WHITE £6.99

Belmonte Marlborough Sauvignon   NEW ZEALAND
Blanc 2002
The textbook is a dull tome at the best of times and
whilst this specimen does not exactly throw it out of
the window it does have its own translation – and this
is all to the good. Thus though we get gooseberry
(what Marlborough Sauvignon Blanc would be
complete without it) we find a touch of raspberry to the

citricity which gives it great appeal. I would serve this wine with smoked fish or scallops with bacon bits. Also at E-tailers (Virgin Wines).

16

WHITE £3.99

Espiral Macabeo/Chardonnay 2001 SPAIN

What a delicious bargain we have here. It offers the tang of lemon and satsuma fruit, lightly coagulated with a hint of lime zest. It is a superb glugging bottle and a wine for a wide variety of fish and light poultry dishes, tuna salad and vegetarian dishes (like a bean salad).

16

RED £5.03

Argento Cabernet Sauvignon 2002 ARGENTINA

This is a looser, less compacted wine than previous vintages which rated higher. Is it affection, not a rational brain, which keeps it at a high 16? Nope. This deserves its elevation to the élite raters, though the berries are sweeter and the tannins less raunchy. It is still impressively fruited and balanced. Food? It'll handle lightly spiced chicken dishes quite well.

16

WHITE SPARKLING £24.49

RO de Ruinart Brut NV FRANCE

Very toasty and mature lovely creamy strawberry fruit. An expensive treat.

Available at 67 stores.

16

WHITE £9.03

Sainsbury's Classic Selection Sancerre FRANCE
Fouassier 2002

Expensive but it is in good form, being a 2002, and has an extra layer of nutty richness to it.

16

RED £5.03

Sainsbury's Reserve Selection, Corbières 2001 FRANCE
Extraordinary baked plums, touch of macadamia nut
(roasted) and a creamy intensity balanced by tobacco-
ey tannins. Rustic yes, but pungent.

16

WHITE £2.99

Margaret Island Dry White NV HUNGARY
This is an amazing mouthful for the money and with
its terrific screwcap it'll keep its freshness and zip for
many many months (and it'll even be interesting to
see how it matures if cellared). It offers an immediate
apple/pear/melon fruitiness of some subtlety and
charm and the finish, which renews the pace of the
wine as it touches the throat, is not very far from very
sexy indeed.

16

RED £8.99

Bonterra Vineyards Zinfandel 2000 CALIFORNIA, USA
Delightfully chewy, gently grilled berries with touches
of cinnamon. Has a joyously rich and devil-may-care
fruitiness which, thrown in the face of decades of
European po-facedness from old-world wines which
might try to compete (Rhône, Rioja, Chianti), makes an
eloquent case for this wine's inclusion in any
candidate's list for must-drink-wines with first-class,
elegant Indian, Pakistani and Bangladeshi food without
clumsy spicing. Not a cheap wine but then it isn't a
cheap wine: it doesn't warble or trill, it richly roars.
Also at Waitrose, Majestic, Oddbins and Safeway.

Contrary to what some readers believe, I can look an obscene wine in the face. The other day I visited Selfridges' wine department (in London's finest department and food store) and asked whether the price-ticket on one particular bottle, Screaming Eagle Cabernet Sauvignon, was not a misprint. The sales assistant, who was French, smiled and confirmed that £2,300 was indeed correct. 'Well, of course,' he said, 'it's Californian.'

16

RED £7.99

Ravenswood Lodi Zinfandel 1999   CALIFORNIA, USA

Lodi and Zin were made for one another, it seems to me. The right warm area for the perfect warm red grape which, in the right hands, will express itself sweetly yet dryly and rustically with exuberance and passion. As here where generous berries collude with svelte tannins so we get character with class.

16

WHITE £3.99

Zimmermann Riesling 2002   GERMANY

A brilliant new brand from Germany. Feisty, crisp, fresh and fruity. Excellent with spicy fish dishes. Also at Morrison's

16

WHITE SPARKLING £11.99

Sainsbury's Champagne Blanc de Noirs Brut NV   FRANCE

Delicious. One of the best priced, most satisfyingly rich, yet delicate, of own-label champagnes. In the class of champagnes costing three times as much.

16
WHITE £5.99

Ruppertsberg Riesling 2001 GERMANY

Be daring. Dare to drink this limpid Riesling as an
aperitif and shock your friends who will say 'I didn't
know you went in for sweet wine', but then they will
venture into a glass and a rich, dry, crisp smile of
pleasure will spread over their faces.

16
WHITE £5.03

Grand'Arte Alvarinho Chardonnay 2000 PORTUGAL

Very ripe and soft, a touch of peachy, more than a
touch of pear and lemony, is ideal with Thai fish
dishes (not too spicy).

16
RED £5.99

Viña Albali Valdepeñas Gran Reserva 1995 SPAIN

Very creamy and ripe and much more excitingly textured
and complex than most Riojas at the same price.

16
RED £6.99

Durius Marqués de Griñon Tempranillo 2000 SPAIN

Smells of frying spicy sausages which belie the
immediate delicacy of the berries in the fruit. But then
the soft savoury side of the wine takes over and
caresses the palate.

16
RED £3.99

Prahova Valley Reserve Pinot Noir 2000 ROMANIA

Sweet, touch of good, brisk tannins. Rich and deep and
remarkably priced for genuine Pinot oomph (yet delicacy).
Also at Budgens.

16

RED £8.99

Bonterra Zinfandel, Mendocino   CALIFORNIA, USA
County 1999
Now this is boisterous and tongue-happy, like a puppy
that has breeding to it, some charm, some real gloss
to its coat, and tenderness in its eyes.

16

RED £18.99

Petaluma Coonawarra Cabernet Sauvignon/   AUSTRALIA
Merlot 1999
Intense, very dry (almost like ashes in the mouth as it
quits the throat), but very elegant, classy and compact.
It is expensive but its concentrated, very subtle
tobacco-leaf edge is impressive.
Also at Majestic and Oddbins.

16

WHITE £4.03

Kendermanns Pinot Grigio, Pfalz 2002   GERMANY
'Rulander' they call this grape and it's ineffably
Teutonic, lean, crisp and very refreshing.

16

WHITE £5.99

Dr L Riesling, Mosel-Saar-Ruwer 2002   GERMANY
Delicious touch of honey to citrus and dry under-ripe
gooseberry. Will develop in bottle for 3–8 years to
huge advantage.

16

WHITE £8.99

Dr Loosen Graacher Himmelreich Riesling   GERMANY
Kabinett, Mosel-Saar-Ruwer 2002
Rated for cellaring purposes only as it needs 2–3 years yet
to show its complex potential. Will develop for 12–15 years.
Available in 50 stores.

16

RED £6.03

Carnebay Liggle Old Bush Vine Red 2002   SOUTH AFRICA
I just like the name. And the label. The fruit? Oh yes,
the fruit. In a word it has as much chutzpah as the
rest of the production.

16

RED £16.99

Mount Difficulty Pinot Noir 2001   NEW ZEALAND
This improves in bottle every time I taste it and it is
one of the few Kiwi Pinots to have disciplined tannins
and a lovely gamey dryness.

16

RED £3.99

Sainsbury's Argentinian Bonarda 2002   ARGENTINA
Vivid plums and ripe strawberries. A full-on fruity treat.

16

RED £4.99

Lo Tengo Malbec 2002   ARGENTINA
Great idea by the label designer, nothing strange there,
but the fruit has no gimmicks. It's pure berried delight.

16

RED £5.49

Sainsbury's Reserve Selection Malbec 2002   ARGENTINA
Ripe and rich, very accommodating with a wide range
of dishes (from tandoori chicken to pea soup).

16

RED £7.99

Marqués de Casa Concha Merlot 2001   CHILE
Rich and very layered, ripe berries with a creamy
finish dusted with tannins.

16

RED £4.99

Concha y Toro Casillero del Diablo Carmenere 2001 CHILE
How to be full without being flashy. Lovely brisk
tannins. Gorgeous berries.

16

RED £6.99

Errazuriz Estate Syrah 2001 CHILE
Vivid, vivacious, vital, very, very delicious.

16

RED £7.99

Ravenswood Lodi Zinfandel 2000 CALIFORNIA, USA
Terrific spicy berries and pert tannins.
Also at Waitrose.

16

WHITE £10.99

Villa Maria Wairau Reserve Sauvignon NEW ZEALAND
Blanc 2002
Cellar it for 3–5 years and 20 points will emerge.
Kings Road and Cromwell Road branches only.

16

FORTIFIED (50cl bottle) £4.99

Solear Manzanilla Sherry SPAIN
Terrific textured, bone-dry fruit. Tastes of saline
almonds.

16

FORTIFIED (50cl bottle) £6.99

Torres Muscatel Oro SPAIN
Stunning crème brûlée fruit with a hint of toasty
raspberry. Lovely honied wine to drink with fresh
fruit.

16

FORTIFIED £12.99

Graham's Crusted Port 1999 PORTUGAL

Delicious creamy berries and sweet chocolate tannins (very soft).

Available in 62 stores.

16

FORTIFIED (37.5cl bottle) £9.99

Dow's Bomfim Port 1987 PORTUGAL

Terrific dry berries, chewy tannins and gentle molasses.

16

WHITE £7.03

Nobilo Sauvignon Blanc 2002 NEW ZEALAND

Nobilo gets it right at last (now it's owned by Aussies). The fruit is aromatic and would-be rich, handsomely gooseberryish and it finishes wittily.

16

WHITE £9.03

Fairview Viognier 2002 SOUTH AFRICA

Restrained apricot, touch of grilled nut, hint of citrus. A lovely package capable of developing more exciting in bottle over the next 3 years.

16

RED (3 litre box) £20.15

Lindemans Bin 50 Shiraz 2002 AUSTRALIA

One of the better Aussie reds in a box! Tangy, rich, sanely balanced, eager yet not OTT, and has good tannins of softness yet character. The perfect gift for someone who just wants a glass of sticky, plum-pudding-rich (yet dry) glass of Aussie Shiraz once a day. Also at Tesco.

16

RED £5.49

Inycon Aglianico 2002   SICILY, ITALY

Biting black cherry fruit, a hint of tobacco, and rich raunchy tannins. Very fresh and pert altogether.

16

RED £5.03

Fairview Goats du Roam 2002   SOUTH AFRICA

Tar and plums, roasted edge to the tannins, a finish of morello cherry. Very bright fleshy plums, hint of strawberries with a fine dusting of tannins. An excellent casserole red. Better than any Côtes du Rhône at the same price (under a fiver).
Also at Asda, Booths, Morrison's, Oddbins, Somerfield and Tesco.

SMALL MERCHANTS

ADNAMS WINE MERCHANTS

Sole Bay Brewery,
East Green,
Southwold,
Suffolk IP18 6JW

Tel: (01502) 727222
Fax: (01502) 727223

E-mail: wines@adnams.co.uk
Website: www.adnamswines.co.uk

ARKELL VINTNERS

Arkell's Brewery Ltd,
Stratton St Margaret,
Swindon,
Wiltshire SN2 7RU

Tel: (01793) 823 026

BACCHANALIA

90 Mill Road,
Cambridge CB1 2BD

Tel/Fax: (01223) 576 292

E-mail: paul.bowes@ntlworld.com

BALLANTYNES OF COWBRIDGE

3 Westgate
Cowbridge
South Glamorgan CF71 7AQ

Tel: (01446) 774 840
Fax: (01446) 775 253

E-mail: richard@ballantynes.co.uk
Website: www.ballantynes.co.uk

BENNETS FINE WINES

High Street,
Chipping Campden,
Glos GL55 6AG

Tel: (01386) 840 392

BERRY BROS & RUDD

3 St James Street,
London SW1A 1EG

Tel: (020) 7396 9600 or (0870) 900 4300
Fax: (0870) 900 4301

E-mail: orders@bbr.com
Website: www.bbr.com

BIBENDUM WINE LIMITED

113 Regents Park Road,
London NW1 8UR

Tel: (020) 7449 4120
Fax: (020) 7449 4121

Website: www.bibendumfinewine.co.uk
www.bibendum-wine.co.uk

BIG WINES

Glebe Farm House,
Barlow Drive,
Awsworth,
Nottinghamshire NG16 2RR

Tel: (0115) 849 4041
Fax: (0115) 849 4042

E-mail: big.wines@ntlworld.com

THE BRISTOL WINE COMPANY

Transom House,
Victoria Street,
Bristol BS1 6AH

Tel: (0117) 373 0288
Fax: (0117) 373 0287

E-mail: info@thebristolwinecompany.co.uk
Website: www.thebristolwinecompany.co.uk

D BYRNE & CO.

Victoria Building,
12 King Street,
Clitheroe,
Yorks BB7 2EP

Tel: (01200) 423152

CAMBRIDGE WINE MERCHANTS

32 Bridge Street,
Cambridge CB2 1UT

Tel: (01223) 568991
Fax: (01223) 568992

E-mail: info@cambridgewine.com
Website: www.cambridgewine.com

CORNEY & BARROW

12 Helmet Row,
London EC1V 3TD

Tel: (020) 7539 3200
Fax: (020) 7608 1373

E-mail: wine@corbar.co.uk
Website: www.corneyandbarrow.com

DARTMOUTH VINTNERS LTD
The Butterwalk,
6 Duke Street,
Dartmouth,
South Devon TQ6 9PZ

Tel: (01803) 832 602

DOMAIN DIRECT
8–14 Orsman Road
London N1 6DL

Tel: (020) 7837 1142

FRIARWOOD
26 New Kings Road,
London SW6 4ST

Tel: (020) 7736 2628
Fax: (020) 7731 0411

E-mail: sales@friarwood.com
Website: www.friarwood.com

HALIFAX WINE COMPANY
18 Prescott Street,
Halifax,
West Yorkshire HX1 2LG

Tel: (01422) 256 333

HEDLEY WRIGHT WINE MERCHANTS
11 Twyford Centre,
London Road,
Bishop's Stortford,
Herts CM23 3YT

Tel: (01279) 465 818

E-mail: justin@hedleywright.co.uk
Website: www.hedleywright.co.uk

CHARLES HENNINGS LTD

London House,
Lower Street,
Pulborough,
West Sussex RH20 2BW

Tel: (01798) 343021
Fax: (01798) 343021

E-mail: sales@chu-wine.co.uk
Website: www.chu/wine.co.uk

HICKS & DON

4 Old Station Yard,
Edington,
Westbury,
Wiltshire BA13 4NT

Tel: (01380) 831234
Fax: (01380) 831010

E-mail: mailbox@hicksanddon.co.uk
Website: www.hicksanddon.co.uk

HOULTS WINE MERCHANTS

5 Cherry Tree Walk,
The Calls,
Leeds,
West Yorkshire LS2 7EB

Tel: (01484) 510 700

E-mail: sales@hoults-winemerchants.co.uk
Website: www.hoults-winemerchants.co.uk

IRVINE ROBERTSON WINES LTD

10–11 North Leith Sands,
Edinburgh EH6 4ER

Tel: (0131) 553 3521

LAY & WHEELER

Gosbecks Park,
117 Gosbecks Road,
Colchester,
Essex CO2 9JT

Tel: (0845) 330 1855
Fax: (01206) 560002

E-mail: sales@laywheeler.com
Website: www.laywheeler.com

MILTON SANDFORD WINES LIMITED

The Old Chalk Mine
Warren Row Road
Knowl Hill
Reading,
Berks RG10 9AJ

Tel: (01628) 829449

NIDDERDALE WINES (South Australian specialists)

2a High Street,
Pateley Bridge,
Harrogate,
North Yorkshire HG3 5AW

Tel: (01423) 711 703

E-mail: info@southaustralianwines.com
Website: www.southaustralianwines.com

THE OXFORD WINE CO LTD

The Wine Warehouse,
Standlake,
Witney,
Oxon OX29 7PR

Tel: (018650) 301 144

OZ WINES

68 Heythorpe Street,
London SW18 5BN

Tel: (0845) 4501261

PARTRIDGES

24–25 Drury Lane,
London WC2B 5RJ

Tel: (020) 7240 1336
Fax: (020) 7497 5601

Website: www.partridges.co.uk

THOS PEATLING FINE WINES

Westgate House,
Bury St Edmunds,
Suffolk IP33 1QS
Tel: (01284) 755948
Fax: (01284) 714483

E-mail: sales@thospeatling.co.uk
Website: www.thospeatling.co.uk

PHILGLAS & SWIGGOT

21 Northcote Road,
London SW11 1NG

Tel: (0207) 9244494

CHRISTOPHER PIPER WINES LTD

1 Silver Street,
Ottery St Mary,
Devon EX11 1DB

Tel: (01404) 814139

TERRY PLATT WINE MERCHANTS
Council Street,
Llandudno,
Gwynedd LL30 1ED

Tel: (01492) 874 099
Fax: (01492) 874 788

E-mail: info@terryplattwines.co.uk
Website: www.terryplattwines.co.uk

PORTLAND WINE COMPANY
16 North Parade,
Sale Moor N33 3JS

Tel: (01619) 962 8752

E-mail: info@lcb.com.uk

RAEBURN FINE WINES
21-23 Comely Bank Road,
Edinburgh EH4 1DS

Tel: (0131) 343 1159
Fax: (0131) 332 5166

E-mail: sales@raeburnfinewines.com
Website: www.raeburnfinewines.com

REID WINES LTD
The Mill,
Marsh Lane,
Hallatrow,
Bristol BS39 6EB

Tel: (01761) 452 645

PAUL ROBERTS WINES

4 Grove Avenue,
Moseley,
Birmingham B13 9RU

Tel: (0121) 449 7757

ROBERSONS WINE MERCHANTS

348–354 Kensington High Street,
London W14 8NS

Tel: (0207) 371 2121

SCATCHARD LTD

21 Victoria Street,
Liverpool L1 6BD

Tel/Fax: (0151) 236 2955

E-mail: info@scatchard.com

STEVENS GARNIER

47 West Way,
Oxford OX2 0JF

Tel: (01865) 263300
Fax: (01865) 791594

E-mail: info@ stevensgarnier.co.uk

STRATFORD'S WINE AGENCIES

High Street,
Cookham,
Berkshire SL6 9SQ

Tel: (01628) 810 606

E-mail: sales@stratfordwine.co.uk
Website: www.stratfordwine.co.uk

TRANSATLANTIC WINES
Patrick Whenham-Bossy,
The Magpies,
Eye Kettleby Drive,
Eye Kettleby,
Melton Mowbray,
Leics LE14 2TD

Tel: (01664) 565 013
Fax: (01664) 564 938

E-mail: patrick@transatlantic-wines.co.uk.

TURVILLE VALLEY WINES
The Firs,
Potter Row,
Great Missenden
Bucks HP19 9LT

Tel: (01494) 868818

UNWINS
Birchwood House,
Victoria Road,
Dartford,
Kent DA1 5AJ

Tel: (01322) 272 711
Fax: (01322) 294469

E-mail: admin@unwinswines.co.uk
Website: www.unwins.co.uk

VERITAS WINES
103 Cherry Pinton Road,
Cambridge CB1 7BS

Tel: (01223) 212500

LA VIGNERONNE FINE WINES LTD
105 Old Brompton Road,
London SW7 3LE

Tel: (0207) 5896113

VILLENEUVE WINES
1 Venlaw Court,
Peebles EH45 8AE

Tel: (01721) 722 500

E-mail: wines@villeneuvewines.com
Website: www.villeneuvewines.com

VIN DU VIN
Colthups,
The Street,
Appledore,
Kent TN26 2BX

Tel: (01233) 758727

WILJAY WINES
Unit 7G, Lodge Road,
Staplehurst,
Tonbridge,
Kent TN12 0QW

Tel:(01580) 891 973

E-mail: jenni.wilson@btopenworld.com

WIMBLEDON WINE CELLARS
1 Gladstone Road,
Wimbledon,
London SW19 1QU

Tel: (020) 8540 9979

WINE IN CORNWALL

Nancenoy,
Falmouth,
Cornwall TR11 5RP

Tel: (01326) 340 332

E-mail: sales@wineincornwall.co.uk
Website: www.wineincornwall.co.uk

THE WINE JUNCTION

225a Balham High Road,
London SW17 7BQ

Tel: (020) 8767 4455

THE WINERY

4 Clifton Road,
Maida Vale,
London W9 1SS

Tel: (020) 7286 6475
Fax: (020) 7286 2733

E-mail: dmotion@globalnet.co.uk

THE WRIGHT WINE CO. LTD

The Old Smithy,
Raikes Road,
Skipton,
North Yorkshire BD23 1NP

Tel: (01756) 700 886

NOEL YOUNG WINES

56 High Street,
Trumpington,
Cambridge CB2 2LS

Tel: (01223) 844 744

E-mail: admin@nywines.co.uk
Website: www.nywines.co.uk

For all Small Merchants' wines 15.5 points and under
visit www.superplonk.com

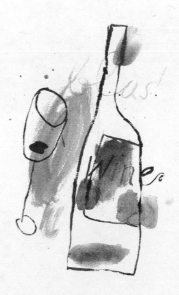

18

Endrizzi Masetto Nero 2000

Adnams

This is one of the most exciting red wines I have tasted all year. It is a blend, a delicious clash forsooth, between the ubiquitous international varieties Cabernet Sauvignon and Merlot and the localised north-eastern Italian varieties Lagrein and Terodelgo. We are, then, talking here about a wine from the Alto-Adige, with its meticulous cities of Bolzano and Trentino, its Hapsburg history, its unique Mediterranean-meets-Alpine climate and some of this is sensed as one smells and tastes the wine and then mulls over its savoury kick. I must admit I took a somewhat lazy attitude to it when the bottle arrived at my home (as bottles do) and I stuck it on the tasting shelf. A few days later my hand fell on it by accident and I opened it and poured it and as the aroma of roasted nuts hit my nostrils and the fruit, fresh and finely toasted raspberry and chocolate, caressed and then aroused my palate and throat it was – and this is not an exaggeration – like my first sight (1968) of Claudia Cardinale in the flesh: serene, polished, tempestuously beautiful. There is nothing artificial in this wine. It is made using extreme organic methods by the estate's owners, Paolo and Christine Endrici, whose care is manifest in every singular drop of this thrilling wine.

18

Casa Lapostolle Cuvée Alexandre Cabernet Sauvignon 1998

Berry Bros & Rudd

Dry catering chocolate, toasted walnuts, rich cassis and plum, with touches of licorice – is this as good as this wine can get? It seems to be mature yet healthy, ripe yet far from sere, and fully in possession of that destiny of all great wine: itself (or rather that self which its maker has in mind for it). A magnificent wine for fresh Italian alpine cheeses and truffle omelette and risotto with wild mushrooms (plenty of Parmesan and a squizzle of green olive oil over it as it sits on the plate). Also at London Stores (Selfridges) and E-tailers (Everywine).

17.5

Montes Alpha M, Santa Cruz 2000

Berry Bros & Rudd

This delicious specimen is a blend of Cabernets Sauvignon and Franc, Merlot and Petit Verdot, and it is a stunning upstaging of the Médoc style. It requires whole decantation and 5–6 hours of breathing to reach an apogee of deliciousness to make Lafite seem like something to drink with merguez.

17.5

Decoy Migration Duckhorn 1999

Lay & Wheeler

This is a stunning blend of Merlot, Cabernet Franc, Cabernet Sauvignon and Petit Verdot which is couth

yet characterful, sweet yet dry, well muscled yet
genteel. It has an intrusive cocoa-coated tannicity, very
luxurious in texture and finishing aplomb. Offers
great finesse yet potency. Very individual stuff, this.
The liquid talks to you. The glass into which it is
poured becomes strangely eloquent (and I have no
doubt that any dregs left over can be used to divine
the future in the manner of those soothsayers who
employ tea-leaves).

17.5   WHITE £19.90

Grosset Piccadilly Chardonnay 2001   AUSTRALIA

*Milton Sandford Wines, Veritas Wines, La Vigneronne,
Philglas & Swiggot, Turville Valley Wines, Vin du Vin,
Bennets Fine Wines, Halifax Wine Company, D Byrne,
Domain Direct*

Toasted citrus, vegetality-edged Ogen melon, and a rich
texture of supreme class. Like a magical Montrachet,
this wine comes even more alive with food – anything
from roast fowl to mushroom risotto – but as a
supreme treat to sip whilst reading a book it is superb.
Also at London Stores (Fortnum & Mason, Harvey
Nichols).

17.5   RED £21.75

Grosset Gaia 2000   AUSTRALIA

*Milton Sandford Wines, Oz Wines, La Vigneronne,
Philglas & Swiggot, Vin du Vin, Bennets Fine Wines,
Halifax Wine Company, D Byrne, Robersons Wine
Merchants, Domain Direct*

A Cabernet Sauvignon, Merlot, Cabernet Franc blend
of wonderfully gently roasted soft berries and very

calm tannins. It oozes class and finesse yet has that subdued power exciting wines have. It both invigorates and caresses the palate.

Also at London Stores (Fortnum & Mason, Harvey Nichols).

17

RED SPARKLING £12.99–£13.99

Chainsaw Sparkling Shiraz, Knappstein 1999   AUSTRALIA

Villeneuve Wines, Noel Young Wines, Wimbledon Wine Cellars, Halifax Wine Company, Portland Wine Company, Nidderdale Fine Wine

No idle name, this. The back label explains how the greatest mass murderer in Australian viticultural history took a chainsaw to the vines in the early 1980s (they were planted in 1969), so Chardonnay could be grafted on instead of the original Shiraz. In 1996 the killer was back in the vineyard, this time with the more benign purpose of reversing what had been done. The chainsaw took off the Chardonnay and Shiraz was re-grafted on. The result is a glorious gamey, spicy, exuberant sparkling red which not only smells and tastes of dry summer pudding but has virulent acids and terrific tannins. With the Christmas fowl stuffed with exotic fruits and spices this wine would be an absolute triumph. Indeed, it is pretty wonderful drinking it as I write this, the crimson bubbles rebuking me for my cowardliness in only having a small glass. But it is lunchtime. I must work through. At dinner tonight, with merguez sausages and onion gravy with green olive oil and garlic in the mashed potatoes, I shall finish the bottle. Or it will finish me. (I don't much care which.)

£2.79 for a Cabernet Sauvignon has to be some kind of
joke, doesn't it? Well, of course it is. We can smile as
we satisfyingly glug, and the Chancellor of the
Exchequer can guffaw as he sneaks off with more
profit from the wine than any participant in its
manufacture, distribution, or sale. But of course this is
a Bulgarian wine, so that's all right then . . .

WHITE SPARKLING (6 bottle case in bond) £135
Henriot Brut Millésimé Champagne 1996   FRANCE
Lay & Wheeler

A great deal of fuss has been made of the 1996
champagne vintage. I judge each wine on its merits,
each bottle on its merits forsooth, and it is unwise to
let this kind of hype go to the head (which is very easy
to allow happen especially if the bottle in question is
the Henriot). Lay & Wheeler themselves made a lot of
fuss of the '96 vintage and echoed the enthusiasm of
the Champenois who apparently did let things go to
their haughty heads with pronouncements about the
'purity' of the vintage, the 'concentration and
complexity' waiting to unfold as the bottles lay in
cellars. I would only agree that, with some examples,
patience is necessary as 2–3 more years in the cellar
are required. However, this specimen is splendidly
immediate, mature and ready to seduce any palate it
touches. It is classic sparkling wine, to my mind, for it
offers beautifully dry crisp fruit with a teasing hint of
melon and a vague suggestion of raspberry. These are
under-ripe characteristics but crucial if a bubbly is to
last the course and not clog the throat after one or two

glasses. I do think this is the best champagne at this retailer and better than all the other 1996s on the list (which includes Duval Leroy Blanc de Chardonnay 14 points, Gosset Grande Millésimé 15 points, Taittinger Brut Millésimé 14 points, Moët et Chandon Millésimé 15.5 points, Veuve Clicquot Vintage Reserve 14.5 points, Louis Roederer Brut 14 points, Bollinger Grande Année 13 points and Bollinger Grande Année Rosé 13 points). In fairness, I do think some of these champagnes need time but even given that condition I am concerned that I would still find the fruit too forward and cloddish, though the Moët et Chandon Millésimé in a couple of years could be a hit. L & W's 1996 champagnes are only just becoming available around now, autumn 2003, when the wines should be shipped. Duty and VAT are charged following clearance from bond. Current rates at time of going to press are (per dozen bottles) table wines: £13.89 + VAT @17.5% (£16.32). Wines will be held in Vinothèque, Lay & Wheeler's storage facility in Burton-on-Trent (so who said beer and champagne don't mix?).

17

WHITE £7.99

Spreitzer Oestricher Doosberg Riesling 2001   AUSTRIA
The Winery

Of course David Motion who runs the joint is discreet and refuses to claim any relationship with Andrew Motion, the silkily attired and velvet-voiced lackey-versifier of the Queen. But you can't fool me. They look, for a start, nothing like one another. This is always a dead give-away. Motion obeys laws. Einstein wrote about it. Don't ask me to explain these mysteries of the universe. However, I can explain David Motion's so-called and dully titled The Winery. It is a quaint shop in Maida Vale in London with the pre-war chemist's shelving still lining the walls and the original Victorian grate in the corner (although this latter fitting has been modernised and has one of those gas fires therein which look as if real coals were burning). This particular example of Mr Motion's buying skill offers dry honey, nuts, hint of fatness (peach, apricot) as it finishes. It possesses a lovely silky texture.

17   WHITE SPARKLING £8.99

Zum Krug Josef Laufer Sekt Privat Cuvée   GERMANY
Brut 2000
The Winery
Amazingly dry yet impishly lemony and elegant.
Superior to hundreds of champagnes, and entirely
original. Superb with food (smoked fish, light poultry
dishes). Beguiling with mood (blue, green, red,
jaundiced).

17   WHITE £11.50

Herrenberg Riesling Trocken Fass Nr. 5 2001   GERMANY
The Winery
Evolves on the taste buds slowly and gorgeously to
reveal dry peach and very dry grapefruit. Will be better
and will age with more cohesion, precision and
sensuality than any white Burgundy and become
perfect (20 points) in 5, 6 years? Maybe earlier. Sorry
for the diffidence on this point.

17

Casa Lapostolle Merlot 2002 CHILE

*Cambridge Wine Merchants, Hicks & Don, Charles
Hennings Ltd, Thos Peatling Fine Wines, Friarwood*
Marvellously couth and civilised tippling here with
superbly soft tannins.
Also stocked at London Stores (Selfridges) and E-
tailers (ChateauOnLine.co.uk, Everywine, European
Wine Growers' Association and Friarwood.

17

Domaine Huet Le Mont Vouvray Demi-Sec 1988 FRANCE
Bibendum, Transatlantic Wines
Kettners in Romilly Street, Soho, was once a place of
pilgrimage, and for a couple of hours on a windy
June afternoon in 2003 it became one again. The
oldest vintage of the wines of the Huet estate I and
other assembled hacks sipped was 1947 but the
venue can claim a lineage which goes back to 1867 (a
year notable, you will recall, for America buying
Alaska). When I once ate at Kettners in the mid
1960s the house white, served en carafe, was Swiss
(at twenty-five bob), and the waiters, venerable
codgers each with the philosophical stoop of the
professional servitor, were a funereal cabaret which
only, in those days, could be matched by the glum
retinue at A L'Ecu de France in Jermyn Street and the
chummier bunch at L'Etoile in Charlotte Street. Many
of these guys actually lived in Soho and their children
went either to the Soho Parish school in Windmill
Street or the Peter Street Primary off Berwick Street

market. How I envied those kids: they had the sauciest tarts in England on their doorstep and the Empire Leicester Square as their local flea-pit. Domaine Huet has long demonstrated the remarkable qualities and diversity of Chenin Blanc and I was privileged to taste many of its wines going back to 1947 at this tasting but only the one above, of the ones I tasted, is available at the moment in the UK.

Huet is a biodynamic estate, some 100 acres in size, and has been biodynamic for many years. Through Gaston Huet, the ex-mayor of Vouvray who died last year aged 92, it developed a reputation for extraordinary wines of longevity, finesse and delightful (and often surprising) versatility. The wines are made from three sites, all individually made and labelled as such, and they are Le Haut-Lieu, Le Clos du Bourg and Le Mont. Now a lot of nonsense is talked about the biodynamic way of raising fruit and it attracts ferocious critics, following as it does the precepts of Rudolf Steiner. It involves astrology and the phases of the moon amongst other derided concepts. However, the wines are wonderful and this 1988, mature and tantalising, with dry honey and peach and a marvellous unguent, yet far from sweet, textured richness is remarkable and for the money not expensive.

After the tasting of the Huet wines in Kettners I went off to the Chueng Cheng Ku Chinese restaurant in Wardour Street, carrying the choicest of the Huet estate wines as mental baggage, and the girls there, who either prepare the food freshly in front of you or push it around on trolleys (making them not only the most acceptable but the fastest of fast food purveyors on the planet), rustled up steamed chickens' feet (with the '62), prawn balls (with the '90), roast duck (with the '97), greens in oyster sauce (with the mousseaux '70) and, to finish (with that '47), a pair of Chinatown's subtlest gift to pâtisserie: freshly made egg tarts with their rarified, flakier form of phyllo. True, the green tea which accompanied this late afternoon lunch was a poor subsitute for the actual physical presence of Chenin Blanc à la Huet but the imagination and the memory are powerful dynamics. I could truly smell and taste each of the selected wines with each of those dishes (only the mousseaux with the bok-choy greens was a bit of a disappointment). Can a wine estate be paid a higher tribute than that its products create so cerebrally vibrant an existence? As a result of which you may be persuaded of two further insights: first, wines that don't live in the glass cannot live in the mind and, second, to be a wine writer it helps if you are more than slightly barmy.

It also might help if I provide a list of the Huet wines Patrick Whenham-Bossy of Transatlantic Wines does stock. Here they are. I have yet to taste them, for this book was going to press within hours of my becoming aware of this retailer's existence, but readers may like to chance their arms with one or other of what are some of the most individually brilliant wines in France.

Sparkling:

1998 Vouvray Pétillant Brut £19.80 (150cl)

1998 Vouvray Mousseux Brut £9.90 (150cl)

Sec:

1993 Vouvray 'Le Haut Lieu' £9.50

1992 Vouvray 'Le Haut Lieu' £11.05 (only 5 bottles)

Demi-Sec:

1998 Vouvray 'Le Mont' £11.25

1995 Vouvray 'Le Haut Lieu' £16.25

1993 Vouvray 'Le Mont' £9.98

1988 Vouvray 'Le Mont' £14.55

1971 Vouvray 'Le Haut Lieu' £37.55

Moelleux:

2001 Vouvray 'Clos de Bourg' £14.35

1996 Vouvray 'Le Mont' 1er Trie £17.75

1993 Vouvray 'Le Haut Lieu' 1er Trie £22.50

1989 Vouvray 'Le Haut Lieu' 1er Trie £51.45

1957 Vouvray 'Le Mont' £49.05

'Less of a blend than a collision of interpretations,' said Vladmir Nabokov referring to someone's attempt to turn *Lolita* into a screenplay. The appropriate blended wine, however, to match Nabokov's wit has eluded me. I have searched for years. I'd love to find to find a wine of which I could say it's less of a blend than a collision of interpretations. Mediocre wines, whatever their blend of grapes, never offer anything as exciting as a collision: a yawning gap rather than a coming together, a flat falling-off as opposed to a impactful striking of surfaces.

16.5

Casa Lapostolle Chardonnay 2002   CHILE

*Partridges, Charles Hennings Ltd, Cambridge Wine
Merchants, Thos Peatling Fine Wines*

The secret of this estate's success, or should I say one
of several secrets, is the ability to choose precisely the
right time to pick its grape so that all the chemical
elements in the berries co-operate to the maximum in
producing a glorious sum of the parts. Here is a
prime example of svelteness and balance to prove it.
Also stocked at London Stores (Selfridges) and E-tailers
(Everywine, European Wine Growers' Association,
Barrels and Bottles, ChateauOnline.co.uk).

16.5

Casa Lapostolle Cabernet Sauvignon 2001   CHILE

*Cambridge Wine Merchants, Charles Hennings Ltd,
Friarwood, Hicks & Don, Thos Peatling Fine Wines*

What more can I add to the words I have expended on
extolling the virtues of this estate's wines and their
popularity with my palate and pocket? This specimen
is utterly smooth yet, paradoxically, rugged.
Also at London Stores (Selfridges, Harrods), Thresher,
and E-tailers (ChateauOnline.co.uk, Everywine, Barrels
and Bottles and European Wine Growers' Association).

16.5

Prinz Riesling Trocken 2001   GERMANY

The Winery

Intense, cultured, haughty, dry – citrus as interpreted
by Schubert.

16.5

**Kruger-Rumpf Munsterer Kapellenberg
Riesling 2000**

The Winery

Utterly delicious dry peach, and pert minerally acidity.
Touch of Charentais melon on the finish. Texture is
first class.

16.5

**Clemens Busch Pundericher Marienburg
Spätlese 2001**

The Winery

Complex tones of spicy apricot, dry peach, lemon and
mango. Texturally superb and still young. Will reach
19 points in 6–7 years.

16.5

Navarrsotillo Noemus Rioja Blanco 2001

The Winery

At last! A great, inexpensive white Rioja! This Viura
grape variety is more sly and silky than Chardonnay.
It offers cobnuts and a hint of satsuma on the finish.
What subtlety yet emphasis! Only the label is horrible
and cheap and will repel snobs (so the price should
stay as absurd as it is).

16.5

**Lay & Wheeler Chilean Merlot, Curico
(Errazuriz) 2001**

Lay & Wheeler

It has a melt-in-the-mouth chocolate richness tempered
by silky tannins. A gorgeous mouthful for the money.

16.5
WHITE £6.95

Lay & Wheeler Sauvignon Blanc, Casablanca CHILE
(Errazuriz) 2002
Lay & Wheeler
Lovely balance of white peach, gooseberry, a hint of
satsuma, and acids. Has a stunning lazy insouciant
finish of white tannins and a touch of white chocolate.

16.5
WHITE £7.75

Pinot Blanc Vieilles Vignes, Meyer-Fonn, FRANCE
Alsace 2001 £7.75
Lay & Wheeler
Delicious! Almost in the class of a fine Tokay-Pinot Gris
is this purposeful Pinot Blanc. The vines are patently
crusty, bad-tempered and ancient and it shows in the
wine with some marvellously well-concentrated apricot
and white peach fruitiness which would be brilliant
with Thai food. It really needs to be treated like a red
wine and wholly decanted 2–3 hours before drinking.

16.5
WHITE £19.75

St Peray La Belle de Mai, Jean-Luc Colombo 2000 FRANCE
Lay & Wheeler
This took some debate to include in this book as some
will find the oakiness of the fruit intimidating and
even a little ill-poised. As the wine strikes the back of
the palate this may appear as a fault and for twenty
quid who wants faults, real or perceived? However, this
barrel-fermented Roussanne's bouquet is compelling
and the fruit is unusually forward and oleaginous. It
really needs to be treated like a red wine and wholly

decanted 2-3 hours before drinking and I have rated it on this basis. Do not buy the wine, open it and drink it straightaway or you will be disappointed.

16.5

RED £16.95
FRANCE

Coin Caché Mas de la Dame Les Baux de Provence 1999

Lay & Wheeler

This estate, owned by Anne Poniatowski and Caroline Missoffe with Jean-Luc Colombo, a Rhône wine maker, helping out as consultant, is patently a passionate business. The wine shows extreme passion in its make-up. It is a 100% Grenache offering vigour and slow-to-evolve tannic civility with a touch of coffee and some light chocolate. There is a devil-may-care undertone which may strike the sensitive drinker as louche and speaking personally I find this hugely appealing. Anne Poniatowski and Caroline Missoffe are sisters, and daughters of Jacques Chatin who bought the 800-acre estate in 1920 (though only around 130 acres are given over to vines, the rest being pine woods, heather, and 62 acres of olive trees). Both sisters, I believe, are married to Paris-based politicians. None of this is remotely apparent in the wine which exudes a parochial indomitability.

16.5

RED £6.99
CHILE

Montes Reserve Cabernet Sauvignon 2001

Hedley Wright Wine Merchants, Arkell Vintners, Christopher Piper Wines, Dartmouth Vintners, Irvine Robertson Wines, Oxford Wine Co., Reid Wines, Wright Wine Co.

This wine has made British medical history. But first: what does it smell and taste like? It smells and tastes like nutty catering chocolate but the bitterness of this is totally modulated by a sweet cassis edge. It is hugely quaffable, beautifully textured, and free of any troublesome jagged edges because its svelte tannins are so caressing. Yet its tannins are what it has made it so popular with the medical profession. For this is the wine prescribed to patients, two glasses a day, in the cardiac ward at Swindon's Great Western Hospital (you don't need directions to find this ward, you can hear the singing down in reception). Now we all know that the antioxidants, the tannins, in red wine help prevent blood clotting and cholesterol build-up and these virtues have long been extolled by wine writers such as myself who have been drinking tannic red wines for 40 years and yet don't look a day over 19 (there's a club, but I'm the only member thus far). I have, though, no idea of the state of my arteries let alone the condition of my so-often-broken heart. Swindon is the first hospital in Europe to put these theories of red wine and heart disease prevention into practice based on the findings of studies which have found that drinking two glasses of red wine a day can cut the chance of having a stroke by 20% and a heart attack by 50%. The hospital's communications manager, Chris Birdsall, has said that 'since the publicity, which has been international, we have had a steady stream of calls from people asking which wine they should be drinking.' Mr Birdsall, an extremely civilised chap by all accounts, revealed that the wine is served in wine glasses and not via intravenous drips, enemas, or plastic cups. Doubtless George Riedel, a man who has designed hundreds of wine glasses for just about every grape variety and drinking situation you can imagine, will now sit down and come up with The British Hospital Glass (Red Wine). I have also been told that the wine is paid for by the hospital's charitable trust, not NHS funds (so put your pen and paper away and write a letter of complaint about something else). The cardiologist behind the scheme believes, according to the BBC website, that 'it will pay off'. This splendid individual, Dr William McCrea, further said: 'Red wine contains antioxidants. These are the chemicals which stop blood clotting and stop the build-up of cholesterol in blood vessels.' One of the patients who has been enjoying his daily tipple, Richard Corcoran, was reported by the BBC to have remarked: 'It feels like warm aspirin. I can feel it going around my system.' Warm aspirin eh? Well, I got through a bottle of the stuff, Mr Corcoran, and I didn't get warm aspirin but I think I know what you mean. Here's looking at you, kid. Long life to you.

16.5 (18.5 in 3-4 years?)   WHITE £12.99–£13.99
Grosset Watervale Riesling 2002   AUSTRALIA
Milton Sandford Wines, Oz Wines, La Vigneronne, Philglas & Swiggot, Turville Valley Wines, Vin du Vin, Robersons, Bennets Fine Wines, Halifax Wine Company, D Byrne, Berry Bros & Rudd
See entry for Grosset Polish Hill Riesling for more on this estate.

This is screwcapped and so will age without hindrance from any cork. It is young but it bursts with potential. It shows great concentration of dry peach and citrus with fine acids and I would expect the texture to develop greater finesse with time. Exactly how good will it get? Here are my reactions to this wine of various vintages tasted in July 2003.

16   Grosset Watervale Riesling 1992. That fatness showing up, suggesting it is past its best but still excellent. Different bottles will vary tremendously, now the wine is this age – that's all because of the cork.

16.5   Grosset Watervale Riesling 1994. Fatter year, more of a toffee-edge, still delicious and purposeful.

18.5   Grosset Watervale Riesling 1997. Superb oleaginous gooseberry, minerals and acidic citrus with layered levels of soft peach (under-ripe).

18   Grosset Watervale Riesling 1998.The oiliness here is more buttery (but not like rich cream, à la Aussie Chardonnay, but more lean and alpine) and there is a gentle toastiness.

17.5   Grosset Watervale Riesling 1999. Petroleum and an oiliness developing.

17   Grosset Watervale Riesling 2000. Crunchier, getting mature – lovely balance and great class.

17   Grosset Watervale Riesling 2001. Screwcap. Gorgeous bite and crunchy minerals and Ogen melon and citrus with a touch of under-ripe gooseberry.

It can be appreciated from the list above that this Riesling has the capacity to develop brilliantly in bottle and the screwcaps of the later vintage will enable this to happen with greater assurance.
Also at London Stores (Fortnum & Mason, Harvey Nichols).

16

WHITE £7.95
NEW ZEALAND

Lay & Wheeler Sauvignon Blanc, Marlborough 2002
Lay & Wheeler
Screwcapped to keep it fresh and pertinent for several years, the wine shows the regulation Kiwi gooseberry fruit but with suggestions of pineapple and orange peel.

I once remarked in my column that though everything else I was sent by wine retailers was susceptible to recycling (including corks and polystyrene containers), the empty bladder of a 3-litre wine box had defeated me. I offered a prize to the reader who came up with the best suggestion and I received a number of responses. None, however, was as ingenious, as simple, and as vital as Ms Anna Weinel's whose e-mail announced: 'I am a speech and language therapist working with people with profound and multiple disabilities. Our department uses the silver bags inside wine boxes to make "pat mats" when doing sensory work with clients. They can be filled with warm water and are then interesting to touch and feel and listen to!'

16   RED £8.95

Vacqueyras Domaine Le Clos des Cazeaux 2000   FRANCE
Lay & Wheeler
Delicious touches of tobacco to ripe berries and firm
tannins. Very well tailored and polished.

16   RED £5.95

Cabernet Franc/Tempranillo, Pla des Pages   SPAIN
Abadal 2000
Lay & Wheeler
A gloriously unpretentious mouthful of ripe plums
(damsons, towards-the-end-of-season)and very supple
tannins.

16   WHITE £6.25

Torrontes Alta Vista, Mendoza 2002   ARGENTINA
Lay & Wheeler
Delicious, restrained spicy and citrus with a background
echo of white peach. A excellent aperitif tipple.

16   WHITE £7.49

Morgenhof 2001   SOUTH AFRICA
The Bristol Wine Company
Delicious pineapple, pear and melon richness. Very
heartening and charming.
Also at London Stores (Harrods) and Booths.

16   WHITE £9.99

Bergdolt Weissburgunder Kabinett Trocken 2001 GERMANY
The Winery
Delicious demure, dry apricot. Almost effortlessly
polite, well-mannered and couth.

16

Penfolds Bin 28 Kalimna Shiraz 2000 AUSTRALIA

Unwins

One of Penfolds' most harmonious, savoury blends of
fruit and tannins. It opens out well after a couple of
hours of breathing (full decantation) to reveal genteel
spice and smooth berries and those lively tannins.
Also at Oddbins, Sainsbury's, Safeway, Somerfield,
Tesco, Majestic and Thresher.

16

WHITE £6.40

Nelsons Creek Sauvignon Blanc 2002 SOUTH AFRICA

Corney & Barrow

A very untypical Sauvignon Blanc which contrives
light under-ripe gooseberry and apricot with some
orange-peel undertone. Elegant, high drinkable,
complete. It is a nicely balanced 12.5% alcohol so it is
a tad lighter than many of its ilk (i.e. new world white
wines).

16

WHITE £3.95

Montagne Noire Marsanne, Vin de Pays d'Oc FRANCE
2001

Lay & Wheeler

This is a label on sale in supermarkets but this blend
is exclusive to this retailer and what a gently funky,
opulent little number it is with oily fruit of intense,
toffee-edged melonosity. With breathing – that is to
say exposure to the air in the glass – some pleasing
citrus develops.

16   RED £8.95

Hautes-Côtes de Beaune Vieilles Vignes,   FRANCE
Nicolas Potel 1999
Lay & Wheeler
One of the few authentically gripping, tannic Beaunes
under a tenner I can comfortably recommend. Has
good cherry fruit, bitter-edged (the way I like it!), and
the wine exudes a great sense of integrity and
wholeness. It is not a flashy Pinot but it has great
charm and elegance and is terrific chilled – it is
certainly better if decanted for an hour before serving.

16   WHITE SPARKLING (6 bottle case in bond) £120.00

Mailly Cuvée La Terre Champagne 1996   FRANCE
Lay & Wheeler
This is one of this retailer's champagnes I prefer. It
has a wonderful teasing ripeness and richness which
finishes crisp and clean. It will improve for several
more years, and develop that vegetality so beloved of
certain British bubbly aficionados, but it is strikingly
good now.

16   RED £10.45

Willow Bridge Shiraz, Winemaker's Reserve   AUSTRALIA
2001
Stevens Garnier
Expensive but impressively complete, gently spicy,
very firmly berried and classy.
Also at London Stores (Fortnum & Mason, Harvey
Nichols).

16 **(18.5** in 3–5 years) WHITE £14.99–£15.99
Grosset Polish Hill Riesling 2002 AUSTRALIA

*Milton Sandford Wines Limited, Oz Wines, La
Vigneronne, Philglas & Swiggot, Turville Valley Wines,
Vin du Vin, Robersons, Bennets Fine Wines, D Byrne,
Halifax Wine Company*

Mr Grosset makes Australasia's most complex and
incisive Rieslings which age with huge distinction,
charm and calm. He is a great enthusiast for
screwcaps and this only adds to the guarantee that he
provides of excitement to come – as with this young
specimen. It can be cellared with confidence, though
its melon, citrus and dry white peach edge can be
enjoyed now (otherwise that 16 rating is a mockery). I
drank it several times last year in Australia and
thought it wonderful, but it went through a quiet
phase in the summer of 2003 but will pick up by late
2003. This wine has a great, great future and it is wise
to consign that future to the certainty of a screwcap
rather than the gamble of a cork. How it might
develop is shown by these tasting notes of previous
vintages, all tasted in July 2003, starting from the
oldest.

18 Grosset Polish Hill Riesling 1992. Amazing life
and vigour here – from citrus and minerals.

17.5 Grosset Polish Hill Riesling 1994. See below for
thoughts on this.

17 Grosset Polish Hill Riesling 1995. Here we get
textured Charentais melon with rich, mature
citrus.

17.5 Grosset Polish Hill Riesling 1996. Lip-smacking minerals and very dry citrus and a hint of orange peel.

18 Grosset Polish Hill Riesling 1997. Stunning oiliness which coats subtle layered citrus, peach, pine nuts and with fine minerals showing up on the finish.

17 Grosset Polish Hill Riesling 1998. Lovely textured citrus and complex soft/hard fruit.

17 Grosset Polish Hill Riesling 1999. Crunchy minerals, hint of oil to the under-ripe citrus.

16.5 Grosset Polish Hill Riesling 2000. Like the 2001 (and also screwcapped) but with more toastiness showing up and the acids have softened.

16.5 Grosset Polish Hill Riesling 2001. Already the richness and complexity of the greatest of Aussie Rieslings is showing its class – dry, elegant, will improve for 20 years more, thanks to that screwcap. This vintage may be available at some of the listed retailers. Berry Bros certainly had some older vintages, a few cases left of, during the summer of 2003.

Jeffrey Grosset's lightly golden Rieslings are legendary in Australia, and his Polish Hill vineyard vines, which produce a sublimely minerally and exquisite liquid of great finesse, are patently planted on complex limestone bases under their top and subsoils. Jeffrey Grosset, when I met him on his home turf a few years back, struck me immediately as an abbot: a person of great inner calm, his resolute beliefs firmly held beneath pale skin which had not seen the sun, it seemed, for decades; a man of piety and utterly controlled vigour. We quickly tasted his wines, no time for vineyard visiting on this trip, and got down to the nitty-gritty of wine banter. He is a highly articulate advocate of screwcaps and both his Polish Hill Riesling and Watervale Riesling (see entry) are so sealed. The latter wine was like a fine Nahe (German wine region) Riesling, with that rich uplift on the finish. The Polish Hill was in a different league, more Rheingau like, with beautifully advanced grapefruit/peach touches, superb acids, and the potential, screwcapped as it is, to develop for 30 years before significantly fading. What were the geological differences between these two sites, I wanted to know? Is there genuinely a case to be made out for the vitality of the terroirs?

I learned that Polish Hill has a sandy top overlaying clay with interspersed shale, then gravel, and then slate. I suspect there must be deep limestone deposits here but it seems Watervale, with its loamy topsoil has underneath some soft calcrete, which is not pure limestone, into which the vines' root systems penetrate. But it isn't only the siting of his vineyards, there's also his meticulously motherly approach to the wine making.

'I have 46 fermentation tanks here so I can pick different vineyard sites, or parts of a vineyard, and vinify separately,' he told me. 'One of the secrets of getting consistency in a small winery is doing

everything in small batches – and blending.'
Some passionate German and French Riesling
growers have been sufficiently aroused by Jeffrey's
wines to visit here: Loosen, Gunderloch, Trimbach
and Bruer amongst them.

'I want the purest expression of the vineyard and the
grape,' he added. And one can go along with this
notion of terroir because it is so readily evident in his
wines and it is he who is controlling it (anyone else
and the wines would be different, this human factor
being the hugely overlooked element in any terroir
assessment). Jeffrey Grosset is a tremendously
thoughtful and concentrated talker on Riesling. And
the wines consummately echo this. In any event, the
Riesling is a most expressive grape, more so perhaps
than any other, and readily offers when fermented
with love the character of the nourishment it has
received as a rooted plant. Perhaps this is the reason
the French do not permit the planting of the Riesling
grape except within 50 miles of the German border
(hence Riesling's confinement to Alsace); were it to
replace Chardonnay in Burgundy, say, or in Chablis,
the notion of terroir might be truly rumbled because
the Riesling would really express geological
differences the Chardonnay cannot, at best, even
vaguely caricature.

Jeffrey made his apologies and left for a business
meeting, which I why there was no time for me to see
the vines, but not before he handed me a bottle of his
'94 Polish Hill. I had expressed a wish to taste a
mature specimen of his and later in my Aussie trip

this magnificent wine, still excitingly evolving with teasing minerals, was part of a unique evening when for the first time in my life, after scores of fruitless attempts, I held a fishing rod at the other end of which was a fish. I drank the wine while I fished (in the Murray River and my single catch was a cod). The wine suits fish, then, admirably. However, I have enjoyed Polish Hill with other dishes (but none, perhaps, so vigorously fresh and alive). Polish Hill Riesling I drank in Sydney with scallops, aubergines and celeriac with a tomato broth which managed to fall in love so deliriously with the Grosset wine that all I had to do was pour it on to my tongue and the liquid did the rest. Dizzy with delight I ordered grilled barramundi to follow with cacciatore sausage, but the sausage was too strong for the delicate fish; however, the roast tomatoes and whole baby fennel with the dish were superb and the wine was delectable. The restaurant was Bel Mondo down by the dockside. In Melbourne I ate at a French bistro called Tabou and my host knew my preferences.

'You're always going on about Grossett's screwcapped Polish Hill Riesling,' he growled, 'so let's have a bottle.'

I also remember another dinner, also at Bel Mondo, with Philip Shaw who at the time was head wine maker at Penfolds. I was reminded of Terence Stamp in his features or Clark Gable without the 'tache. If you dyed Philip's hair black (it is presently the colour of snowmelt) and gave him a pencil moustache then this ex-wine-maker-in-chief could indeed pass for one of those 1930s Hollywood matinee idols who consumed women like I consume Polish Hill Riesling.

'I want to put the fun back into wine making at Penfolds,' he said to me. 'We'd become too formula minded, too corporate. You know, I've already got three of our people, wine makers, to go overseas this year. Some of our people have never been out of their own areas before.'

This is a man who made his reputation at Rosemount, turning out brilliantly successful commercial wines of occasional style and sometimes wit. He had 60 wine makers under him making wine all over Australia for the Penfolds/Rosemount group, with its 20,000 acres of vines, but he wanted to devolve more responsibility to the individuals actually making the wines.

'I want the wine makers to make the wines. I've got rid of all the senior wine makers. If the wine makers in the wineries can make the wines, well then...who needs wine makers over them?'

We were soon seated and Philip ordered a bottle of...well, I never. The generosity of Aussies never ceases to amaze me. Not because they stand you dinner but because of their readiness to drink one another's wines rather than always indulging in their own. So it is that Philip did not order a Penfolds wine or even a Rosemount wine ('this is something I knocked up a little earlier' sort of thing). He ordered my favourite Aussie Riesling: Grosset's Polish Hill Riesling 2002 with its delicious taint-free screwcap. Dead wine writers, it follows from this, are not found

in heaven. They have no need of heaven; heaven has
no place for them. Why repeat the experience they
have enjoyed on earth? When we die we wine hacks
visit hell. And for the first time we experience what's
it's like to pay for something.

Also at London Stores (Fortnum & Mason, Harvey
Nichols).

The critical community attending wine went into a
bathetic lather in 2002, behind closed internet screens,
regarding scoring and rating systems. Few wine writers
have numerical notation as their critical epicentre, but I
regard it as an essential dynamic because it gives the
reader something tangible beyond the paucities of
language, something which indelibly fixes the critic's
worth of the wine. The American luxury-wine magus,
Robert Parker, is also a devotee. His 100-point
maximum system has become notorious and Bordeaux
château proprietors whose wines attain less than 90-
point scores lose not only face but custom. They crush
the grapes, then along comes Mr Parker to crush them.

However, one reason why a rating system (though
mine, unlike Mr Parker's, is based firmly on value-for-
money) seems to me to be so valuable, apart from the
assurance it gives the reader, is the focus it gives the
critic. I may well describe an Aussie Shiraz as having
the aroma of a sumo wrestler's jockstrap, but if the
wine carries the imprimatur of 17.5 points out of 20
then there can be no doubt it has attractive weight in
all other departments except price.

16

Grosset Sémillon/Sauvignon Blanc 2002   AUSTRALIA

Milton Sandford Wines, Oz Wines, La Vigneronne,
Philglas & Swiggot, Turville Valley Wines, Vin du Vin,
Robersons, Bennets Fine Wines, Halifax Wine Company,
D Byrne, Berry Bros & Rudd

Yet another healthy, screwcapped liquid from Mr
Grosset. Lovely lashings of under-ripe gooseberry and
mineralised melon make this a classic blend to my
mind and it will age, and put on points, with great
ease over the next few years and at 6 or 7 years of age
will be sublime.

Also at London Stores (Harvey Nichols).

16

Wakefield Shiraz 2002   AUSTRALIA

Stratford's, Wiljay Wines, Wine Junction, Wright Wine
Company, Raeburn Fine Wines, Hoults Wine Merchants,
Big Wines, Portland Wine Cellars, Paul Roberts,
Ballantynes of Cowbridge, Scathard, Nidderdale Fine
Wines, Bacchanalia, Wine in Cornwall, Terry Platt Wine
Merchants, Unwins

Has interestingly characterful berries with subtle
coriander/paprika edging. This spicing is far from
OTT, almost genteel, certainly polite, and it's nicely
calmed by the savoury tannins. This vintage of this
wine is claimed to represent one of its best ever and
may, in the words of Mitchell Taylor, the managing
director of Wakefield, 'eclipse the previous great red
vintage of 1998'. Adam Eggins, the wine maker, is
silent on the matter (but then I did not ask him), but

his effort is claimed by the producer to offer 'aromas of plum, cinnamon, liquorice [sic], and spice with creamy nuances of vanilla oak, chocolate and coffee.' I wasn't sure about the chocolate and failed to find the coffee, and I did look hard, but perhaps readers possessed of longer noses and more enquiring palates than mine, would get in touch with their findings.

Also at Oddbins and E-tailers (European Wine Growers' Association).

SOMERFIELD

Somerfield House,
Whitchurch Lane,
Bristol BS14 0TJ

Tel: (0117) 935 9359
Fax: (0117) 978 0629

E-mail: customer.service@somerfield.co.uk
Website: www.somerfield.co.uk

For Somerfield wines 15.5 points and under visit
www.superplonk.com

17

RED £4.99

Santa Julia Oaked Tempranillo 2001 ARGENTINA
Drink it by Christmas 2003! The wine is superbly
immediate, complex and bold with various
berries, nuts, gravy-like tannins and a dry, hearty
finish.
Also at Tesco.

17

WHITE £5.99

Fairview Chardonnay 2001 SOUTH AFRICA
Best white wine at Somerfield's? Probably: rich,
developed, mature, smoky, classy deep, vegetal yet
fruity, dry yet full of itself, full of itself yet subtle.

16.5

WHITE £5.99

Somerfield Gewürztraminer d'Alsace 2001 FRANCE
Gorgeous, rich, balsamic-textured richness yet not
OTT-ness. Very elegant and self-sufficient.

16.5

WHITE SPARKLING £6.99

Somerfield Vintage Cava Brut 1998 SPAIN
One of the most stylish cavas around. Beautifully
mature yet crisp. Knocks a lot of grand marque
champagnes into a cocked chapeau.

16.5

WHITE £3.99

Zagara Cateratto/Chardonnay 2001 SICILY, ITALY
Superb oily consistency – rich gooseberry, melon,
lemon and a hint of orange – delicious, classy,
elegant, food friendly.

16.5

RED £4.99

Argento Malbec 2002 ARGENTINA

Superb under-a-fiver class and precision. Lovely top-class tannins and roasted berries of real weight and wit.

Also at Budgens.

16.5

RED £5.99

Fairview Shiraz 2001 SOUTH AFRICA

Lovely lush berries with intelligent tannins.

Also at Tesco.

16

RED £9.99

Penfolds Bin 28 Kalimna Shiraz 2000 AUSTRALIA

One of Penfolds' most harmonious, savoury blends of fruit and tannins. It opens out well after a couple of hours of breathing (full decantation) to reveal genteel spice and smooth berries and those lively tannins. This is one of those wines which wrote its own 16-point rating, no second thoughts: just the afterthought that how perfect such a red would be to drink with spicy food (excellent, therefore, for a BYOB treat).

Also at Oddbins, Sainsbury's, Safeway, Thresher, Majestic, Tesco and Small Merchants (Unwins).

16

RED SPARKLING £7.99

Banrock Station Sparkling Shiraz NV AUSTRALIA

Still a great wine – a red bubbly no less – to have with the Christmas bird.

Also at Sainsbury's, Waitrose and Morrisons.

16 WHITE £4.99

Somerfield Domaine Ste-Agathe, Vin de Pays FRANCE
d'Oc 2001
Superbly well textured and chewy (touch of white
tannin on the finish) Lovely mature fruit.

---

16 RED £3.99

Fairview Goats du Roam 2002 SOUTH AFRICA
Tar and plums, roasted edge to the tannins, a finish of
morello cherry. Very bright fleshy plums, hint of
strawberries with a fine dusting of tannins. An
excellent casserole red. Better than any Côtes du
Rhône at the same price (under a fiver).
Also at Asda, Booths, Morrison's, Oddbins, Tesco and
Sainsbury's.

---

16 WHITE £3.99

Somerfield Chilean Chardonnay 2002 CHILE
At last! A high-rating Somerfield own-label white.

How would you like your cornflakes to taste of the
cardboard they came in? Would you take kindly to
your baked beans tasting of tin? How about the
prospect of your lunchtime snack having the delicious
tang of cellophane? I suggest there would not be a
sane Briton who would tolerate any of this. So why do
we stomach all of the deficiencies detailed
above when it comes to wine? Wine, that is, which is
sealed with a cork fashioned from a piece of tree bark.
It is a scandal.

16
RED £4.99
Infierno Merlot Monastrell 2000   SPAIN
Very rich and savoury, good roasted edge to the tannins.

16
RED £4.99
Inycon Aglianico 2001   SICILY, ITALY
Grilled berries, early tannins, touch of herb (sage?).

16
RED £5.99
Familia Lucchese Accademia del Sole,   SICILY, ITALY
Nero d'Avola/Cabernet Sauvignon 2001
Cross between California and the southern Rhône in
feel. So we get rustic herbiness and briskness with
restrained class – which does get submerged in
challenging tannins on the finish.

16
RED £5.99
Trulli Premium Selection Old Vine Zinfandel 1999   ITALY
Lipsmackingly savoury and well-tailored – warm,
generous berries and soft, finely scattered tannins.

16
RED £6.49
Porcupine Ridge Cabernet Sauvignon 2001   SOUTH AFRICA
Gripping yet graceful, dashing yet delicate, rich and
deep yet subtle.

16
RED £7.99
Normans Old Vine Shiraz 1999   AUSTRALIA
An adult edge to the herbs and jam here – and decent
tannins.

16

RED £9.99

Evans & Tate Margaret River Shiraz 2000　AUSTRALIA

Energetic and mouth-filling fruit hits the tastebuds
deliciously and softly.

16

WHITE DESSERT　(50cl bottle) £4.99

Muscat de Frontignan NV　FRANCE

Delicious crème brûlée and honey specimen.

16

RED £4.99

Santa Julia Tempranillo 2002　ARGENTINA

Delicious fat fruit saved from obesity by deft tannins.
Elegant, easy to quaff, rich and savoury.

TESCO

Head Office:
Tesco House,
PO Box 18,
Delamare Road,
Cheshunt, Hertfordshire EN8 9SL

Tel: (01992) 632222

Customer Services helpline:
Tel: (0800) 505555

Email: customer.service@tesco.co.uk
Website: www.tesco.com

For Tesco wines 15.5 points and under visit
www.superplonk.com

18

St Hallett Old Block Shiraz, Barossa 1999   AUSTRALIA
Superb. Can bat for the planet as the Shiraz
representative. Huge licorice, chocolate, cocoa, roasted
nutty fruit with fine tannins – at the peak of its
drinkability.

17.5

WHITE £4.99

Tesco Finest Chilean Chardonnay Reserve 2001   CHILE
This is part of Tesco's so-called Finest range. This one
is certainly a worthy inclusion. It offers quite superb
toasty, classy fruit with touches of mango and apricot
and perfect acidic balance. Very elegant. Very
emphatically stylish.

17.5

RED £9.99

Errazuriz Syrah Reserva 1999   CHILE
What a scrumptious red! It seems to combine the
most telling features of the world's greatest wines.
Thus it has Barolo's richness, Châteauneuf's savoury
cosiness, St Emilion's smooth leatheriness, Rhône's
earthiness, Coonawarra's hint of mintiness and, yet,
it's uniquely, marvellously Chilean.

17.5

WHITE £5.99

Errazuriz Chardonnay 2001   CHILE
Scrumptiously complete, opulently ripe and rich yet
balanced and well in control of its toasty melon,
raspberry, apricot and citrus richness. Great texture on
the finish, great style all round.

17.5

Tim Adams Clare Valley Riesling 2002   AUSTRALIA
Screwcapped and brilliantly mature already. Has
superb lemon and chalk richness with dry melon and
a touch of grilled nut. Yes, I say it's mature, but it will
improve and it will reach 20 points in 5-10 years.

17.5

RED £7.99

'Q' Tempranillo La Agricola 2000   ARGENTINA
What a wonderful wine. Huge yet full of finesse,
complex fruits, complete and utterly bewitchingly
delicious structure. Offers the full throatedness of a
great Médoc with the funkiness of a non run-of-the-
mill Rioja.

17.5

FORTIFIED £10.69

Gonzalez Byass Noe Sherry   SPAIN
No vintage but aged at least 30 years. The appearance
in the glass is like the remains of a drained car sump
– oily and dull. The aroma is of baked molasses and
apple crumble. The texture is of axle grease, and the
finish is of condensed milk, Cretan honey and Italian
figs baked in the sun. Pour it over ice-cream (or on
the tongue directly for maximum sybaritic effect).

17.5

RED £9.92

Penfolds Bin 128 Coonawarra Shiraz 2000   AUSTRALIA
What a masterpiece of coagulated richness, roasted,
berried depth, yet elegance. It really is on top drinking
form, complex and complete.

17.5   RED £5.99

Errazuriz Merlot 2001   CHILE

The succulence of the pert berries is beautifully
counterpointed by rich tannins of great couthness.
Also at Thresher.

17   RED £8.95

Jacobs Creek Reserve Shiraz 1999   AUSTRALIA

Better than a Barolo on this showing (and a third of
the price). Enormous strength of character here and
tannic elegance.

17   WHITE £7.99

Tim Adams Sémillon 2000   AUSTRALIA

Gorgeous, tasty, tangy fruit of great elegance and
textured bite. Complex, rich yet delicate, controlled
and beautifully individual. A triumph. Will age well
for 3–4 years more.

17   RED £6.99

Tesco Finest McLaren Vale Shiraz 1999   AUSTRALIA

Great maturity of fruit here and sublime drinkability.
The berries are rich, tangy, thick and sexy, and the
tannins touchingly sympathetic.

17   RED £8.99

Familia Zuccardi Q Tempranillo 2002   ARGENTINA

Makes most Riojas seem like fruit juices in
comparison. It has frightening fruit, terrifying chocolate
tannins and heaps of herbs. A wonderful thick, potent,
deep brew of tongue-lashing scrumptiousness.

17

Tesco Picajuan Peak Sangiovese 2002   ARGENTINA

Makes most Chiantis seem green and mean. Has
beautifully tanned berries, a hint of chocolate, a touch
of licorice, and the roasted tannins are subtle yet
discernible. A stunning wine for the money.

17

Penfolds Thomas Hyland Chardonnay 2002   AUSTRALIA

I have not been hugely impressed, thus far, by Gordon
Ramsay's restaurant at Claridges. Someone took me
there for my birthday last year and I did have an
amusing conversation with the man himself (about
playing schoolboy football in London and Glasgow),
but though his food was good it was not always
thrilling or consistent.

And then Penfolds decided to launch its new Thomas
Hyland range of wines at the restaurant (on the day
the company's CEO resigned which added a further
droll element to proceedings, as the news broke in the
middle of the first course). This first course
announced itself as 'ravioli of tiger prawns and hand-
dived sea scallops with a lemongrass vinaigrette'. This
deliciously smoky wine was served with it. Composed
of fruit from the Adelaide Hills and Eden Valley, it has
a decided Californian feel (the 8 months in French
oak helps) and its musky richness was a shrewd foil to
the 'hand-dived' scallops. Indeed, it was a superb
marriage.

Also at Majestic.

17

WHITE £4.99

Tempus Two Chardonnay 2002　　AUSTRALIA

Stunningly smooth yet ruffled, potent yet delicate, rich
yet demure. Has lovely gooseberry, pineapple, lemon
and gunsmoke complexities, and the finish has a hint
of orange. Needs to be drunk well chilled.

17

WHITE £6.99

Chapel Hill Unwooded Chardonnay 2001　　AUSTRALIA

Sheer satin-textured class in a glass. Offers dry citrus,
soft apricot and melon, a hint of nut. The luxurious
texture caresses, not merely refreshes.

17

RED £6.99

Valdivieso Cabernet Sauvignon Reserve 1999　　CHILE

Delicious grip to some delightfully witty berries
offering tobacco and cocoa. Stern but relaxed tannins.

17

WHITE £6.99

Yalumba Y Series Viognier 2002　　AUSTRALIA

Not as crunchy or concentrated as the previous vintage
but still a well-tailored specimen. Gorgeous apricot fruit-
cake of a wine leavened with a hint of fig and fine
citrussy acids, scrumptious citrus, mango and pineapple
with apricot on the finish. Classy and complete.
Also at Sainsbury's and Waitrose.

17

RED £4.99

Santa Julia Oaked Tempranillo 2001　　ARGENTINA

Delicious degrees of plummy depths are struck here.
Brilliant soft tannins and textured berries.
Also at Somerfield.

16.5   WHITE £4.99

Torres Viña Esmeralda 2002   SPAIN

Screwcapped freshness sealed in so the spicy pear and
lemon will develop well for several years in the bottle.
The Gewürztraminer and Muscat blend of grapes allows
spiciness which is fresh, aromatic and dry with citrus,
raspberry and floral hints. There is a touch of honey
banana on the finish. Congratulations, Miguel (Torres),
for sticking your neck out and putting a screwcap on it.
Also at Thresher and Waitrose.

16.5   RED £6.49

La Palméria Merlot Reserve 2001   CHILE

Superb, genteel leather coated with plums, licorice
and tannins.
Richly rewarding tippling here.

16.5   RED £4.99

Valdivieso Merlot 2001   CHILE

Lovely cherries and plums with soft, supple tannins
providing a fluent backdrop.

16.5   WHITE £4.99

Santa Julia Viognier 2002   ARGENTINA

Wonderful apricot fruit, dry, with a touch of grilled
sesame seed. Lovely, warmly textured yet crisp white
wine: elegant, purposeful, polished.

16.5   RED £8.99

Tim Adams Shiraz 2001   AUSTRALIA

Touches of mint and black olive to the berries provide

great intrigue and complexity. Roasted berries and high-class tannins here.

16.5 RED £4.99

Tesco Finest Australian Reserve Shiraz 2001 AUSTRALIA

How is it that Tesco's own-label Aussie wines are so much sexier, richer, more pungent, more vibrantly and, above all, so elegantly tannic than brands at the same price (or more)? The answer must be Mr Phil Reedman who handles Tesco's Aussie buying out of Adelaide, and is the only UK supermarket employee to work like this. Take a bow, Phil.

16.5 WHITE £5.99

St Hallett Chardonnay 2002 AUSTRALIA

The texture is glorious, thickly knitted and comely. The gentle plumpness of the melon/lemon/ peach fruit is subtle yet emphatic. A terrific Chardonnay.

There is something about champagne which gets up my nose big time and it isn't the bubbles or the bouquet. The product is often raw, the prices are scandalous, and the po-faced producers take themselves so seriously they invite derision. If I had to spend my life exclusively in such a milieu I'd rebel and retire to Tashkent and devote my life to translating the novels of Iris Murdoch into Middle Kingdom hieroglyphs (and, concurrently, Uzbek, just to keep the locals amused).

16.5

Tesco Finest Late-picked Verdicchio 2000   ITALY

Superb! Lovely dry apricot and apple, pear and citrus.
The result is a gorgeous, well-knitted, textured white
wine with aplomb and style.

16.5

WHITE £9.99

Leo Buring Special Release Eden Valley   AUSTRALIA
Riesling 2000

Young, capable of maturing beautifully for 10 to 12 to
15 years. Already assertively lemony, apricotty and
delicious.

16.5

WHITE £4.99

Tesco Finest Great Southern Riesling 2002   AUSTRALIA

Screwcapped and all the better for it. Beautiful tangy
citrus, soft pear and pineapple here. But hold on! Wait
5–6 years, let the fruit concentrate itself even more
and an 18.5 point will emerge . . . perhaps even higher.
Is this a revolution or what? A world in which under-
a-fiver wines can be laid down for so long is a huge
improvement on anything that's gone before, and it's
all thanks to the screwcap.

16.5

WHITE £14.99

Leasingham Classic Clare Riesling 1998   AUSTRALIA

Grand stuff from Ms Thompson (this wine's maker).
Good, mature, nicely textured, ripe, exciting grapefruit
richness. Will cellar well for a decade.

16.5

RED £5.49

Tesco Finest South African Shiraz/ SOUTH AFRICA
Cabernet 2002
Brisk tannins of a chewy intensity, lovely deep
bustling berries, and a savoury undertone to a rich
purposeful finish.

16.5

RED £3.99

Tesco Picajuan Peak Bonarda 2002 ARGENTINA
Remarkably well-clotted berries and cream, a hint of
cocoa, and a lava-like consistency as it coagulates in
the throat. Wonderful with spicy food.

16.5

WHITE £4.99

Montana Marlborough Riesling 2002 NEW ZEALAND
Superbly well packed with ripe peach, melon, lemon
and citrus. Very elegant and rich, yet has a finish of
great finesse.

16.5

RED £5.99

Fairview Shiraz 2001 SOUTH AFRICA
Works deliciously slowly as the fruit moves like
warm tar across the tastebuds revealing roast plums,
licorice, nuts, raspberries and rich, soupy tannins.
Also at Somerfield.

16.5

ROSÉ £3.99

Tesco Chilean Cabernet Sauvignon Rosé NV CHILE
One of the best rosés around with its seriously dry
cherry/plum fruit and touch of tannin to its pineapple
and raspberry finish.

16.5

RED £4.99

Cono Sur Merlot 2002 CHILE

It's all of a piece you see, that's what makes it so lovely,
from nose to throat, and such astounding value.
Spreads like some amazing brand of juice (dry) on the
tongue and the actual berry has yet to be classified
(strawb and black is more or less about right).
Also at Majestic.

16

RED £4.99

Cono Sur Cabernet Sauvignon 2001 CHILE
Dried plum and pepper fruit with stiff tannins.

16

RED £4.99

Tesco Finest Chilean Merlot Reserve 2001 CHILE
Delicious sweet coffee fruit with dry, disciplined tannins.

16

RED £3.99

Tesco Chilean Carmenere NV CHILE
A superb tipple to chuck down with spicy food. But
that is not to say this wine is sweet – it has attitude,
dryness and stealthy tannins.

16

RED £5.99

Luis Felipe Edwards Carmenere 2001 CHILE
Sheer velvet chocolate with hints of raspberry and
grilled plum. Very, very delicious.

16

WHITE £2.97

Tesco Chilean White NV CHILE
Screwcapped freshness of deliciousness and wit.

Lovely aromatic, chewy gooseberry and a hint of
calamine. Dry, serious, elegant.

16   WHITE £3.99

Tesco Chilean Chardonnay NV   CHILE
Good melony ripeness with excellent citrussy balance.

16   WHITE £4.48

Cono Sur Chardonnay 2001   CHILE
Delicious oily ripeness, melon/pear/lemon fruit, well
knitted and tenacious, with a hint of grilled nut.

16   WHITE £3.47

Tesco Chilean Sauvignon Blanc NV   CHILE
Ripe gooseberry with citrus. Classic recipe. Fantastic
price.

16   WHITE (half bottle) £4.99

Maikammerer Mandelhohe Beerenauslese 1999 GERMANY
Snap it up now and cellar it for 4–10 years. It's
honeyed and peachy now, with a crème caramel
undertone, but with age it'll be even more complex
and tantalising. You can't easily get your tongue round
the name to pronounce it but you can, I assure you,
with great fluidity get your tongue around the fruit.

16   WHITE £3.99

Devil's Rock Riesling 2001   GERMANY
Gorgeous! The best vintage yet. Lovely ripe melon and
grapefruit with good classy acids. Hint of spicy pear
on the finish.

16
RED £4.99
Orobio Tempranillo Rioja 2001   SPAIN
Excellent balance of savoury cherries and berries with
tannins which lengthen the experience considerably.

16
WHITE £4.49
Torres Viña Sol 2002   SPAIN
Fine vintage this. Offers chalky melon (Ogen) and
good citrus balance.

16
WHITE £5.99
Campillo Barrel Fermented Rioja 2001   SPAIN
Deliciously controlled fruit of woody melon, raspberry
and pineapple. Excellent stealthy acids. Positive texture.

16
RED £6.99
Ravenswood Vintners Blend Zinfandel   CALIFORNIA, USA
2001
Very jammy but very attractively so, for its sweetness
is perfectly balanced by the earthy tannins.

16
WHITE £5.97
Gallo Turning Leaf Chardonnay 2001   CALIFORNIA, USA
Specially screwcapped for Tesco and a ripe, rich
specimen it is, with very melony, mango-edged fruit.

16
WHITE £9.99
Gallo Coastal Chardonnay 2000   CALIFORNIA, USA
Very classy, rich yet delicate. Has tenacious citrus/pear/
Charentais melon fruit with grilled nut. Very elegant.

16

ROSÉ £5.99

Fetzer Syrah Rosé 2002   CALIFORNIA, USA

Screwcapped – especially for picnics? Perhaps. The
result is excellent with furiously cherry-ripe fruit with
raspberry and pineapple.

16

WHITE £4.49

La Gioiosa Pinot Grigio 2002   ITALY

Delicious! Remarkably elegant citrus with a touch of
toasted almond.

16

RED (3 litre box) £19.99

Lindemans Bin 50 Shiraz 2002   AUSTRALIA

One of the better Aussie reds in a box! Tangy, rich,
sanely balanced, eager yet not OTT, and has good
tannins of softness yet character.] The perfect gift for
someone who just wants a glass of sticky, plum-
pudding-rich (yet dry) glass of Aussie Shiraz once a
day.
Also at Sainsbury's.

16

WHITE (3 litre box) £13.99

Tesco Australian Chardonnay NV   AUSTRALIA

Very convincing, surprisingly mature and delicious
toasty fruit of class, crunchiness and concentration.

16

RED (3 litre box) £14.99

Tesco Chilean Cabernet Sauvignon NV   CHILE

Dry, slightly spicy and very slow-to-evolve tobacco-
edged berries. Very classily correct.

16
                                                  WHITE (3 litre box) £12.99

Tesco Côtes de Gascogne NV   FRANCE

Terrific wine for the money. Lovely spicy pear and pineapple with a floral undertone. Unpretentious and engaging.

16
                                                    RED (3 litre box) £12.99

Organic Tempranillo La Mancha NV   SPAIN

Vanillary, ripe, very dry, deeply engaging fruit of earthy integrity.

16
                                                 WHITE £14.99
                      (2 x 1.5 litres in a single box with 2 taps)

Duo Chardonnay: French Chardonnay and   FRANCE/CHILE
Chilean Chardonnay NV

Much better wines than when first launched, this novel idea unites French Chardonnay and Chilean Chardonnay in separate compartments in a single box. The French is dry and classily complete with a lovely firm texture (on first tasting it was far less gripping). The Chilean is ripe, exotically tinged with pineapple, and finishes with citrus. I suppose the Chilean just about edges in terms of texture, but the whole cheeky idea rates what it does worthily.

16
                                                  RED £18.99

Ascheri Vigna dei Pola Barolo 1998   ITALY

Complex licorice, toasted tannins, plums, cherries and a hint of wild raspberry. Impressively itself and haughtily so. Yes, it's a weight on the pocket but equally it's a weight on the palate.

16   RED £4.99
                                                      ITALY
Tesco Finest Italian Merlot 2000
Very chewy, rich and raunchy with bitingly classy
tannins and plummy fruit of depth and lingering
richness.

16   RED £7.99
                                                      ITALY
Tesco Finest Chianti Classico Riserva 1999
Clinging tannins of great tenacity. The fruit suggests
roasted plum and raspberry, a touch of cherry as it
finishes. Good earthy backbone.

16   RED £3.99
                                                      ITALY
Villa Pigna Rosso Piceno Superiore 1999
Surprisingly assertive and rococo. Fine plums and
intricate tannins.

16   RED £3.99
                                                      ITALY
Tesco Primitivo/Sangiovese 2001
Yes, it's brash and vivid but I love the roller-coaster
way the roasted plums go up and down, playing
footloose and fancy free with the strident tannins.

16   WHITE £3.25
                                                      ITALY
Villa Jolanda Moscato d'Asti NV
Outrageous that a wine so spicily simplistic and
brilliant should be in this book, but just call me
soppily sentimental. Best, I suppose, well chilled in
the back garden with friends on a humid evening. It
reminds me of my mother: warm, big-hearted,
instantly refreshing (and, like her, slightly pétillant).

There are still waiters who assume that it is the man,
or the men, in the party who must be handed the wine
list and the first glass to taste, and cough up the
wherewithal at the end of the meal. I have developed a
simple strategy to deal with offenders which I have
persuaded my female hosts to adopt and which I urge
all women readers to follow: do not, under any
circumstances, leave a tip and make it plain why you
are doing this.

16

WHITE £8.49

Gavi di Gavi La Meirana 2002   ITALY

Delicious, crisp lemon. A brilliant fish and shellfish
wine. Lovely citrus specimen.

16

WHITE £4.99

Lamberti Pinot Grigio 2002   ITALY

It has a nervous edge of lemon and greengage with a
very classy undertone of roasted bread.

16

WHITE £3.46

Tesco Orvieto Classico Abboccato 2002   ITALY

Very attractive pear and pineapple richness with good
acids providing balance and poise.

16

WHITE £4.99

Inycon Chardonnay 2001   SICILY, ITALY

Lovely oily apricot, pineapple, toasty melon and soft
acids (if acids can be termed soft). The texture and
that oil are the exciting things here. Deliciously rich
yet not OTT, this is one of the smartest white wines

(modern) to come out of Sicily. Lifts a bad mood, and
lifts good food (fish, poultry, risottos, pasta).
Also at Morrison's.

16

WHITE £5.99

Montana Sauvignon Blanc 2002   NEW ZEALAND
Very rich gooseberry and lemon complexities with
touches of minerality.

16

WHITE £7.92

Villa Maria Private Bin Sauvignon   NEW ZEALAND
Blanc 2002
To really appreciate this wine at its rating, do not
unscrew its cap for 18 months to 2 years. The citrus
brilliance of the wine will develop beautifully. Tangy
and very forwardly gooseberryish, but better tasted in
a year, and then in the years to come, as its screwcap
permits such slow delicate maturation. (Indeed, it will
age interestingly for 3 decades but not everyone will
find the interest uplifting by then).
Also at Majestic.

16

RED £4.99

Fairview Goats du Roam 2002   SOUTH AFRICA
Tar and plums, roasted edge to the tannins, a finish of
morello cherry. Very bright fleshy plums, hint of
strawberries with a fine dusting of tannins. An
excellent casserole red. Better than any Côtes du
Rhône at the same price (under a fiver).
Also at Asda, Booths, Morrison's, Somerfield,
Oddbins and Sainsbury's.

16   RED £4.99

Tesco Finest South African Reserve   SOUTH AFRICA
Cabernet Sauvignon/Shiraz 2001
Lovely spicy, mouth-tinglingly rich fruit of great
pizazz and chutzpah. Full of vibrant sensuality.

16   WHITE £6.49

Hardy's Varietal Range Reserve   AUSTRALIA
Chardonnay 2001
Delicious peachiness to the regulation melon and
lemon. Excellent forthright texture. Screwcapped, so
it'll stay fresh for many years and develop attractively
along the way.

16   WHITE £6.99

Rosemount Estate Diamond Riesling 2002   AUSTRALIA
The screwcap keeps in the fresh grapefruit and lime
fruit.

16   WHITE £8.49

JL Wolf Wachenheimer Riesling 2001   GERMANY
Young peach and fresh lemon edge to a curiously
forward Riesling. Will cellar well for 3–8 years.

16   WHITE £12.99

Dr Loosen Graacher Himmelreich Riesling   GERMANY
Spätlese, Mosel-Saar-Ruwer 2002
Delicious subtle layers of sweet peach and lychee, but
they are so adolescent. It's surely a shame not to cellar
this for 3–5 years further.

16

Redbank Sunday Morning Pinot Gris 2002 AUSTRALIA
Young but delightfully active on the palate with its
apricot, gooseberry and lemon.

16
WHITE £6.99

Yalumba Barossa Chardonnay 2002 AUSTRALIA
A demure, classy Aussie of elegance and easy
quaffability.

16
ROSÉ £6.99

Antipodean Sangiovese Rosé 2002 AUSTRALIA
One of the more deliciously textured rosés I've tasted.
Strawberry with lemon is the theme.

16
WHITE £4.99

Tesco Finest Reserve Australian Sauvignon AUSTRALIA
Blanc 2002
Vigorous spicy gooseberry. Great with Thai fish dishes.

16
WHITE £6.49

Hardy's Varietal Range Reserve Sauvignon AUSTRALIA
Blanc/Sémillon 2001
Delicious gooseberry and apricot. Screwcap.

16
WHITE £5.49

Peter Lehmann Sémillon 2002 AUSTRALIA
What a wine to cellar for 3–6 years! Already showing
deft, dry peach and pear. Screwcapped, so it can't
suffer from cork taint or quickly lose its freshness.

16

WHITE £5.99

Rosemount Estate Traminer Riesling 2002   AUSTRALIA
Great fruity form and will cellar for 5–6 years. It's a
touch sweet and honeyed but it's balanced and has
good acids. Superb with Chinese food. Screwcapped.

16

WHITE £8.99

Ca' dei Frati Lugana 2001   ITALY
An apricot-scented and -fruited wine of considerable
finesse.

16

WHITE (3 litre box) £11.49

Tesco Argentinean White NV   ARGENTINA
Take it to the Chinese or Thai BYOB and enjoy
yourself with its grapefruit and honey fruit (dry).

16

RED £6.49

Corbières Reserve Ancien Comte 2001   FRANCE
Chewy, ripe, textured, deep – a lovely tense duel
between the berries and the tannins which is match
drawn (deliciously).

16

RED £3.99

Santa Julia Fuzion Tempranillo/Malbec 2002   ARGENTINA
A bargain! Lovely ripe berries, brisk (but soft) tannins
and a faint touch of spice.

16

RED £5.99

Alamos Malbec 2002   ARGENTINA
More lush than previous vintages and more clinging in
the throat. Very firm, rich, potent, broad and clotted.

16

Penfolds Thomas Hyland Cabernet Sauvignon 2001

I am fond of red wine and fish but I had never thought that an Aussie Cabernet like this would go so brilliantly with rare salmon. This dish (see earlier entry for Hyland wine) was described by its chef as a 'fillet of salmon on a bed of braised baby gem lettuce with tomato butter sauce', and the sweetness in the sauce and the perfect condition of the salmon made this one of the best red wine/fish pairings I've had. The wine has lithe tannins (Penfolds do love adding them – a trick they picked up in Bordeaux), excellently structured and textured, and they permit the wine to flow to a most satisfying finish (with or without fish).

16

Jacobs Creek Reserve Chardonnay 2001   AUSTRALIA

Lovely dry apricot, toasty melon and dry citrus fruit. Very finely tailored and classy.

16

Penfolds Rawson's Retreat Riesling 2001   AUSTRALIA

Brilliant screwcapped freshness and dry nuttiness here. Has petroleum undertones developing and a citrus richness already tangy. Will age 10–12 years easily.

16

Oxford Landing Sauvignon Blanc 2002   AUSTRALIA

Lovely controlled grassiness and yet soft melon approachability with a gooseberry finish. A truly delicious fish wine (and for the cook to sip whilst preparing it).

16   WHITE £4.99

Brown Brothers Dry Muscat 2002   AUSTRALIA
Deliciously dry, very elegant and demure spice fruit. A superb aperitif of great style.
Also at Asda.

16   WHITE £5.99

Lindemans Bin 95 Sauvignon Blanc 2002   AUSTRALIA
Screwcapped toastiness and very dry under-ripe gooseberry richness. Goodness, I'd love to drink this wine in 8 years to see if it's reached 19 points.

16   RED £3.99

Tesco Picajuan Peak Malbec 2002   ARGENTINA
Lip-smackingly licorice rich and blackberryish. Gorgeous texture and tension (between the elements of fruit and acid and tannins).

16   RED £4.99

Tesco Finest Argentinean Malbec Reserve 2002   ARGENTINA
Dry yet full of vibrant fruit. Superb casserole-friendly bottle.

16   WHITE £3.48

Tesco Picajuan Peak Chardonnay 2002   ARGENTINA
What incredible value for money. Rich, opulent, sly and eager-to-please peach, pear and citrus fruit. Huge charm.

16 RED (1.5 litres £5.95) £2.99

Tesco Australian Red NV AUSTRALIA

Tarry, plummy, rich and well polished. An amazing
wine for the money. The tannins are like ruffled velvet
patches on the corduroy-textured fruit.

16 RED £3.48

Tesco Australian Shiraz/Cabernet AUSTRALIA
Sauvignon NV

Mad isn't it? A wine this cheap being so drinkably
complete, well berried and so succulently kitted out
with tannins.

I remember the £4 bottle of Château Pétrus 1949
offered by the hotel I stayed in on my first honeymoon
in the late 1960s. A bottle of this claret of that vintage
went for several thousand pounds at auction last year.
A rational visitor from another planet would surely
remark how much the liquid must have improved in
that time to have added so spectacularly to its value
but as you and I know the wine did not improve.
Indeed, it was doubtless considerably more of a
tannically tantalising masterpiece twenty years after its
manufacture than it was at fifty-two. What had
happened to the wine was the fanaticism of the
international collectors' market where things are not
appreciated for what they intrinsically are as
performers on the senses but as symbols of status. Is
this the age we live in? If so, then I hope this book is
an attempt to construct a bulwark against it.

16

RED £6.97

Penfolds Koonunga Hill Shiraz/Cabernet 2001   AUSTRALIA
Has a lovely minty, blackberry richness. Excellent
tannins too.

16

RED £4.99

Banrock Station Cabernet Sauvignon 2001   AUSTRALIA
Lovely rich and berried and quite fantastically
pleasingly plump, yet not inelegant.

16

RED £4.99

Tesco Finest Reserve Cabernet Sauvignon   AUSTRALIA
2000
Has tar, mint, herbs, berries, tannins and it's all
married together thickly and richly.

16

RED £6.99

Tesco Finest Coonawarra Cabernet Sauvignon   AUSTRALIA
1999
Perfect maturity and ripeness with hints of mint and
sage to the vibrant berries.

16

RED £9.99

Chapel Hill McLaren Vale/Coonawarra   AUSTRALIA
Cabernet Sauvignon 2000
Very dry yet very fruity. And the dryness never wavers
even as the berries thicken and get richer on the tongue.

16

RED £3.77

Tesco Australian Shiraz NV   AUSTRALIA
Juicy but has good tannins to keep it serious and
seriously quaffable. Amazing value for money.

16

RED £7.49
AUSTRALIA

Rosemount Shiraz 2001

Drink it soon (by Christmas 2003). The tannins are
keeping the sweaty plums and dry berries in order –
but they won't last forever (not with a cork seal).

16

RED £7.99
AUSTRALIA

Brown Brothers Shiraz, Victoria 2000

Minty, ripe, finely dusted with lingering licorice-edged
tannins. A handsomely textured red.

16

RED £7.99
AUSTRALIA

St Hallett Faith Shiraz 2001

It's so delicious it melts the heart. It's sheer toasted
berries and velvet tannins.

16

RED £5.94
AUSTRALIA

Jacobs Creek Merlot 2001

Juicy and infinitely curry-friendly but also very
complex as it hits the throat, and the tannins lie
resplendently on the memory.

16

WHITE £5.95
AUSTRALIA

Rosemount Sémillon/Chardonnay 2002

Good fatness of fruit here with a charming toasty
undertone with a touch of toffee cream. Screwcapped
to keep it perky for years.

16

WHITE £3.48
AUSTRALIA

Tesco Australian Chardonnay NV

Delicious toasty melon, hint of citrus, touch of grilled
walnut as it finishes. Dry elegant, astounding value
for money.

16

WHITE £5.97

Penfolds Koonunga Hill Chardonnay 2001   AUSTRALIA
Very elegant, mature, and toasty. Better than a
thousand white Burgundies at five times the price.

16

WHITE £5.99

Tesco Finest Padthaway Chardonnay 2001   AUSTRALIA
Remarkably chewily textured and rich, yet has great
finesse and patience. A civilised wine with lingering
charms.

16

WHITE £5.99

Lindemans Bin 665 Chardonnay 2002   AUSTRALIA
Fresh, dry, reliable and classy. Drier than earlier
vintages and it will mature more slowly, thanks to its
screwcap, but it is delicious now. Will improve in 3–4
years' time to rate considerably higher.

16

WHITE £6.94

Rosemount Chardonnay 2002   AUSTRALIA
Flatters to deceive as it opens, for it seems about to
engulf the palate, but it settles down to parade peach
and citrus fruit – and pleasantly restrained it is by the
time it decides to finish.

16

RED £4.99

Tesco Finest Côtes du Rhône-Villages, Domaine   FRANCE
Le Grand Rétour 2001
Terrific texture and sticky toffee tannins with good
grilled berries.

16

RED £9.49

Perrin Vacqueyras 2000   FRANCE
Sweet licorice and dry berries, firm tannins, roasted
undertone.

16

WHITE DESSERT (37.5cl bottle) £4.49

Muscat de Beaumes de Venise NV   FRANCE
Lovely ripe pineapple and honey with a touch of toffee
apple. Superb with fresh fruit at the end of a meal.

16

WHITE £5.99

Tesco Finest Alsace Gewürztraminer 2001   FRANCE
Rosy fruit of perfume and spice. Superb with Peking
duck.

16

WHITE SPARKLING £11.99

Tesco Blanc de Noirs Champagne NV   FRANCE
Delicious strawberry subtleties and crisp lemon
edging. Classic specimen, and finer than many
champagnes at four times the price.

16

WHITE SPARKLING £12.99

Tesco Premier Cru Champagne Brut NV   FRANCE
Has a softer, richer edge than the Blanc de Noirs and
is arguably better with food.

16

WHITE SPARKLING £14.99

Tesco Blanc de Blancs Champagne NV   FRANCE
Full yet subtle, delicate yet emphatic, decisive yet
stealthy. More than a hint of spice and melon here
(not to mention paradox).

16

RED £9.99

Penfolds Bin 28 Kalimna Shiraz 2000 AUSTRALIA

One of Penfolds' most harmonious, savoury blends of fruit and tannins. It opens out well after a couple of hours of breathing (full decantation) to reveal genteel spice and smooth berries and those lively tannins. This is one of those wines which wrote its own 16-point rating, no second thoughts: just the afterthought that how perfect such a red would be to drink with spicy food (excellent, therefore, for a BYOB treat). Also at Safeway, Sainsbury's, Somerfield, Thresher, Oddbins, Majestic and Small Merchants (Unwins).

THRESHER

Enjoyment Hall,
Bessemer Road,
Welwyn Garden City,
Hertfordshire AL7 1BL

Tel: (01707) 387200
Fax: (01707) 387416

For Thresher wines 15.5 points and under visit
www.superplonk.com

Currently this retailer, in addition to Thresher, still
operates under various fascias – Wine Rack, Bottoms
Up, Victoria Wine, Haddows in Scotland –
and some of the wines below will be
found there. However, it is
anticipated that very soon the
majority of the shops will be
all, thank the good Lord for
simplifying my working
life, called Thresher.

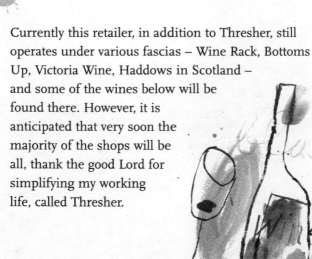

17.5

RED £9.99

Vacqueyras Les Christians Perrin 2001 FRANCE

A 80% Grenache, 20% Syrah blend which really does
clobber the tastebuds with great clods of roasted fruit
and deep chocolate tannins. Stupendous stuff.

17.5

RED £6.99

Casa Lapostolle Cabernet Sauvignon 2000 CHILE

Dry chocolate, touch of bell pepper and black pepper,
beautifully silky yet assertive tannins and a dry, cassis
finish. Impressively textured and fruited, this has
liveliness yet finesse. It went splendidly with coq au
vin blanc I knocked up with shiitake mushrooms and
baby turnips – the gaminess of the dish brought out
the feral side of the wine.
Also at London Stores (Selfridges, Harrods) and E-
tailers (Virgin Wines, ChateauOnline.co.uk).

17.5

RED £5.99

Errazuriz Merlot 2001 CHILE

This red offers you the luxury of drinking vinified Gucci
leather loafers with ruffled velvet stitching. It's all
texture, this glorious liquid. The price is, frankly,
absurd, laughable, crazy – though Merlot growers in
other countries may not find it quite so amusing as that.
Also at Tesco.

17.5

RED £6.99

Errazuriz Syrah 2001 CHILE

Utterly beguiling smoky berries with the tannins
roasted to a turn. There are no Aussie Shirazes at this

price in the same textured class. I do believe that if Chile could turn out several dozen Shirazes like this at this price a shiver would not just go down the Aussies' backs but Rhône producers also.

17.5

WHITE £7.99

Villa Maria Sauvignon Blanc 2002   NEW ZEALAND

Screwcapped and all the better for it. Superb extruded crushed gooseberry fruit here with lime and minerals.

We wine writers become a trifle barmy. We spend a large proportion of our lives spitting wine out: the precise opposite of what sane drinkers do. If not expectorating, or indeed having just done so, we then muse over what food a wine might accompany, what precise dish it will perfectly accompany perhaps, not just the specific regional cuisine which it might suit.

It is not enough to find wines to go with dishes, however. We must find wines to go with every human activity. I have, in my time, not just matched wines with scores of dishes (and written a book on it), but found wines to suit certain novels (and written two articles on it), wines to go with romantic interludes (several articles when I was wine editor of *Cosmo* though I refrained from nominating the perfect wine for actual congress on the grounds that the research was too daunting to contemplate), the wines to suit barbecues and to enjoy after mowing a lawn, the wines to have to hand when preparing food, the wines to take to the cinema (which my local flea-pit allows), and the wines to go with certain pieces of classical music (to which end I compiled a cd for Deutsche Grammophon).

Will develop excitingly in bottle for some years yet.
Lovely fresh finesse now. Concentrated vegetality in
the future.
Also at Sainsbury's.

17
RED £8.99

Château La Clotte-Fontaine, Cremailh 2001 FRANCE
Superb clotted plum and cream fruit with a dusting of
cocoa powder which lingers to coat the very rich
tannins. A terrific wine of great class.

17
WHITE £5.99

Vouvray Coteaux Tufiers 2001 FRANCE
Wonderful texture and tangy tangerine, lemon, ripe
Ogen melon and pineapple – with a dry honey edge.
Will cellar brilliantly for years. This is a hugely
underrated appellation, Vouvray, and this specimen
offers a treat at a risible price.

17
WHITE £6.99

Villa Maria Riesling 2002 NEW ZEALAND
Screwcap! Don't you just love the idea? All that
freshness and flavour trapped, to develop at its own
pace, unhurried and untainted by a cork. The result is
opulence yet restraint (melon/pear/citrus) in this
specimen.
Also at Morrison's and Sainsbury's.

17
RED £6.99

Les Favorites Merlot Réserve 2000 FRANCE
Superb leathery fruit, cherries and berries, with fine
roasted tannins. The texture is outstanding. This is one

of the new-style, new-world-in-feel-and-shape Merlots
coming out of southern France, from the previously
despised boondocks, and I must say it beats many a
much vaunted St-Emilion for textured vivacity.

16.5 WHITE £6.99

Les Favorites Chardonnay Réserve 2001 FRANCE
As good, as arboreal, as advanced as many a white
Burgundy (an exceptional, rare example of course).

16.5 WHITE £5.49

Concha y Toro Casillero del Diablo Sauvignon CHILE
Blanc 2002
Delicious fresh melon and lemon with a touch of
gooseberry. Very classy, elegant, stylish from nose to
throat.
Also at Majestic.

16.5 WHITE £8.99

Pewsey Vale Eden Valley Riesling 2000 AUSTRALIA
Beautifully artistic from nose to throat: petrol, limes,
dry peach, and minerals and it's only a few years old.
Will it reach 19 points in 5 years? Could be.

16.5 WHITE £5.99

Torres Viña Esmeralda 2002 SPAIN
Screwcapped freshness sealed in so the spicy pear and
lemon will develop well for several years in the bottle.
The Gewürztraminer and Muscat blend of grapes
allows spiciness which is fresh, aromatic and dry with
citrus, raspberry and floral hints. There is a touch of

honey banana on the finish. Congratulations, Miguel
(Torres), for sticking your neck out and putting a
screwcap on it.
Also at Tesco and Waitrose.

16.5
RED £4.99

Concha y Toro Casillero del Diablo Cabernet   CHILE
Sauvignon 2002
One of the world's most elegant Cabs under a fiver.
Takes you from nose to throat in superior upholstered
comfort. It's the chewiness of the tannins I love – they
will not be shifted and are almost protean as they shift
and shape and linger. Superb edge to the chewy
tannins gives the wine breadth and depth. Terrific
tension between the tannins and the berries, which
lingers lushly, yet responsibly.
Also at Sainsbury's and Waitrose.

16.5
WHITE £6.99

Josefinegrund Trittenheimer Apotheke   GERMANY
Riesling Spätlese 1994
Delicious citrus and gently spicy peach just beginning
to turn petrolly and classic. Touch of honey is
balanced with a mineral undertone.

16.5
RED £6.99

Durius Marqués de Griñon Tempranillo 2001   SPAIN
Gorgeous tannins to lovely brisk cherries and plums.
A hint of chocolate to the rich berries. Shows just how
civilised and polished (yet characterful) the
Tempranillo grape can become. Beautiful plump, soft

texture here. Flashy, rich, textured, gripping and, for the price, a steal.

Also at Morrison's, Budgens, Majestic and Sainsbury's.

16.5   RED £6.99

Hoya de Cadeñas Reserva 1998   SPAIN

Has a ripe undertone of vanilla and cherry, very beautifully co-ordinated with the encroaching tannins. Hint of black olive here.

16.5   RED £6.99

Casa Lapostolle Cabernet Sauvignon 2001   CHILE

What more can I add to the words I have expended on extolling the virtues of this estate's wines and their popularity with my palate and pocket? This specimen is utterly smooth yet, paradoxically, rugged.

Also available at London Stores (Selfridges, Harrods), Small Merchants (Friarwood, Cambridge Wine Merchants, Hicks & Don, Thos Peatling Fine Wines, Charles Hennings Ltd) and E-tailers (Barrels and Bottles, ChateauOnline.co.uk, Everywine).

16.5   WHITE £5.99

Touraine Sauvignon Blanc, Domaine   FRANCE
Pré-Baron 2002

Better, crisper, more structured and more tantalisingly tangier than many a Sancerre.

16   WHITE £4.99

Concha y Toro Casillero del Diablo   CHILE
Chardonnay 2001

Delicate, gently textured, slightly smoky melon and lemon. Very elegant and understated.

16

WHITE £6.99

Cave de Turckheim Tokay-Pinot Gris, Alsace FRANCE
2001
Lovely crisp, tangy apricot and citrus. Very complete,
elegant wine.

16

RED £3.99

Côtes du Ventoux La Mission 2001 FRANCE
Delightfully couth and calm, nothing too sweaty or
rustic here. Has delicious cherry/chocolate fruit and
firm tannins.

16

RED £7.49

Château de Grand Prébois, Côtes du Rhône FRANCE
1999
Brilliantly lingering mouthful of plums,
chocolate, woodsmoke and very thick, but soft,
tannins.

16

RED £5.99

Valpolicella Superiore Zenato 2000 ITALY
Has very nice cherries with a touch of roasted
loganberry and slow-to-evolve tannins. Wonderful
chilled, with cold meats.

16

RED £5.99

Ermitage du Pic Saint-Loup Réserve, Coteaux FRANCE
du Languedoc 2001
Delicious frisky fruit with dry tannins.

16
RED £6.99
Durius Marqués de Griñon Rioja 2001 SPAIN
Always one of the smoothest, most elegant, satisfying
and civilised of Riojas – and certainly the most
elegant. Has character as well as class.
Also at Morrison's.

16
RED £5.99
Canaletto Nero d'Avola/Syrah 2002 SICILY, ITALY
Firm cherry fruit with good tannins which develop
slowly, deliciously.

16
RED £9.99
Monteguelfo Chianti Classico Riserva 1999 ITALY
One of the most polished yet characterful Chiantis
I've tasted this year. Soft yet warm tannins to really
good berries.

16
RED £5.99
Little Boomey Merlot 2001 AUSTRALIA
It's different, delicate, determined to please. The fruit
is very soft and plummy, the tannins a pushover.

16
RED £9.99
Neffiez Cuvée Balthazar, Coteaux du FRANCE
Languedoc 2001
Most curious baked fruit, warm tannins, and a texture
which clings like ruffled satin.

16
RED £3.99
Hilltop Riverview Merlot/Cabernet 2001 HUNGARY
Nice gruff tannins and firm berries.

16

RED £6.99

St Hallett Barossa Cabernet/Shiraz 2001   AUSTRALIA
It's what Oz does best: jammy berries with full but
not raw tannins.

16

RED £7.99

Wynn's Coonawarra Shiraz 2001   AUSTRALIA
Minty, hint of oil to the berries. Fine tannins with a
touch of cassis and a great texture.

16

RED £9.99

St Hallett Barossa Shiraz 2000   AUSTRALIA
Has a complete approach to palate seduction: it lays
out all its wares fully and deeply, from nose to throat.

16

RED £9.99

Escudo Rojo 2000   CHILE
Curiously spicy and wacky. Has delicious burned
berries, leafy tannins, and a rich roasted finish.

16

WHITE £4.99

Villiera Chenin Blanc 2002   SOUTH AFRICA
A rich wine of dry apricot and melon with citrus.
Brilliant with Thai food.

16

RED £9.99

Penfolds Bin 28 Kalimna Shiraz 2000   AUSTRALIA
One of Penfolds' most harmonious, savoury blends of
fruit and tannins. It opens out well after a couple of
hours of breathing (full decantation) to reveal genteel
spice and smooth berries and those lively tannins.

This is one of those wines which wrote its own 16-point rating, no second thoughts: just the afterthought that how perfect such a red would be to drink with spicy food (excellent, therefore, for a BYOB treat). Also at Sainsbury's, Somerfield, Safeway, Oddbins, Majestic, Tesco and Small Merchants (Unwins).

16

WHITE SPARKLING £14.99

Jean de Praisac NV   FRANCE

The real thing. Beautifully crisp and clean. Absolutely delicious. What makes it a classic is because it is all suggestiveness, slyness, understatement. It is glorious dryness elevated to something beyond words (or my ability to find such, at any rate).

16

WHITE £4.99

Kendermans Organic White 2001   GERMANY

A delicious grapefruit-tinged, clean white wine of consummate quaffability.

16

WHITE £6.99

Booarra Chenin/Verdelho 2002   AUSTRALIA

Screwcapped and so it will age with distinction as well as it will gush from the bottle fresh and untainted. Has lovely bitter-lemon and pineapple undertones of great charm.

16

WHITE £6.99

Houghton HWB 2002   AUSTRALIA

It was called Houghton White Burgundy (hence HWB), but EU regulations put a stop to such copycat and misleading goings-on and so it was compelled to

call it something or hide what HWB once stood for. It
is Burgundian, fresh and gently vegetal in feel, but it
is doubtful whether any grapes of Burgundian origin
play any part in the wine.

16

WHITE £7.99

Vin Five Collection Sémillon/Sauvignon 2002   AUSTRALIA
Crisp, fresh, crunchy gooseberry, pineapple and pear
fruit.

16

RED £4.99

Santo Cristo Tempranillo/Garnacha, Campo de   SPAIN
Borja 2002
Wild cherry, roasted nuts, good plummy finish.

16

RED £5.99

Domaine de la Thebaide, Minervois 2001   FRANCE
Rustic couthness and charm. Delicious grilled berries
with svelte tannins. This is one of those country reds
which the Midi is now turning out to compete with
the best from the new world.

16

RED £5.49

Laurent Miquel Syrah 2002   FRANCE
Harmony from vigorous plums, roasted berries and a
touch of juiciness with the tannins. It is a terrific
casserole red.

16

RED £7.99

Perrin Nature, Côtes du Rhône 2001   FRANCE
Brilliant lipsmacking jamminess with the stealthy
tannins making a late, but welcome, appearance.

WAITROSE

Head Office:
Doncaster Road,
Southern Industrial Area,
Bracknell, Berkshire RG12 8YA

Tel:(01344)424680

WAITROSE WINE DIRECT

Freepost SW1647
Bracknell,
Berkshire RG12 8HX

Tel:(0800)188881
Fax:(0800)188888

Email: customerservice@waitrose.co.uk
Website: www.waitrose.com

Helpline: (0800)188884
(open Monday-Friday 7am–10pm,
Saturday 7am–8pm,
Sunday 10am–5pm)

20

White dessert £170.00

**Château d'Yquem Sauternes
1er Grand Cru Classé 1997** FRANCE

Simply a perfect wine. Complex, vivid, provocative yet
caressing, it is a statement of humankind's creative
genius (but that is not to say this wine has anything to
do with artistic expression). The liquid is not mono-
dimensionally sweet but full of myriad butterscotch,
soft and hard fruit flavours and combines delicacy
with magnificently textured, satiny richness yet
subtlety. It is of course young and can be laid down
for many years (as few as 5, as many as 20 and more)
but when I drank it, sipping a small glass with some
fruit and soft goat's cheese, I was ravished by its
pertinacity, and its youth was beguiling, not gauche.
Available only in Canary Wharf and Kingston-on-
Thames branches. Half bottles at some Sainsbury's.

18.5

RED £35.00

Montes Folly Syrah 2000 CHILE

Magnificent mocha coffee, herbs, berries tantalisingly
roasted yet fresh, and tannins like boulders – this is
an awesome Syrah of world-class texture and
complexity. It seizes the mind as much as it does the
palate.

18.5

RED £12.99

**Marqués de Griñon Dominio de Valdepusa Syrah
2000** SPAIN

One of Spain's sexiest reds with its complex layers of
fruit which linger for minutes. It has the magic of an

awesome texture, superb knitted tannins, and a finish
of quite surprising delicacy yet weight. I found a mild
curry-style dish ruffled its surface, but with gentler
fare, a roast chicken or roast cod, it kept its cool.

18.5

WHITE £9.99

Yalumba Eden Valley Viognier 2001 AUSTRALIA

About as magnificent as Viognier can get with its
apricotty ripeness, touch of Alfonso mango, citrus and
toasted sesame seeds. Why I chickened out of giving it
20 points, I don't know. (Well, I do, now I can write
this in the calm of the morning and the evening's
bottle lies empty and sullen, rebuking me for daring
to hand it a mere 18.5 points. Such is this wine's class
that it can induce feelings like that.)
Also at Safeway.

18.5

WHITE £9.99

Domaine de la Baume Blanc Viognier/ FRANCE
Chardonnay, Vin de Pays d'Oc 2000

Magnificent chewy, minerally creamy, rich, firm white
wine of complexity, clout, concentration and class. I
must say I would prefer to drink this wine than a
thousand white Burgundies at three to five times the
price.

18

RED £35.00

Montes Folly Santa Cruz 2000 CHILE

A 100% Syrah to make Grange, the Aussies' self-
proclaimed top Syrah, seem like gnat's piss mark two.
The level of cherries, liquorice, chocolate and cassis in
this wine is scrumptiously, robustly world class. I can do

without Santa Claus at Christmas but I'm very happy to welcome Santa Cruz with the festive fowl suitably stuffed with truffles and with the appropriate sauce. Canary Wharf branch only.

17.5   WHITE DESSERT (37.5cl bottle) £11.99
Château Doisy-Daëne Sauternes 2ème Grand   FRANCE
Cru Classé 2000
Magnificent youth! Oily, tenacious, rich, honeyed, assertive and superbly 'textured' – this is a great pudding wine.

One of the ideas which a nervy Auntie refused to allow me to develop when I presented a wine series on BBC2 some years back involved swapping labels on bottles of wine so that tasters (and I mean experienced ones) would be confronted by bottles of Château Margaux or Domaine de la Romanée-Conti, but the liquid inside would be something far cheaper and less grand. I wished to explore my belief that even so-called experts are swayed by what is outside the bottle, specifically the label, to the extent that their tasting faculties and subsequent judgements are affected. I now learn that a sly fellow called Frederic Brochet has done exactly that in Bordeaux. According to the Cape magazine *Wine*, Monsieur Brochet got together over 50 local experts and let them taste a range of Cru Classé clarets and then put the same liquids into bottles from no-account vineyards and sat back and watched 80% of these soi-disant experts totally change their ratings and views when the same wine was in a different bottle.

17.5   WHITE DESSERT (50cl bottle) £8.99
Domaine des Forges, Coteaux du Layon Chaume   FRANCE
2001
Wickedly sweet and thick, yet hugely insouciant and
elegant. I rarely taste such couthness in a sweet wine,
for the honeyed side of such wines always
predominate, but here the wine reveals mango and
cream and thus balance.

17.5   WHITE £22.95
Chablis Grand Cru Vaudésir, J-M Brocard   FRANCE
2000
It is – and I say it through gritted teeth – a classic,
world-class Chardonnay. Crisp, minerally, delicate – it's
almost as great as Riesling in this example. Why
gritted teeth? I've been off Chablis for years, finding so
few bottles justifying their prices. But this one does.

17.5   WHITE £9.99
Catena Agrelo Vineyards Chardonnay 2001   ARGENTINA
Tannins! Ah yes! The fruit is creamy, yet dry, and
shows spicy apricot and very subtle tangerine acidity.

17.5   RED £6.99
Porcupine Ridge Syrah 2002   SOUTH AFRICA
Boekenhoutskloof, where this wine is grown and
made, is a winery set snugly beneath an outcrop of
rocky hills (almost pink in the sun when I went there
in February 2003). The sight makes an instant
impression. As does this wine's maker, Marc Kent. He
looks like the sort of hippie I lived near in Greenwich

Village in 1969 and he is just as affable. Nothing disagreeable seems to nest in his beard and certainly not on his tasting-room table. This example of his oenological prowess offers superb chocolate-drenched berries and deft tannins interwoven with touches of roasted macadamia nut, burned cream and herbs. I drank it with my lunch on the winery's terrace, hard by the boules court. The food was a take-away, prepared by sous-chef Vanie Padayachee of Le Quartier Français restaurant in Franschhoek, and it was magnificent. The chicken liver pâté I would kill to be able to make so light yet so intense (20 points out of 20 for that contribution, Vanie).

17.5   RED £10.99
Domaine La Colombette Lledoner Pelut 2000   FRANCE
A mouthful of liquid chocolate with strawberry, pear and plums. Wonderful classy texture and richness. It has a classy texture and richness due to its extraordinary grape, the Lledoner Pelut of the Minervois.

17.5   RED £15.00
Villa Maria Reserve Merlot/Cabernet 1998   NEW ZEALAND
Superb maturity of fruit here. Cocoa, herbs, chocolate, tobacco, cassis – it has it all.

17.5   WHITE SPARKLING £19.99
Waitrose Brut Vintage Champagne 1996   FRANCE
A superb 65 %Pinot Noir, 35% Chardonnay blend of such toast elegance and bite, it makes a mockery of Krug. It is of the highest, silky, class.

17.5   WHITE £9.49

Bouchard Finlayson Crocodile's Lair   SOUTH AFRICA
Chardonnay 2001
Makes any white Burgundy for the same money,
green. The fruit here is smoky, dry, rich yet delicate,
dainty yet decisive – and superbly textured.

17.5   WHITE £5.99

Basedow Barossa Valley Sémillon 2001   AUSTRALIA
A great Aussie contribution to civilised tippling. The
oily citrus and sinuous pineapple fruity sensations
continue gloriously.

17.5   RED £12.99

Katnook Estate Cabernet Sauvignon 1999   AUSTRALIA
This is one of Australia's smoothest, most polished
Cabs, classic Coonawarra Cabernet. That is to say
minty, crisp and yet soft, energetic yet demure, rich
yet subtle. You travel in plushly upholstered comfort,
catching the whiff of mint and crushed blackberries.
Drink with a pea risotto – wonderful!!!
Also available at Oddbins and The Wine Society.

17   RED £24.00

Boekenhoutskloof Syrah 2000   SOUTH AFRICA
Superb toffee-edged fruit of cassis and brilliantly
tailored tannins. One of the new world's greatest
expressions of this group (see entry further back for
further remarks about the maker of this wine and the
winery).

17   FORTIFIED (half bottle) £6.49
Henriques & Henriques Monte Seco Madeira   PORTUGAL
One of civilisation's most cryptic conundrums.
Is it dry? Is it sweet? Is it. . . what? It is in fact,
cooked fruit which manages to be dry, elegant and
curiously consoling. It is utterly delicious and
wonderful to sit down with, a glass in one hand, a
book in the other, and a bowl of nuts to the side,
Together they combine to make one of life's greatest
pleasures.

17   WHITE SPARKLING £16.99
Le Mesnil Blanc de Blancs Grand Cru Brut NV   FRANCE
Champagne
A 100 % Chardonnay from a fine co-operative, whose
growers produce Grand Cru status grapes, from one
of the six Grand Cru villages in the Côtes de Blancs.
Much of their vin clair goes to the old-established
champagne houses for their tête de cuvée blends, to
give them staying power. The cuvée is based on 1998
vintage, with some 1997. The same wine, Waitrose
tells me, is the house champagne at La Gavroche –
which is London's greatest French restaurant – where
it goes for £40 a bottle.

17   WHITE £17.49
Cloudy Bay Te Koko 2000   NEW ZEALAND
A wacky expression of Sauvignon Blanc: grapefruit,
tobacco, apricots and dry spice. More wines should be
as individual, as challenging as this.

17

RED £4.99

Tautavel Côtes de Roussillon-Villages 2001   FRANCE
Amazing grilled chocolate fruit with nuts and hearty
tannins. Gripping, gorgeous, game (and even a little
gamey).

17

RED £6.99

Mont Gras Cabernet Sauvignon/Syrah Reserva   CHILE
2000
What generous berries here. They provide minutes of
languorous richness and tannin-touched tantalising
fruit.

17

RED £7.49

Mont Gras Limited Edition Cabernet Sauvignon/   CHILE
Merlot 2000
Simply gorgeous from the tip of the nose to the back
of the throat. Sweet nut chocolate and tannins in
tandem – and they perform beautifully.

17

RED £8.99

Norton Malbec Reserve 2000   ARGENTINA
Quite superb. Manages to be plump yet delicate, rich
yet subtle – lovely texture to the fruit, quite lovely.

17

RED £9.99

Norton Privada 2000   ARGENTINA
Richly endowed with roasted berries and firm, deep
tannins. Lashes the tongue with exciting fruit and
leaves behind nothing but sensual memories.
Also at Safeway.

17 RED £5.99

Tria Syrah 2002 SICILY, ITALY

Superb texture and high-class berried fruit. Delicious
roasted berries and urgent tannins. Utterly
remarkable wine for the money.

17 RED £14.99

Château Tour Simard Saint-Emilion Grand Cru FRANCE
1998
Superbly mature claret bustling and bursting with
burned berries and grilled tannins. An expensive treat.

17 WHITE £13.45

Henschke Louis Sémillon 2001 AUSTRALIA

Very, very classy fruit: melon, lemon, peach and dry paw-
paw. Superbly well textured and elegant. A real treat.

17 WHITE £6.99

Yalumba Y Series Viognier 2002 AUSTRALIA

Not as crunchy or concentrated as the previous vintage
but still a well-tailored specimen. Gorgeous apricot fruit-
cake of a wine leavened with a hint of fig and fine
citrussy acids, scrumptious citrus, mango and pineapple
with apricot on the finish. Classy and complete.
Also at Sainsbury's and Tesco.

17 WHITE £5.49

Lugana Villa Flora 2002 ITALY

Wonderful vintage to this perennial work of
craftsmanship from Zenato. A lovely dry wine of
staggering layers of pear, pineapple, lychee and citrus.
Stunningly well textured.

WHITE £7.99

Warwick Estate Chardonnay 2001   SOUTH AFRICA

This is one of the Cape's most fluent solutions to the
Chardonnay dilemma (Chardonnay grape equals
neutral fruit and therefore this requires intense winemaker commitment, yet how to make the wine exciting
without being heavy-handed or brutal?). It is a little old-
style in feel, with its subtle vegetality, and it has a
Burgundy touch to it (insulting until I add that this is
not modern white Burgundy I refer to here but the
magical potions of the wines of the 50s and 60s –
grown before the area became both a cultural and
agricultural desert with the exception of exquisite oases
like Comte de Lafon). The wine, however, does have a
modern citrus undertone, albeit subtle, and this, with
the satiny texture, makes for an elegant wine which is
finely dry with a lightly grilled sesame-seed edge. It will
improve if sympathetically cellared for 18 months to 3
years, though after this only old soaks in club chairs
will approve of it as they rant against modern youth.

WHITE £5.69

Château Saint-Jean-des-Graves 2001   FRANCE

Superb class here: textured, sensual, perfumed, fruity
yet dry and delicate. A lovely Bordeaux blanc of great
finesse.

WHITE £7.99

Château Carsin Cuvée Prestige 2001   FRANCE

Superb marriage of wood, fruit and acids. World-class
texture and elemental tension.

17   WHITE £9.95

Clos d'Yvigne Cuvée Saint Nicholas, Bergerac   FRANCE
2000

Anyone who has ever dreamed of owning a patch
of vines in France and making wine should read
Patricia Atkinson's book *The Ripening Sun* (Century,
£12.99). The title seems as banal as a cornflakes
slogan but it refers to the author's own maturing as
much as her grapes'. Ms Atkinson is an author of
stout and manifold resources and she will doubtless
inspire the dreamers because, against seemingly
impossible odds (she didn't speak French, lousy
marriage, knew nothing about oenology), she has
conjured wines of great finesse from her hectares,
Clos d'Yvigne in the Côtes de Bergerac. Three of the
fruits of her devoted labours are now on sale in the
UK. Cuvée Nicholas Bergerac is a blend of
Sauvignon, Sémillon and Muscadelle grapes,
fermented in French oak barrels and unfiltered. It
has a gently oily texture, sinuous and sensual, and it
offers crushed under-ripe Charentais melon,
grapefruit, thyme, and a touch of lemon and orange
peel on the finish. It is a seriously scrumptious white
wine of considerable class and demeanour. *The
Ripening Sun* is a more passionate tale than Anna
Karenina's and all the more moving for being non-
fiction and all the more incredible for never using the
words romance, love or sex. This inspiring and
delicate story (as delicate as the Atkinson wines) is
one of the most attractively written and
unpretentious stories of *la vrai vie rustique française*

and surely the most striking since Peter Mayle's.
Indeed, *mangez votre coeur dehors, Pete mon vieux,
vous avez rencontrez votre allumette.*
Also at Booths.

17

WHITE £7.99

Jordan Estate Chardonnay 2002   SOUTH AFRICA

The petite Jordans (Kathy and Gary) exude
enthusiasm and integrity (somewhat akin to their
wines) and they learned their craft, as a married
couple, at Davis University in California – a grove of
academe renowned for turning out many state-of-the-
art wine makers. It was Gary's dad who bought the
vineyard originally, as a place to build a house and get
away from the family shoe business (the Jordan great-
grandfather coming from Groby, now a suburb of
Leicester, the footwear manufactory of the UK). This
Chardonnay shows creamily, dreamily delicious fruit
which dries out to reveal toffee, pineapple, melon and
a touch of grilled nut.
Also at Booths.

17

WHITE £5.99

Gracia Chardonnay Reserva Ausente 2001   CHILE

Stunning oily pineapple and lime which slowly,
deliciously slowly, goes creamy and smoky in the throat.

17

RED £11.99

Montes Alpha Syrah, Colchagua 2000/2001   CHILE

Both vintages of this wine are, unusually, rated
similarly though there are differences too subtle to
remark on at this point in time (it requires opening

for a fewer hours for the differences to become
apparent – the '01 has fresher and plummier fruit).
The wine is gently spicy with classy damson fruit, and
shows the house style of tannicity with finesse.
The '00, though, has several oddities (freshness,
eagerness, lack of pretension) but one overriding
virtue. It is gorgeous! All over! I would rather this
Syrah than many of the Aussies' much-vaunted
legends (like Grange or Hill of Grace), for it is not
only massively cheaper but massively sexier.
Also available at Morrisons, Sainsbury's (not the
2001) and Majestic.

17 RED £6.99

Norton Barrel Select Malbec 2000 ARGENTINA
Wonderful relaxed, roasted berries with smoky tannins,
hint of cigar, touch of cocoa. Terrific class and style.
Also at Safeway and Sainsbury's.

16.5 RED £4.99

Concha y Toro Casillero del Diablo Cabernet CHILE
Sauvignon 2002
One of the world's most elegant Cabs under a fiver.
Takes you from nose to throat in superior upholstered
comfort. It's the chewiness of the tannins I love –
they will not be shifted and are almost protean as they
shift and shape and linger. Superb edge to the chewy
tannins gives the wine breadth and depth. Terrific
tension between the tannins and the berries, which
lingers lushly, yet responsibly.
Also at Sainsbury's and Thresher.

16.5

RED £5.99

SPAIN

Mas Collet Celler de Capcanes 2000
Unctuously oily and yet seriously prim, the chocolate-tinged roasted berries course sveltely over the tastebuds in a patchwork of flavours.
Also at Booths.

16.5

RED £4.99

ITALY

Da Luca Primitivo Merlot 2002
Fills every nook and cranny of the senses with rich, chocolate fruit with burned nuts and herbs.

16.5

RED £5.99

GREECE

Tsantali Cabernet Sauvignon 2000
Organic Cabernet of huge tannic complexity and richness. Roasted berries with earth, herbs and a magnificent texture.

16.5

RED £3.99

CHILE

San Andres Carmenere/Cabernet Sauvignon 2002
Superb energy and élan here. The earthy berries go sweet and delicious, the tannins turn savoury and pliant.

16.5

RED £6.99

AUSTRALIA

Rutherglen Estates Durif 2002
Lovely screwcapped red of daring tannins and delicious plummy fruit. The colour for a start blinds the eye so rich is it and it heralds fruit as svelte as satin yet ruffled with voluptuous tannins. This vibrant red is my

idea of liquid which turns the merest balti into a treat, and it is perfect for BYOB restaurants because it has a screwcap and so cannot be tainted by any cork.

16.5   £7.99

Domaine de Courtilles, Corbières 2000   FRANCE
You munch your way through this wine, rather than glugging: wonderful grip and dash to the savoury berries.

16.5   RED £3.99

La Cité Cabernet Sauvignon, Vin de Pays   FRANCE
d'Oc 2001
Superb depth to the tannins, terrific pace to the tightly pressed berries.

Richard Riddiford, the managing director of Palliser Estate wines in New Zealand, told me this. 'I was in Taiwan a short time ago showing retailers my wines. A businessman took me out to dinner. He asks me, "Do you like Chateau Pétrus?" I say, "Well, yes, wouldn't anyone?" He says OK and orders a bottle of the 1982 vintage and a bottle of Coca-Cola. Don't ask me how many thousands of Kiwi dollars the Pétrus must have cost. He pours me a glass. It's wonderful. Into his glass of the Pétrus he pours some of the Coke. I stare in disbelief. I ask, "What's with the Coke?" He says, "I don't like the taste of the wine." And he turns the bottle round so the label can be seen by diners at other tables.'

16.5

RED £7.99

Les Vieilles Vignes de Château Maris 2001 FRANCE
Develops deliciously, insidiously slowly on the palate
to spring surprise after surprise – the throat is
stunned.

16.5

RED £8.95

Clos d'Yvigne Rouge et Noir, Bergerac 2000 FRANCE
The blend here is Merlot and Cabernet, unfiltered, and
the liquid is deep red with royal purple edges. The
aroma is of crushed berries with a touch of earth, some
herb (rosemary?) and a very subtle undertone of black
olive. The fruit, as it floods the mouth, is generous with
tannins which allow for a decidedly polished finish to
coagulate in the throat. It is not a showy red, rather
genteel really, Bordeaux in feel (with that ineffable
sense of luxury blessed examples of such wines exude),
and there is a nonchalant air as it quits the throat and
one is left with those tannins as they expire . . . and one
feels deliciously satisfied yet ready for more. Of course,
and this must be admitted by the taster, the effect of the
wine was enhanced by his reading, as he drank his way
through the bottle, the book written by its maker,
Patricia Atkinson. For more details about Ms Atkinson
and her vines, see entry further back.

16.5

RED £8.69

Château La Fleur Chambeau Lussac-Saint- FRANCE
Emilion 2001
Unusually chewy toothsome Saint-Em – hints of
chocolate and rose petals. Very crunchy fruit.

16.5   RED £6.99

Peter Lehmann Clancy's Shiraz/Cabernet   AUSTRALIA
Sauvignon/Merlot/Cabernet Franc 2001
Terrific buzz to this wine. The blend is seamless,
exciting, deep and full yet dry and firm, and the finish
is pure hedonism.

16.5   RED SPARKLING £26.00

Leasingham Classic Clare Sparkling Shiraz   AUSTRALIA
1994
About as fine as sparkling Shiraz gets. Superbly
textured, tannicity world class, and with delicious
berried-plum fruit, toasty and complex.

16.5   WHITE £24.99

Chablis Grand Cru Bougros, Domaine William   FRANCE
Fèvre 2000
Simply superb texture and dryness. Minimalist
elegance of superior style.

16.5   FORTIFIED £5.95

Waitrose Solera Jerezana Rich Cream Sherry   SPAIN
The colour of engine oil and as clotted and viscous,
this gorgeous wine seduces with toasted berries and
molasses. But it is far from over-sweet.

16.5   FORTIFIED £5.95

Waitrose Solera Jerezana Dry Amontillado Sherry   SPAIN
The whiff of oxidised treacle is a big come-on. And it
doesn't let the palate down either with its thickly
textured, dry-treacle fruit of originality and dry wit.

16.5 ROSÉ £3.29

River Route Merlot ROMANIA (BOTTLED IN GERMANY)
Rosé 2002
Impressively chewy and strawberry-edged, it
offers real rosé richness yet subtlety, dryness and
elegance.

16.5 WHITE SPARKLING £4.99

Waitrose Cava Brut NV SPAIN
Simply gorgeous blend of 40% Macabeo, 20%
Parellada and 40% Xarel-lo grapes with which
no champagne can compete. Dry, elegant,
complete.

16.5 WHITE £3.99

Waitrose Touraine Sauvignon Blanc 2002 FRANCE
Gorgeous gooseberry, grapefruit and lime freshness.
A wonderfully tangy specimen.

16.5 WHITE £6.99

Villa Maria Private Bin Pinot Gris, NEW ZEALAND
Marlborough 2002
Screwcapped spice and mellow honeydew melon.
Lovely wine to drink with oriental food and it'll cellar
for a decade.

16.5 WHITE £7.99

Montana Reserve Gewürztraminer 2002 NEW ZEALAND
Very cultured, plum-in-the-mouth elocution here. It
speaks with polish and wry soft vowels.

16.5   WHITE £8.99

Steenberg Sauvignon Blanc 2002   SOUTH AFRICA
Eat your heart out, Sancerre! This gorgeus, tannic,
rich yet demure, complex wine throbs with crisp fruit
and tangy acids. High-class stuff indeed.

16.5   WHITE £7.99

Steenberg Sémillon 2002   SOUTH AFRICA
Has a lovely turn of creamy pace as it caresses the
tastebuds before nailing the throat with complex
vegetality.

16.5   WHITE £2.99

Trinacria Bianco 2002   SICILY, ITALY
Gorgeous smoky, slightly charred gooseberries and
pear with fine citrus. A soft yet dry wine of great class
(for the money a miracle).

16.5   WHITE £4.99

Soave Classico, Vigneto Colombara 2002   ITALY
Brilliant gooseberry finish to grapefruit and citrus fruit.

16.5   WHITE £4.99

La Baume Viognier, Vin de Pays d'Oc 2002   FRANCE
Screwcapped apricots and citrus, beautifully modulated
and modest – yet thrillingly sensual and fruity.

16.5   WHITE £6.99

Saint-Véran Les Plantes Cave de Prisse 2002   FRANCE
Stunningly tangy and complete. Lovely citrus and
under-ripe melon fruit.

16.5

WHITE £6.49

Riesling Bassermann-Jordan, Pfalz 2001 GERMANY
Delicious dry honey and citrus with gentle minerals.
Will rate even higher if laid down for 2–6 years.

16.5

WHITE £5.49

Torres Viña Esmeralda 2002 SPAIN
Screwcapped freshness sealed in so the spicy pear and
lemon will develop well for several years in the bottle.
The Gewürztraminer and Muscat blend of grapes
allows spiciness which is fresh, aromatic and dry with
citrus, raspberry and floral hints. There is a touch of
honey banana on the finish. Congratulations, Miguel
(Torres), for putting a screwcap on it.
Also at Tesco and Thresher.

16.5

WHITE £4.99

Concha y Toro Casillero del Diablo CHILE
Chardonnay 2002
Has a lovely undertone of creamy mango and
balanced pineapple.
Also at Majestic.

16

RED £8.99

Bonterra Vineyards Zinfandel 2000 CALIFORNIA
Delightfully chewy, gently grilled berries with touches
of cinnamon. Has a joyously rich and devil-may-care
fruitiness which, thrown in the face of decades of
European po-facedness from old-world wines which
might try to compete (Rhône, Rioja, Chianti), makes an
eloquent case for this wine's inclusion in any

candidate's list for must-drink-wines with first-class, elegant Indian, Pakistani and Bangladeshi food without clumsy spicing. Not a cheap wine but then it isn't a cheep wine: it doesn't warble or trill, it richly roars. Also available at Majestic, Oddbins, Safeway and Sainsbury's.

16

RED £6.99

Château de Targe Saumur-Champigny 2000   FRANCE
Light raspberry and herby strawberry fruit. Utterly delicious chilled with fish.

16

RED £5.69

Château Haut d'Allard, Côtes de Bourg 2001   FRANCE
A most accommodatingly cheery claret – dry plums, berries and a hint of bracken.

16

RED £7.99

Château Segonzac, Premières Côtes de Blaye 2001   FRANCE
The delicious bit comes when the tannins melt and the toasted raspberries ring out.

16

RED £8.49

Seigneurs d'Aiguilhe, Côtes de Castillon 2000   FRANCE
Delightfully complete wine with roasted berries and rich, dry tannins. Classy and concentrated.

16

RED £6.49

La Cuvée Mythique, Vin de Pays d'Oc 2001   FRANCE
Smooth yet characterful, fruity yet subtle, rich yet has finesse with flavour. Delicious warmth here with firm berries and chocolate-edged tannins.
Also at Morrison's and Safeway.

16

RED £5.99

FRANCE

Ermitage du Pic Saint-Loup, Coteaux du Languedoc 2001
Hint of tobacco to prime berries with good, firm tannins.

16

RED £6.99

FRANCE

Château Cazal-Viel, Cuvée des Fées, Saint Chinian 2000
Very smooth strawberries and raspberries. The tannins cruise in.

16

RED £5.99

FRANCE

Chapoutier Organic Côtes du Rhône 2001
The smoothest of the smooth (style of Rhône red). But there are some hints of rustic heritage (be grateful).

16

RED £6.99

PORTUGAL

Trincadeira J P Ramos 2001
Delicious tobacco-scented berries (strawberries and raspberries) with roasted plums and tannins.

16

RED £4.99

SPAIN

Monasterio de Santa Ana Monastrell 2002
Strikingly biscuity tannins, hint of strawberry jam, and an excellent firm finish.

16

RED (3 litre box) £14.99

SPAIN

Eden Collection Tempranillo NV
Real quality tannins here and well-tailored, rich berries. I've not tasted a better red in a box.

Why are so many people so sniffy about wine boxes?
Boxes cannot suffer from cork taint, they offer 3 litres
of wine in a drinkable state for a month or more once
the tap's been turned for the first time, and the quality
of the liquid inside the bag in the box is, nowadays,
better than it has ever been. Those who darkly mutter
than such a method of containing wine is horribly
modern and brash, and that wine should come in
heavy glass bottles and be sealed with that wretched
stuff from cork oaks, seem to forget that in fact the
bag-in-box wine is a superb, technologically-more-
perfect development of the ancient animal wine-skin
with its dodgy wooden peg stopper. The wine box is,
therefore, more traditional than any bottle.

16   RED £6.99
                                          SPAIN
Finca Sobreno Crianza 1999
Marvellously mature and gripping fruit. A complex
lingering red of character and concentration.

16   RED £7.99
                                          SPAIN
Rivola Abadia Retuerta, Castilla y Leon 2000
Compacted strawberries and plums with tannins
which dry out to reveal a cocoa undertone.

16   RED £5.99
Excelsior Estate Paddock Shiraz 2002   SOUTH AFRICA
Rich and very soft, yet has lovely incisive tannins
which congeal in the throat to reveal chocolate and
cream with grilled cobnuts.

16

RED £6.99

Diemersfontein Shiraz 2002   SOUTH AFRICA

Let it breathe, wholly decanted, 3–4 hours beforehand
to fully appreciate the chutzpah of the roasted berries.
I met David Sonnenberg of Diemersfontein one
evening in the Cape and the abiding memory of the
evening, forgetting the roaring braai (so necessary on
such a chilly night), was the various friendly
arguments which raged, the openness of Mr
Sonnenberg and other wine makers who were there
and the spirit with which they questioned me on my
likes and dislikes. The wines I tasted were all well
made, no obvious wine-making boobs, but I felt if an
overall criticism can be levelled (from which I would
wholly exempt the generally marvellous
Diemersfontein line-up), it was the lack of balancing
acids to compensate for the generous fruit. All the
wines showed an impressive warmth of fruit,
testimony to the extraordinarily cosy growing
conditions in the Cape, but balance is everything in a
wine – sugar, acid, tannin etc. – and the overall
elegance of a wine, and its poise on the tastebuds, is
how, surely, we all judge a wine whether we articulate
it like this or not. A person who has never run a race
in his or her life can appreciate an athlete who runs
beautifully; and it is the same with wine. Poise,
balance, sheer beauty of texture – *'her limbs moved like*
polished pistons on the track carrying her rapidly and
silkily from start to finish ahead of everyone else and
leaving an indelible impression of power and grace in the
mind for evermore' – is how a great wine performs.

Many people consider it snobbish to argue that the shape of a wine glass drastically alters the way the liquid inside performs on the nose and palate. Now, thanks to the University of Tennessee, we have been furnished with scientific proof. By pouring Merlot into different-shaped glasses - a champagne flute, a large-bowled Bordeaux glass, and a martini glass (those reverse-Madonna-bra shaped ones which usually contain a cocktail stick and an olive) – researchers demonstrated that a crucial acid present in wine, a phenolic compound called gallic acid, decreased and softened better in the Bordeaux glass and it was also this glass which had higher concentrations of important esters called catechin gallates. Thus the perfume of the wine in the last-named glass was the more pronounced.

It is easy to reach such findings yourself. You hardly need boffins. At a splendid book signing and wine tasting at Ottakar's bookshop in Norwich, I was able to prove to the assembled host that the wine in my glass was superior to the wine in theirs even though it was the same liquid. The reason? Ottakar's had undemocratically (but exquisitely thoughtfully) supplied me with a large glass with a bowled middle and a tapering top and everyone else with those pathetic 1960s gin-and-tonic-style glasses called Paris goblets. When everyone smelled the Midi Syrah/Grenache blend in my glass it was evident that the wine was twice if not three times sexier as a result of its enhanced aroma and greater depth of flavour.

16

Spice Route Pinotage 2000

You can sling this wine into action with Indian, Pakistani and Bangladeshi cuisine, or employ it with more classic dinner-party fare like roast lamb with garlic. I drank it, along with several other wines, at an alfresco lunch with its maker, Charl du Plessis and estate owner Charles Back, some little while past beside the converted tobacco shed which is the Spice Route winery. There is a large tree there, dangerously fecund (very hard fruit kept falling), and under this Diane Back, Charles's wife, had miraculously appeared and was setting out a feast on a wobbly table. However, before I could devour anything Mr du Plessis took me for a tour of the winery. Spice Route reds have become one of the most impressive range of Cape wines on sale in the UK and when Mr du Plessis showed me how carefully the basket press squeezes the grapes and how meticulously the band of women on the sorting table select the healthy grapes and weed out anything suspect, it was easy to understand why.

'I pay the women 350 rand a week during the harvest season to sort grapes,' explains Charles. 'It's about what a male truck-driver gets. Some of the co-ops here should employ people like that. We have this huge untapped labour force. Who needs machinery when we have so many people wanting to work?'

Charles would like to make a job for everyone who hasn't got one. In South Africa as a whole that's millions of people. He scorns those who use mechanical harvesters when he believes people should be employed, because they need work.

Lunch is a gracious, though at times windy, affair (I speak of the prevailing breeze), and several of the Back estate cheeses are on display for me to try as well as superb stuffed bread, olives, figs and various cold meats. At times, it's hard work doing my job.
Also at Booths.

16

RED £6.99

Ravenswood Vintners Blend Zinfandel   CALIFORNIA, USA
2000
Juicy but judicious. Finely tempered tannins with generous berries.

16

RED £7.99

Ravenswood Lodi Zinfandel 2000   CALIFORNIA, USA
Terrific spicy berries and pert tannins.
Also at Sainsbury's.

16

RED £4.99

L A Cetto Petite Syrah 2000   MEXICO
Baked apple and apricot intrude amongst the rich berries. This really is a bargain red from an unsung wine region. However, if it makes you feel better you can console yourself with knowing it is grown in Baja California (part of Mey-hee-co).

16

RED £6.99

Cono Sur Merlot Reserve 2001   CHILE
Very firm and jammy but does not lose control of itself. Enthusiasm with finesse is the order of the day here.

16   RED £5.99

Flichman Shiraz Reserva 2001   ARGENTINA

Exotic, ripe, big, rich, devious and worth every farthing.

16   RED £4.99

Banrock Station Petit Verdot 2002   AUSTRALIA

Very jammy but, miraculously, the tannins keep it
seriously drinkable and firm on the finish.

16   RED £7.99

Peter Lehmann Shiraz 2001   AUSTRALIA

A superb savoury soup of roasted blackberries and
plums.

16   RED £12.99

Château Reynella Basket Pressed Shiraz 2000   AUSTRALIA

How to make a sweet red dry. How to make grown
grapes cry. Okay, so thirteen quid makes you think.
But so does the liquid inside the bottle.

16   WHITE £9.99

Craggy Range Old Renwick Sauvignon   NEW ZEALAND
Blanc 2002

Screwcapped, svelte, tangy, very concentrated
gooseberry classiness.

16   WHITE SPARKLING £4.99

Chapel Hill Chardonnay/Pinot Noir NV   HUNGARY

More crisp and concentrated, with a genuine posh
Pinot (wild raspberry) undertone, than many a
champagne at five times the price.

16   WHITE SPARKLING £5.49
Prosecco La Marcha NV   ITALY
Beautifully dry and subtle. Has superb strawberry
shading and finesse. This is a lovely tipple and as an
aperitif before a posh dinner party it works wonders
(for its gently raffish, though civilised, air strikes
exactly the right note).

16   WHITE SPARKLING £11.99
Waitrose Blanc de Noirs NV Champagne   FRANCE
One of the best supermarket blanc de noirs. Has
restrained richness (dry raspberries) and a lovely
lingering elegance.

16   WHITE SPARKLING (magnum) £29.99
Waitrose Brut NV Champagne   FRANCE
A magnum (two bottles) for a special occasion and
very fine stuff it is. Has the classic dry finish yet offers
wild raspberry and citrus.

16   WHITE SPARKLING £15.99
Waitrose Blanc de Blancs NV Champagne   FRANCE
Lovely lemony fruit with a touch of white chocolate
(dry and very, very subtle).

16   WHITE SPARKLING £18.99
Fleury Père et Fils Brut NV Champagne (Organic)   FRANCE
A 90% Pinot Noir, 10% Chardonnay, mostly from
Monsieur Fleury's own vineyards in the Côtes des
Bars, with a little from neighbours, whom he has
persuaded to go organic. He follows bio-dynamic

principles, and the wine is unfiltered. Based on the
1997 (35%) and 1998 (65%) vintages, and disgorged
in March 2000, this is a champagne of exceptional
balance of demure fruit, dry yet concentrated. It would
benefit from 2–3 years more cellaring even.

16　　　　　　　　　　　　　　RED SPARKLING　£7.99
Banrock Station Sparkling Shiraz NV　　AUSTRALIA
Still a great wine – a red bubbly no less – to have with the
Christmas bird.
Also at Morrison's, Sainsbury's and Somerfield.

16　　　　　　　　　　　　　　　　FORTIFIED　£4.89
Waitrose Fino Sherry　　　　　　　　　SPAIN
Terrific value for money for the aficionado of saline,
bone-dry fino.

16　　　　　　　　　　　　　　　　FORTIFIED　£5.95
Waitrose Solera Jerezana Oloroso Sherry　　SPAIN
A wonderful dry-yet-rich aperitif. A single glass does
what other wines take a bottle to do.

16　　　　　　　　　　　　　　　　　ROSÉ　£3.29
Cuvée Fleur Rosé, Vin de Pays de l'Hérault 2002　　FRANCE
An exceedingly cheerful, cherry-edged rosé of great
charm. Has finesse and class and truly makes a
mockery of rosés priced twice and three times as much.

16　　　　　　　　　　　　　　　　　ROSÉ　£6.99
Château de Caraguilhes Rosé, Corbières 2003　　FRANCE
A most elegant and lingering rosé, handsomely
textured and rich.

16
              RED £25.00

Turriga Argiolas 1998   SARDINIA, ITALY
Very cooked fruit of plums, cherries and herbs which
turns lingering and chocolatey on the very dry tannic
finish.

16
              RED £16.00

Suckfizzle Cabernet Sauvignon 2000   AUSTRALIA
Dry, herby, vegetal, individual, delicious.

16
              RED £20.00

Frog's Leap Zinfandel 1999   CALIFORNIA, USA
An organic red of elegance and finely textured blackberry fruit. The tannins tease and tug at the same time.

16
              WHITE £27.99

Chablis Grand Cru Valmur, Domaine William   FRANCE
Fèvre 2000
Classic! Dry, vegetal, finely tailored and pressed as
neatly as you could wish.

16
              WHITE £4.99

Mâcon-Villages Chardonnay, Cave de Prisse 2002   FRANCE
First-class minor white Burgundy. What a year 2002
was for Chardonnay in northern France!

16
              WHITE £26.00

Chassagne-Montrachet   FRANCE
1er Cru Morgeot Clos Pitois 2000
What a treat! This has the class to deliver vegetal
creamy tannins (yes!) attached to textured melon,
lemon and gooseberry. Classic white Burgundy.

16

WHITE £4.99

FRANCE

Muscat Sec Domaine Lafage, Vin de Pays des Côtes Catalanes 2002

Develops slowly on the tongue to reveal spice, dry pear and citrus. A gorgeous aperitif wine.

16

WHITE £3.99

HUNGARY

Riverview Sauvignon Blanc 2002

Delicious, very dry, marvellously chewy gooseberries and hints of spice and rhubarb.
Also at Safeway.

16

WHITE £5.99

ITALY

Tria Grillo 2002

What a lovely change from Chardonnay: pear and lemon peel coated in dry peach.

16

WHITE £5.99

SOUTH AFRICA

Thabani Sauvignon Blanc 2002

Chewy and ripe yet classy and elegant. Unusual solution to the Sauvignon riddle in that the gooseberry is thick and leavened by lime zest.

16

WHITE £4.49

SOUTH AFRICA

Danie de Wet Unoaked Chardonnay 2002

Wonderful style of white, where Chablis meets the lower Hunter Valley to produce an untrammelled Chardonnay of wit and great presence on the tongue.

16

WHITE £14.99

Kumala Journey's End Chardonnay 2002   SOUTH AFRICA
Rich, toffee-edged fruit of impudence and oleaginous
charm.

16

WHITE £14.99

Forrester Meinert Chenin Blanc 2001   SOUTH AFRICA
Like a dry dessert wine, this wine, a Beerenauslese
trocken forsooth, so impertinently rich and fruity is it.
You ask what is a Beerenauslese trocken? The answer
is a German wine picked very late with hugely sweet
berries but which is vinified dry.

16

WHITE £7.49

Wente Chardonnay 2001   CALIFORNIA, USA
Most unusually sticky and rich – peach, pineapple,
citrus and mango – and brilliant with Chinese duck
and plum sauce.

16

RED £2.99

Cuvée Chasseur, Vin de Pays de l'Hérault 2002   FRANCE
One of the l'Hérault's most absurdly under-priced red
wines. Classy, dry and very well balanced. Excellent
from nose to throat.

16

WHITE £5.99

Terrazas Alto Chardonnay 2002   ARGENTINA
Decidedly elegant yet fruity performance. Really turns
it on in the throat.

16

WHITE £7.99

One Tree Unoaked Chardonnay 2002 AUSTRALIA

Screwcapped richness of such tenacity it has to be
thrown in the ring against rich, Thai food.

16

WHITE £2.99

Broken Bridge Chardonnay/ AUSTRALIA (UK BOTTLED)
Colombard 2002

Superb value for money. Has the texture of a wine
costing three times the price. The fruit is sticky and
warm, though not uncomfortably humid.

16

WHITE £4.99

Peter Lehmann Chenin Blanc 2002 AUSTRALIA

Screwcapped freshness yet softness. Lovely textured
ripeness and class.

16

WHITE £4.99

First Step Chardonnay 2002 AUSTRALIA

Dry yet very rich and broad. Brilliant with spicy food.

16

WHITE £5.49

Jacob's Creek Dry Riesling 2002 AUSTRALIA

Screwcapped and eminently cellar worthy. In 5 years'
time, at 18 points, it'll shock people.

16

WHITE £6.99

Leasingham Bin 7 Clare Valley Riesling 2002 AUSTRALIA

Be alerted to the tremendous cellaring potential of
this wonderful wine, because its screwcap will
preserve its freshness for many years. Give it 3–6
years to really show what it can do, though it is tasty

enough now, but in 5 years it'll rate 18 and in 10 years maybe 20. . . . (well, it's possible).

---

16   WHITE   £8.99

Nepenthe Lenswood Riesling, Adelaide Hills 2002 AUSTRALIA
Another brilliant screwcapped Aussie Riesling capable of developing in bottle for years.
The 2001 is available at Oddbins.

---

16   WHITE   £7.99

Nepenthe Lenswood Sauvignon Blanc, Adelaide AUSTRALIA
Hills 2002
I do like Nepenthe whites (not so crazy about the reds). This crisp, tangy specimen is screwcapped and will last for several years.
The 2001 is available at Oddbins.

---

16   WHITE   £9.99

Katnook Estate Coonawarra Sauvignon Blanc AUSTRALIA
2002
Chewy, very dry, hugely elegant and deliciously understated.

---

16   WHITE   £8.99

Penfold's Chardonnay, Clare Valley 2002 AUSTRALIA
Dry, peach/pineapple and melon. Very elegant and incisive.

I wish all the wines in this book were screwcapped, so that every bottle tasted the same as the one I rated. With cork, however, there is no guarantee of this. Only screwcaps can guarantee uniformity and this is why I am 100% in favour of them.

16   WHITE £9.99

Gewürztraminer Classique Josmeyer 2001   FRANCE
Rose petals, lychee, dry mango and orange peel –
exciting enough for anyone, this beautiful Alsatian.

16   WHITE £5.79

Ruppertsberger Nussbien Riesling, Pfalz 2001   GERMANY
The new wave of German wines arrives! Textured,
elegant, comprehensively delicious and
comprehensible.

16   WHITE £9.99

Hallgartener Jungfer Riesling Auslese,   GERMANY
Hans Lang 1999
Lovely grapefruit to the honey and it will get better
over the next 3–10 years.

16   WHITE DESSERT (50cl bottle) £6.99

Château Les Sablines, Monbazillac 1998   FRANCE
Liquidised toffee-apple and mango. Wonderful ice-
cream wine.

16   WHITE £5.29

Cheverny Le Vieux Clos Delaille 2002   FRANCE
Fresh and cutting as a spring early morning. Great
fish wine.

16   WHITE £9.49

Sancerre Domaine Naudet 2002   FRANCE
Deliciously chewy Sancerre. Almost like the old days!
Tangy and terrific and tantalisingly gooseberryish.

16

WHITE £9.95

Pouilly-Fumé Châtelain 2002   FRANCE

Superb old-style, tannic gooseberry. Real excitement
here.

16

WHITE £3.69

Le Pujalet, Vin de Pays du Gers 2002   FRANCE

Lovely pear and apricot fruit, quite deliciously
harmonised.

16

WHITE £3.99

Domaine de Planterieu, Vin de Pays des Côtes   FRANCE
de Gascogne 2002

Finely wrought pineapple and citrus.

16

WHITE £6.99

Petit Chablis La Chablisienne 2002   FRANCE

A screwcapped masterpiece of Chardonnay precision.
Lovely dry pear/melon fruit with a stunning crisp
finish.

16

WHITE £7.99

Chablis La Chablisienne 2002   FRANCE

Lovely chewy fruit which continues to be crisp on the
outside.

16

WHITE £4.99

Moulin des Cailloux Sauvignon Blanc, Côtes de   FRANCE
Duras 2002

Screwcapped gooseberry, in fine chewy fettle.

16

WHITE £6.69

Château Thieuley 2002   FRANCE

Remarkably fruity yet dry. Very elegant and complex.

16

RED £5.99

Finca Flichman Reserve Shiraz 2001   ARGENTINA

Lipsmackin' berries, good firm tannins (well
integrated), and finish with a gentle roasted edge. It
exudes class and precision but does not lack character.
It did strike me as an exotic Rhône in style and
certainly, at that price, is richly competitive with the
Aussie specimens of the Shiraz grape.

16

WHITE £7.49

Wente Livermore Chardonnay 2001   CALIFORNIA, USA

Economical with the truth (the liquid contains 3%
Pinot Blanc), it is not economical with its rich
pear/peach fruitiness. It is an unusually combative
Chardonnay blend, with few striking acids, but offers
tremendous gusto with oriental food and it has been
rated on this basis. Thai fishcakes, for example, or
tandoori prawns would bring out the best in the wine.
Wente is a huge producer, owning some 3000 acres of
vines in the Livermore Valley, San Francisco Bay and
Monterey, and it started with 47 acres when Herr
Wente came over from Germany to plant vines.
Forever the State of opportunity, California. (And the
fourth generation of Wentes are still enjoying it
amongst the vines.)

THE WINE SOCIETY

Members' Shop and HQ:
Gunnels Wood Road,
Stevenage, Hertfordshire SG1 2BG

Tel enquiries: (01438) 741177

E-mail: memberservice@thewinesociety.com.
Website: www.thewinesociety.com

Prices quoted are per bottle and per case. Cases can be mixed and orders over £75 are delivered free.

The first surprise on entering The Wine Society's offices at 10.30am in Stevenage is that five women, sitting in an ante-room, are playing cards. Further incongruities (to enhance the gender bias) strike the observer as he notices no money, no cigarette smoke, no drink, and no attempt by any player to keep her cards close to her chest. Yet how can this be? Why is this absurd shuffle taking place? This is a venerable society, a mail-order wine club which has been at it since 1874, and customers are not customers but shareholders and have to pay £40 to be elected upon proposal by an existing member (easily arranged). There are, it seems, 200,000 of these, though only 90,000 are active, and with every obituary in *The Times* another member pops his clogs (and his single share passes to his heirs).

As I leave the card game and pass along the corridor
to the tasting room the Society's Mr Pierre Mansour,
who has picked me up from the station, explains: 'It is
a French lesson. The woman dealing is our French
teacher.' Ah, of course. At The Wine Society, French
counts for a lot. The list is heavily biased in favour of
that wine nation though other countries, as we shall
discover, appear. I tasted 60 wines from around the
world on my visit, and plan to taste more. And if you
protest that you have no interest in joining a snotty
men's club I agree with you, but The Wine Society is
no such thing. The Society's joining fee is not a mail-
order bribe but confers genuine shareholder status
and the profits, such as they are (for it lacks avaricious
ownership or shareholders in it for fat divis), are
ploughed back and help maintain very competitive
prices.

20

FORTIFIED £8.95 ▪ £106.00

The Society's Exhibition Viejo Oloroso Dulce Sherry

SPAIN

This is what angels use as an underarm deodorant. The smell of this wine is alone worth the entrance money. The fruit is composed of toasted nuts and raspberry with honeyed, spicy peach and the finish is of burned tarte tatin. This is a miracle of a wine of integrity, character and wondrous lushness (and absurdly good value for money). Its sweetness develops with such complex stealth that you quite forget this is 20% alcohol.

The wine was created in 1999 to celebrate the Society's 125th anniversary. It is produced by Sanchez Romate, a family company some 93 years older than The Society with a very traditional outlook (which means meticulous attention to the peculiarities of sherry). This oloroso dulce is blended from wines of up to 15 years old, all from 100% Palomino vines. The Palomino grape is, upon immediate vinification (or indeed tasting on the vine), the world's least prepossessing. However, the magic of Jerez, with its unique airborne yeasts and blending heritage, turns a mean acidic grape into an elixir. The final trick in its maufacture was the addition of so-called 'vino de color'. This ancient process, written up by Pliny and Virgil, involves turning syrup into a wine to provide the final blend not just with colour but with the ability to age for decades.

18

WHITE £8.95 ∎ £106.00

Kaseler Nies'chen Riesling Spätlese, Reichgraf GERMANY
van Kesselstatt 1999
This is what world-class German Riesling is all about in
disciplined hedonism – sensuality by numbers. You
have to admire it: disciplined dry honey mingling with
peach, apricot, tangy raspberry and fine acids holding it
together. Will age for 10–15 years and reach 20 points.

18

WHITE £17

Gewürztraminer Kappelweg Rolly Gassmann, FRANCE
Alsace 2001
Intense perfume of rose petals and spice which leads
to stunning dryness with concentrated richness yet
finesse, showing a variety of under-ripe fruits with
minerals. An utterly remarkable white wine.

17.5

RED £12.99 ∎ £154.00

Katnook Estate Cabernet Sauvignon 1999 AUSTRALIA
This is one of Australia's smoothest, most polished Cabs,
classic Coonawarra Cabernet. That is to say minty, crisp and
yet soft, energetic yet demure, rich yet subtle. You travel in
plushly upholstered comfort, catching the whiff of mint and
crushed blackberries. Drink with a pea risotto – wonderful!!!
Also at Oddbins and Waitrose.

17.5

WHITE £8.95 ∎ £103.00

Wither Hills Chardonnay 2000 NEW ZEALAND
Burned, buttery, creamy, brash – and lovely from nose
to throat. It's a celebration of life. The wine leaves the
impression of toasted cobnuts and toffee.

17.5 RED £7.95 ■ £94.00

The Society's St-Emilion 1998 FRANCE

A blend of 80% Merlot, 20% Cabernet Franc of great
style. Amazingly rich and chocolate-edged fruit of great
class and fruity concentration. Very classy and deep, it
offers berries in beautifully roasted array and firm
tannins of wit and weight. Decant 2 hours before serving.

17.5 RED £9.95 ■ £118.00

The Society's Exhibition Chilean Merlot 2000 CHILE

Superb texture here offering gaminess and great
depth of berried fruit with a hint of cocoa. The wine is
very complex, complete and cultured (thus a great
conversation piece).

17 RED £7.59 ■ £88.00

Vergelegan Mill Race Cabernet/ SOUTH AFRICA
Merlot 2000

Superb roasted strawberries and blackberries with
tannins of great strength (to begin with) and then
molar-crunching intensity.

17 FORTIFIED £9.50 ■ £112.00

The Society's LBV Port 1997 PORTUGAL

Better than many a vintage port. It has a gorgeous
texture, gripping and exact, and sweet plummy fruit
leavened by chocolate tannins.

17 WHITE £8.95 ■ £106.00

Grüner Veltliner Langenreserve Scheiben AUSTRIA
Leth 2001

Superbly aromatic, structured, balanced and more

elegant than a thousand white Burgundies. Dry yet
fruity (gently baked gooseberry and intensely dry
apricot – both very subtle). This is a very fine wine.

17   RED £6.95 ▪ £82.00

Château Clos du Notaire, Côtes de Bourg 2000   FRANCE
Delicious well-ordered claret offering subtle layers of
tobacco, chocolate, wasted berries and gripping,
tenacious tannins.

17   RED £7.95 ▪ £94.00

Vinsobres Côtes du Rhône-Villages Jaume 1999   FRANCE
Glues the teeth together so rich and mouth-filling is
it. Offers berries with chocolate, texture with a thorny
side, and tannins with great grip.

16.5   WHITE £8.95 ▪ £106.00

Neudorf Marlborough Sauvignon   NEW ZEALAND
Blanc 2002
One of the most complete (yet subtle) Sauvignon Blancs
in existence. The texture is of ruffled silk .The fruit of
calm Charentais melon, lemon with dry, very faint
mango to finish. With its delicious screwcap it will
gently and graciously age for many years and become
more and more interesting before a peak is reached and
around, oh, 8–10 years? Something like that.

16.5   WHITE £4.25 ▪ £49.00

The Society's Ruppertsberg Trocken 2001   GERMANY
A Riesling/Sylvaner/Gewürztraminer (10% only)
blend of great wit and elegance, and what a beautifully

dry, incisive blend it is. It offers under-ripe fruit, a
hint of citrus and seasoned nut – and a finish of great
finesse.

16

WHITE £5.95 ■ £70.00

The Society's Vin d'Alsace 2001 FRANCE

Deliciously French, earthy with touches of citrus and
dry melon, this is country wine, minerally and dry,
drinking as firm and charming as it gets in north-
eastern France.

16

WHITE £4.95 ■ £58.00

Douglas Green Chardonnay 2002 SOUTH AFRICA

Very attractive tailored-patchwork citrus on ruffled
velvet melon and crushed gooseberry. Has real fruit,
elegantly and purposefully polished.

Château Cheval-Blanc 1947? I drank it in Hennekey's
wine bar in Marylebone High Street for 73/6 in 1966.
Auction price today? Maybe 1500 quid. Maybe more.
Château Pétrus 1949? Four quid on my first
honeymoon at the Miners' Arms in Priddy in Somerset
in the late 1960s. Auction price today? You might find
an oriental tycoon prepared to part with five grand to
take the bottle off your hands (if it was part of an
impeccably cellared case). People who tell me I'm just
a superplonker who doesn't know about great wine,
fine wine, expensive wine, don't know the half of it. I
know all about great wine. It taught me not to confuse
it with merely greatly expensive wine.

16   WHITE £7.50 ■ £88.00

Madfish Unwooded Chardonnay 2002   AUSTRALIA
Good balance of lingering dry citrus and peach. Very
firm and elegant.

16   WHITE £9.75 ■ £115.00

Pazo de Senorans Albarino 2001   SPAIN
Something different and individual. Apricot/peach
dryness revealing another layer of nuttiness. Miguel
Torres, the great Catalan wine maker, entrepreneur,
linguist and tennis player, told me he reckons the
Albarino grape is related to the Riesling vines left
behind by pilgrims centuries ago on the road to
Santiago di Compostela. He may be right.

16   RED £4.95 ■ £58.00

The Society's Chilean Merlot 2000   CHILE
Delicious jammy berries with a tangy, though refined
edge, to the tannins. Very classy.

16   RED £9.50 ■ £112.00

Wirra Wirra Church Block Cabernet Sauvignon/
Shiraz/ Merlot 2000   AUSTRALIA
Juicy, but has lovely charred tannins to keep it
disciplined and from going sloppy or soppy.

16   RED £4.50 ■ £49.00

Domaine de Limbardie 2002   FRANCE
Lovely roasted berries with deep tannins. Classic
rustic richness with an urbane polish.

16

RED £6.75 ▪ £79.00

The Society's Crozes-Hermitage NV   FRANCE

Luxurious jammy Crozes which then turns tarry and
urgently tannic and gently spicy.

16

RED £7.95 ▪ £94.00

Côtes du Rhône Réserve Personnelle 1999   FRANCE

How to be sweet (yet dry), cute (yet muscular) and full
of yourself but subtle. A delicious Côtes du Rhône.

16

RED £8.95 ▪ £106.00

Gigondas, La Tour Sarrazine, Clos de Cazaux 1998 FRANCE

Mature, spicy, dry, deep, vegetal, splendid, grouchy,
individual, and beginning to go downhill as the
tannins are beginning to feel stretched to me. Drink
by Christmas 2003 – unless, that is, you like your
wine with the bloom of its youth totally departed.

16

WHITE DESSERT £14.50 ▪ £172.00

The Society's Exhibition Sauternes 2001   FRANCE

Delicious honey and crème brûlée rich fruit with the
texture of custard. Very young, complex, finely
balanced and best left in the cellar for 5–10 years.

YAPP BROTHERS

Mere,
Wiltshire BA12 6OY

Tel: (01747) 860 423
Fax: (01747) 860 929

Email: sales@yapp.co.uk.
Website: www.yapp.co.uk.

Open 9am to 6pm Monday to Saturday. Delivery
nationwide, single case £5, 2 or more cases free
delivery on mainland UK (with the exception of post
codes FK 18–21, IV 20, IV 30–32, IV 36, AB 38 and
PH 19–26).

For Yapp wines 15.5 points and under visit
www.superplonk.com

When I first met Jason Yapp, son of Robin Yapp who
founded Yapp Brothers, he was extremely unsteady
on his feet and uttering unintelligible gobbledegook.
He was, it might be said, a wine merchant to the
manner born. How he has grown since 1970! He was
able, this very June, to stand steady as a rock, twiddle
a corkscrew and open a range of glorious wines, and
talk complete sense.

However, 34 years ago it was his dad who gave me insight into those generous and life-enhancing – and in those days obscure – liquids which come from the Rhône and the Loire. Yapp père was a dentist. Now most people go to a dentist, it is fair to say, because they have a dental problem, but I went to him because I wanted to get my teeth into his wines. In 1970, having read in the Sunday's *Observer*, via wine journalist Cyril Ray, of the existence of this wine-dealing dentist, I resolved to visit. I telephoned (Mere 423, I've never forgotten it) and was given elaborate instructions. I purchased an Ordnance Survey map, and my then wife, who could drive, filled her Hillman Husky with petrol. The next Saturday we set off.

There was no-one remotely like Yapp in those days and there is no-one quite like the firm today (though his delightfully illustrated list today is signed not just by Robin but by wife Judith, son Jason and Tom Ashworth). Robin's trail-blazing endeavours deepened my knowledge and expanded my vinous horizons but today he no longer operates on teeth or out of a garage as he did when he started. He has a handsome wine business which still specialises in wines from the Loire and the Rhône with additions from Champagne, Provence, south-west France and even Australia. Robin did not fully hang up his drill until 1986. Yapp Brothers, as it was and is still called (though the brother, now dead, was a doctor based in Paris and played little part in the business), was born

in 1969 in the days when only 10% of the populace
drank wine, supermarkets were grocers who stocked
no bottle more ambitious than Cyprus sherry, and
wine shops, except for honourable exceptions like the
fledgling Oddbins or Peter Dominic (with its 50 or
60 wine shops), were mostly dingy off-licences
staffed by critters who often couldn't be fagged to
remove the Woodbines they had adhering to their
lower lips when they served you – this being choice
filth from the boondocks of Spain and Italy, perhaps
Yugoslavia or, if you had chanced upon a truly
adventurous branch, a sweet white wine from South
Africa.

It was well into Sunday before we returned to our
London flat, our heads still muzzy, the Husky's boot
full of, the rear seats crushed under, as many cases of
wine as that modestly capacious vehicle could
envelop.

Oh yes, we found Robin Yapp's house all right, met
the mewling Jason, and purchased the wine from the
garage. The problem – delicious, dangerous, de
rigueur – was getting away sober. As we
emerged from the Yapp house in the middle of the
afternoon after a filling lunch round the kitchen
table, having indulged ourselves with all manner of
wines Robin had generously opened, my wife
announced, once all the wine had been heaved
aboard and we sat in the car, that she was in no fit
state to drive home. We spent the night in the nearest
local inn.

This June I enjoyed another filling lunch chez Yapp. But this time I took a train, my time, and notes. These latter follow.

18.5

RED £8.25

Cépage Carignan Domaine Ferrer Ribière 2001   FRANCE
From 124-year-old vines, so they've seen a thing or
two, but have they ever produced rustic perfection like
this before? You can eat the tannins and smoke the
tobacco in this stunning red.

18.5

RED £9.50

Vacqueyras Cuvée Spéciale 1998   FRANCE
Superb, dry, mature, great vintage, perfectly tailored
berries with herbs and chocolate.

18

RED £7.50

Mont Caume Cabernet Sauvignon 2000   FRANCE
Magnificent burned fruit, lovely chewy texture, superb
tannins and a stunning finish of huge warmth.

18

RED £10.95

Collioure La Pinède Domaine de la Tour Vieille   FRANCE
2001
Balsam textured yet dry and cocoa edged with hints of
coriander, black olive and tobacco. The tannins are
wonderful too.

17.5

WHITE £10.75

Gewürztraminer Charles Schleret 1999   FRANCE
The smell is pure Deep Secret red roses, the fruit
has a touch of Turkish delight with a very dry
floral undertone, and there is a gloriously delicate
finish.

17　　　　　　　　　WHITE DESSERT (half bottle) £5.75

Monbazillac Domaine de l'Ancienne Cure 2000　　FRANCE
Wonderfully subtle yet emphatic. Gorgeous honeyed
peach and raspberry with toasted seeds. A wonderful
wine to enjoy with fresh fruit.

17　　　　　　　　　　　　　　RED £15.25

Brezeme Eugène de Monicault 1998　　　FRANCE
It proceeds delicately at first then the roasted berries
and great tannins strike.

17　　　　　　　　　　　　　WHITE £11.65

Cassis Clos Ste-Magdeleine 2000　　　FRANCE
Decant it 2–3 hours beforehand to allow the gloriously
oily, perfumed, pear/spice fruit to flower fully.

17　　　　　　　　　　　　　RED £8.75

Chinon L'Arpenty 2002　　　FRANCE
Superb stealth to the roasted, herby fruit which
evolves like lava on the tongue. A gripping book and a
bottle of this gripping wine and life can seem very
special indeed.

16.5　　　　　　　　　　　RED £8.25
Saumur Champigny Domaine Filiatreau 2001　　FRANCE
Stunningly dry and herbily rich. Lovely berried fruit
here which combines potency with delicacy.

16.5　　　　　　　　　　WHITE £6.75
Cuvée L'Orangerie, Savoie NV　　　FRANCE
Wonderful aromatic orange blossom and citrus.

16.5
RED £6.25
FRANCE

Saint Pourcain La Ficelle 2002
The greatest label in France. And the Gamay and
Pinot Noir fruit is tremendous also. Gorgeous sticky
fruit with a lovely roasted undertone.

16.5
RED £11.95
FRANCE

Crozes-Hermitage Alain Graillot 2001
Beautifully rich yet immensely delicate – roasted,
berried, tannicly teasing.

16.5
WHITE £15.25
FRANCE

**Cépage Viognier Le Pied Samson Georges
Vernay 2002**
Intense apricot/pear fruit of great dryness. Great
finesse and subtlety.

16.5
WHITE £8.75
FRANCE

Chinon Château de Ligre 2002
Highly individual, very dry peach, with lingering, dry
minerals.

16.5
WHITE £11.75
FRANCE

Savennières Château de la Bizolière 1999
Very mature, rich, oily fruit, oxidised in style but very
'classy' – and the finish is toasty.

16.5
WHITE £8.75
FRANCE

Jurançon Domaine Bellegarde 2001
Superb, dry, gently medicinal richness yet very
delicate pear/mineral finish.

16

WHITE £7.65
FRANCE

Montlouis Les Liards 2002
Unusual soft, dry peach with a touch of grilled nut.

16

WHITE £6.95
FRANCE

Coteaux d'Aix, Château des Gavelles 2000
Dry, gently anise-edged citrus and vague herb.
Haughty and very French.

16

WHITE £14.95
FRANCE

Bellet Domaine de la Source 2001
Expensive, ineffably Provençal dryness and
herbiness.

16

ROSÉ £8.95
FRANCE

Bourgueil Pierre-Jacques Druet 2000
Very unusual 100% Cab. Franc rosé of great dryness
and deftness.

16

ROSÉ £7.50
FRANCE

Lirac La Fermade 2001
Beautifully dry cherries, herbs and nut fruit. Very
elegant and stylish.

16

RED £5.85
FRANCE

Gamay de l'Ardèche 2001
Very odd rustic tippling, burned mulberry fruit, fresh
and plummy – and it really appreciates being served
chilled.

16   RED £14.75

Irouléguy Cuvée Bixintxo 2000   FRANCE

A 100% Tannat-graped wine of tannic precision yet
plummily fruited delicacy.

16   RED £25.00

Hermitage Pascal Frères 1993   FRANCE

Mature fruit characters of complex fruit at its peak.
Roasted plums and very imaginative tannins. A lot of
dosh but a lot of wine (just about).

Malcolm Gluck as your personal wine consultant. 23p a week.

There is a catch (isn't there always?). The catch is you require a computer and internet access. The rest follows as effortlessly as night follows day.

If you visit **superplonk.com**, described by more than one of its thousands of subscribers as 'the most comprehensive, the most detailed, the most rewarding and the most advanced wine website in the world', you will find plenty: reviews of over 10,000 wines on sale in the UK, daily news on the latest bargains, loads of articles about wine, and a very active Forum where views, often controversial, are exchanged. There is a powerful search capability at your disposal to find all the wines Malcolm Gluck has tasted, including all those not covered in this book.

However, you can also become a privileged user of the website, by forking out £14.95 a year for the new *Clos Encounters* service. This not only permits you unlimited email access to Malcolm G, 'ask me anything you like' he says, but the chance to get the very latest wine news and the opportunity to win some very cool prizes (like an all-expenses-paid holiday in Champagne or a £500 case of superposh wine).

However, for readers of this book there is a special offer. You can sign up for *Clos Encounters* for £2.50 off the normal price (hence 23p a week). Just enter the code SP2004X when you subscribe.

Equally, can you name any other website which offers a fantastic service direct to your mobile phone? With **superplonk.com**'s new World of Wine SMS service you get weekly tips on matching food and wine, the low-down on the latest trends in wine, and an exclusive Superplonk Wine of the Week – all beamed directly to your phone. To start your World of Wine subscription simply send 'wine' to 82128.

You can also get access to Superplonk's Wine Finder on your mobile phone any where, any time. The Mobile Wine Finder lets you search for the top Superplonk wines by country, retailer, wine type and price via an easy-to-use SMS application. In the supermarket, or searching the restaurant wine list, simply send 'Superplonk' to 82128 and then respond to the text message questions to find the perfect Superplonk.

For more details and costs of both these remarkable, state-of-the-art new services visit www.superplonk.com/mobile.

INDEX OF WINE NAMES

The **bold** numeral denotes the rating of the wine.

C

M

INDEX OF WINE TYPES

The **bold** numeral denotes the rating of the wine.

FORTIFIED

A

Asda LBV Port 1996, **17**, *Asda*, 10

B

Blandy's Madeira Malmsey 1978, **20**, *Sainsbury's*, 161–2

D

Dow's Bomfim Port 1987, **16**, *Sainsbury's*, 190
Dow's Vintage Port 1983, **16**, *Sainsbury's*, 182

F

Fletchers Amontillado Sherry, **16**, *Aldi*, 5
Fletchers Cream Sherry, **16**, *Aldi*, 5

G

Gonzalez Byass Noe Sherry, **17.5**, *Tesco*, 250
Graham's Crusted Port 1999, **16**, *Sainsbury's*, 190
Graham's Malvedos Vintage Port 1995, **17.5**, *Sainsbury's*, 166

H

Henriques & Henriques Monte Seco Madeira, **17**, *Waitrose*, 299

S

Sainsbury's Finest Reserve Port, **16**, *Sainsbury's*, 181
Sainsbury's Rich Cream Sherry, **16.5**, *Sainsbury's*, 172
Solear Manzanilla Sherry, **16**, *Sainsbury's*, 189

T

The Society's Exhibition Viejo Oloroso Dulce Sherry, **20**, *Wine Society*, 333

The Society's LBV Port 1997, **17**, *Wine Society*, 335
Torres Muscatel Oro, **16**, *Sainsbury's*, 189

W

Waitrose Fino Sherry, **16**, *Waitrose*, 322
Waitrose Solera Jerezana Rich Cream Sherry, **16.5**, *Waitrose*, 309
Waitrose Solera Jerezana Dry Amontillado Sherry, **16.5**, *Waitrose*, 309
Waitrose Solera Jerezana Oloroso Sherry, **16**, *Waitrose*, 322

RED

A

Abadia Real Vino de la Tierra, Castilla y Leon 2000, **16.5**, *Majestic*, 76
Alamos Bonarda 2001, **16**, *Booths*, 31
Alamos Bonarda 2002, **16**, *Booths*, 26
Alamos Malbec 2002, **16**, *Tesco*, 268
Alentejo Reserva 2000, **16**, *Majestic*, 88
Amarone della Valpolicella Classico, Azienda Agricola Brigaldara 1999, **17.5**, *Booths*, 21
Amativo 2000, **16**, *Sainsbury's*, 175
Anciennes Vignes Carigan, Vin de Pays de l'Aude 2001, **16.5**, *Safeway*, 145
Antony's Yard, Graham Beck 2001, **16**, *Majestic*, 89
Apaltagua Carmenere 2001, **16.5**, *Booths*, 24
Aradon Rioja 2002, **16**, *Oddbins*, 129
Argento Bonarda 2002, **16**, *Safeway*, 151
Argento Malbec 2002, **16.5**, *Budgens*, Somerfield, 38, 242
Ascheri Vigna dei Pola Barolo 1998, **16**, *Tesco*, 262
Asda Chilean Cabernet Sauvignon 2001, **16**, *Asda*, 15
Asda Chilean Merlot 2002, **16**, *Asda*, 14
Asda Claret Red NV, **16**, *Asda*, 11–12
Asda Corbières NV, **16**, *Asda*, 12
Asda French Cabernet Sauvignon, Vin de Pays d'Oc NV, **16**, *Asda*, 17

WHITE

H

I